FINISH
STRONG

GRACE THAT YOU MAY FINISH THE RACE

Dr. James A.
Scudder

Victory In Grace Ministries
60 Quentin Road
Lake Zurich, IL 60047
1-800-78-GRACE
www.victoryingrace.org

Dedication

To all the dear people of Quentin Road Bible Baptist Church who have stuck with me throughout these years. And to my dear wife, Linda, our two children, their spouses, and my four grandchildren, Amy, Erica, Jamie, and Amanda.

Acknowledgements

I also want to express my heartfelt appreciation for the many people who have helped this book become a reality. My wonderful daughter, Julie, was my editor. She spent hundreds of hours taking my writing and making it readable. Without her dedication and skill, *Finish Strong* would never have crossed the finish line. My son, Jim, and daughter-in-law, Karen, oversaw the proofing and publishing. Many incredible church members proofed the project, including Karen Vacko, Lauren Reyes, Jane Vasquez, Mike Floyd, Cameron Edwards, and Barb Vanden Bosch. Special thanks to Kari Kumura for designing the layout and the beautiful cover. This book would never have been possible without these talented and dedicated people.

Endorsements

Dr. James Scudder has founded and built one of the great churches and ministries in the history of American Christianity. Its influence is felt on radio and television, in the schools held on premise, in the deliberations of local and national government, and in the lives of multitudes within its reach. As I eagerly read the original text of *Finish Strong*, I instinctively reflected on my personal observations of this man and his noble work.

Dr. Scudder is gifted with the ability to make the message of the gospel and Biblical Christian service plain and clear. There are no "uncertain sounds" about his message or his convictions. From the Christ-centered spirit of the services, [to] the style and majesty of the music, to the empowerment of the message, being present in the Quentin Road Bible Baptist Church is a moving New Testament experience.

Each weekday, radio and television carry the message of this great church coast to coast. Their preschool ministry is the largest in America, and their Dayspring [Bible] College and Seminary trains students for Christian service to "the regions beyond." The halls of Congress and the politicians of Chicago are conscious of his opinions. He has carried out the full spectrum in his ministry, and has laid the foundations for its ongoing impact.

This book details the steps of faith Dr. Scudder took in carrying out the Great Commission. The rest of us can hereby be encouraged to obediently follow Christ and to *Finish Strong*.

Dr. Carl E. Baugh,
Founder and Director, Creation Evidence Museum—Glen Rose, Texas

---

I am honored to recommend and endorse this excellent book because it is a book of real-life, modern-day miracles! It tells how God used one man who had a godly vision to press on, persevere, and finish strong, fulfilling the ministry that God had called him to. My good friend, James Scudder, has not stopped in over 40 years proclaiming a clear message of the amazing gospel of God's grace—the passion of his heart. *Finish Strong* will bless you mightily.

Dr. Art Rorheim
Founder of AWANA Clubs, International

The famed atheist and economist Ayn Rand was often asked about producing an autobiography, or at least an authorized biography of her life. She routinely replied that someone should publish all of her writings in one volume and put a page at the end that said, "And she meant it."

When reading *Finish Strong* by Dr. James Scudder, one is immediately struck by how the doctrine of grace has influenced all of his life. He truly "means it." *Finish Strong* has four main themes. First, it is the story of Dr. Scudder's life. It is an intriguing story. Secondly, the book covers the history of the Quentin Road Baptist Church. It traces the story of the church from its founding in Chicago until its present role as a local church with an international ministry. Thirdly, woven throughout the book are doctrinal expositions of grace—a very clear doctrine of grace. A fourth theme is the constant encouragement of preachers and servants of the Lord about how to face discouragements, survive them, and finish strong. All four themes in one compelling narrative.

In a day when so many preachers are "falling by the wayside," Dr. Scudder offers massive amounts of encouragement. In a day of confusion about salvation, Dr. Scudder offers Biblical clarity. Anyone who knows Dr. Scudder can picture him expounding the doctrine of grace with great clarity and passion. The story of his life and ministry demonstrates that "he means it." This book displays his spirit of devotion, his sense of determination, and his passion for souls. It does so in a way to encourage others to the same sense of ministry.

Anyone looking for encouragement in a day of great discouragement would do well to read *Finish Strong*.

Dr. Phil Stringer
Senior Pastor of Ravenswood Baptist Church—Chicago, Illinois

This work is long overdue. I, and I am sure many others, have wanted to know more about the history behind the prominent Quentin Road Bible Baptist Church. Here it is by the one who was used by God to found and pastor this Christ-honoring church. Currently [Dr. Scudder's] son, Jim Scudder, Jr., is the executive pastor, doing a grand job, and following in his dad's train.

There are 32 short chapters here. Each of these is intended to give encouragement to pastors, church leaders, and individual Christians as they flesh out the marvelous grace of God to the finish line.

Quentin Road Bible Baptist Church sees to it that its ministry reaches out to the community in many ways, to those outside the church as well as those inside.

It is my desire that this written testimony will encourage the reader to start strong in God's grace [and to] continue strong in His grace so that he or she can finish strong by God's grace and for His glory.

Dr. Robert P. Lightner
Professor Emeritus of Systematic Theology at Dallas Theological Seminary

What a treasure! *Finish Strong* provides priceless insight from someone who has been through the mountains and valleys of a local church ministry with a global outreach. Dr. Scudder's passion to help Christians understand and realize the power of God's Word in their [lives] is exemplified by a life anchored in the promises of God. If you're looking for a proven pattern, look no further; it's here for the taking. I truly believe that God's most amazing works don't happen by accident or through random people. They are planned and orchestrated by His perfect hand through men like Dr. Scudder who say, "Lord, whatever I have, it's all Yours." Many men are willing to say these words, but so few are willing to pay the price through gut-wrenching work to see it through. *Finish Strong* is a thrilling journey to travel; and I believe every reader will be encouraged by the reality that God is still very much at work, if we'll only have the faith to keep going. May every reader discover what my dearest friend and mentor has spent his life proclaiming: the greatest life in the world is found in Christ!

Rev. Paul Julian
Ministry Coordinator at Quentin Road Bible Baptist Church

Table of Contents

Foreword   9

Introduction   11

Section 1: Amazing Grace! How Sweet the Sound

 Chapter 1 — Grace for the Race   14

 Chapter 2 — The Vicious, Spiritual Cycle   23

 Chapter 3 — Hope No Matter What   33

 Chapter 4 — Suffering for a Purpose   41

 Chapter 5 — Detours Are Good   52

 Chapter 6 — The Light   63

 Chapter 7 — Why a Clear Gospel?   79

 Chapter 8 — Avoiding an Unclear Message   87

 Chapter 9 — Can You Call God Off?   99

 Chapter 10 — Eternal Insecurity   105

 Chapter 11 — Called to Serve   111

Section 2: 'Twas Grace That Taught Me

 Chapter 12 — Faith in a Big God   122

 Chapter 13 — A Passion for Souls   131

 Chapter 14 — Operation What's Next   138

 Chapter 15 — More Precious Than Gold   146

 Chapter 16 — Determination in the Power of God   157

 Chapter 17 — Despair Is Not a Factor   169

 Chapter 18 — Facing Forward   177

 Chapter 19 — God Blesses Obedience   187

Section 3: Through Many Dangers, Toils, and Snares

    Chapter 20—A Life Full of Purpose   198

    Chapter 21—Managing, Planning, and Volunteers   207

    Chapter 22—Confidence in God's Plan   216

    Chapter 23—The Key to Success   225

    Chapter 24—Church Growth   236

Section 4: When We've Been There 10,000 Years

    Chapter 25—Burn Out or Rust Out   246

    Chapter 26—God Recycles People   254

    Chapter 27—Thankful or Thankless?   263

    Chapter 28—Continue in the Work   277

    Chapter 29—Pour Courage into Others   291

    Chapter 30—The Sign of the Moose   298

    Chapter 31—Peace When You Need It   307

    Chapter 32—How to Finish Strong   318

Appendix A   330

Notes   333

Foreword

Finish Strong, by Dr. James A. Scudder, is an unusual and important book. It is unusual and important because it supplies truth about the essential relationship between the believer, his church, and his pastor that most books about Christian living neglect to teach.

The average author who writes about the Christian life or spiritual growth seems to think that believers can grow to spiritual maturity and Christlikeness without a good, local church and the ministry of a faithful pastor. Hypothetically, I suppose that this is possible (if no church is available), but it is surely not the norm and almost never happens in real life. For every Christian who becomes spiritual "on his own," there are thousands who never become spiritual; because either willfully or in ignorance, they have failed to unite with a good, local church and enjoy the blessings of the ministry of a godly pastor.

God Himself created the Church, both universal and local. He expressly forbids believers to forsake the assembly. He declares that He gave to the Church gifted men, among them pastor-teachers. These gifted men were given for the perfecting of the saints—so that the saints could become mature—yet books written about the spiritual life tend to leave the Church and its pastors out of the equation.

In Acts 20 and in 1 Peter 5, Paul and Peter, respectively, told the elders and overseers of the church to *poimen*, that is, to shepherd their sheep. They are to lead, feed, shelter, protect from wolves and false shepherds, keep from straying, and so on. In other places the members of the flock are told to follow, imitate, honor, and obey their shepherds. These passages and others in the New Testament clearly teach that the local church and its pastor are an essential part of God's plan for Christian living and the accomplishment of God's goals for the Church.

In *Finish Strong*, you will find teaching, admonition, and exhortation regarding the individual's spiritual life, the role of the pastor, and the duties of the church intertwined as they should be. True spirituality cannot be separated from faithfulness to the local church and its pastor.

Dr. Scudder is eminently qualified to write on this subject. In over 40 years of ministry in the same church, he has sought to know, obey, and teach the Word of God. He has preached with the expectation that God's people would respond positively to the ministry of the Word. When necessary, he has reproved and rebuked, both from the pulpit and in the office. A pastor is a shepherd; his job is to lead his flock and care for his sheep. Dr. Scudder has led and cared. Quentin Road Bible Baptist Church has followed, and God has blessed.

Dr. Scudder has faced just about every kind of attack that the devil has in his arsenal, but has not been defeated. "The greater the testing, the greater the blessing" has become a watchword at Quentin Road. We have seen it proven true in our pastor's life and ministry time and again. Dr. Scudder wants to finish his race and finish strong. The race is not yet over. Our prayer for him is that he will have many more years of ministry, and that he will be strong to the end.

I heartily recommend this book to men who have answered God's call to the pastorate. It's a tough job; but you, too, can succeed. I also commend this book to individual believers, that they may become genuinely mature in Christ as they are blessed by their pastor's ministry and are used by God for His work in their local church.

Dr. Michael T. Floyd
Academic Dean
Dayspring Bible College & Seminary
Longtime associate and friend of Dr. Scudder.

Introduction

Finish Strong. Perhaps you wonder why I would write a book with this title. The answer is simple: this is my goal. Sometimes when I look at churches across the country, I see the pastors and congregations struggling. They don't know what to do to get back on track and see new growth. Many churches have tried to solve this problem by adopting the worldly system to get people. This solution will never work. As the Body of Christ, we have to press toward the mark of the high calling of Christ Jesus. *Finish Strong* is full of practical ways to do this which will enrich your ministry, your personal life, and spiritual life.

Over 41 years ago, the Lord asked my wife and me to the Chicago area to start a church. Countless times through the years which followed, I wanted to give up and quit. But the one thing that motivated me was what Christ did for me on the cross. He never gave up on me, so how could I give up on the work He gave me to do?

People ask, "Are there real miracles today?" The answer is yes. In these pages, you will see some of the greatest miracles in the world. I share my heart the best way I know how as we went from a struggling church in a small storefront to a church that has the largest Christian preschool in America with an average of 1,400 students per year. We have a worldwide TV ministry, a Bible college with a new campus, and 43 acres at our main church which will seat over 3,000 people. These are miracles, no question about it.

I want to thank all the people in our church and my family, especially my daughter Julie, for all they've done to make *Finish Strong* a reality.

For all the pastors, laypeople, and believers who read this book, it is my deepest desire that you discover there are way more blessings than testings, and there is no greater life than to be in a local church. I hope pastors will be encouraged not to give up, and all believers will realize how great it is to serve in a biblically oriented church.

From someone who wanted to quit on every Monday, I know what it is like to need an extra dose of encouragement. The key was when I understood that it wasn't necessarily wrong to want to quit, but it was wrong to actually quit.

My prayer is that this book will help you finish strong.

Section 1

Amazing Grace! how sweet the sound —
That saved a wretch like me!
I once was lost but now am found,
Was blind, but now I see.

Chapter 1
Grace for the Race

Thou therefore, my son, be strong in the grace that is in Christ Jesus. 2 Timothy 2:1

The size of the steel beams for our new, multi-purpose facility astounded all of us. One hundred twenty feet across, each beam weighed 8,000 lbs. The beams supporting the outside of the structure weighed 8,500 lbs. We had known their size when they were ordered, but there is a difference between knowing this information and seeing them up close and personal. The massive, dark red beams on the truck looked like a skyscraper from the Chicago skyline dumped on its side.

The truck driver smirked at the crane we had rented. "No way are you going to get those beams off this truck with that puny thing," he said, shaking his head.

He was right. We rented a larger crane and were finally able to get the beams off the truck. But now the real problem loomed. How in the world would we get the beams up and set? This 76,000-square-foot building would contain a 3,500-seat auditorium, swimming pool, many classrooms, a full-service food serving area, commercial kitchen, McDonald's-style playland, and more. Members of our congregation had determined to build the entire new facility themselves, from the steel beams, to the electric, to the plumbing. This would save millions of dollars and help the church continue for future generations. While we had built a couple of our previous buildings ourselves, nothing compared to the size of this structure. We were now at our fourth location and fifth building project since we'd started the church in inner-city Chicago in 1971.

This building project had trouble right from the start. We had problems receiving permits, pouring concrete, and getting the steel to arrive in the first place. The beams were supposed to come in the summer when it would have been easier to build; but they hadn't come until the beginning of the long, cold, Chicago winter.

This unprecedented event marked a step of faith. It would require every drop of strength. We were a group of common people trying to do something on a huge scale and make a difference. We were gung ho, excited, and couldn't wait. The frosty, November morning didn't faze us, nor the fact that most likely we would freeze throughout the winter during construction. Nothing mattered except getting the building built.

But the problem lay before us in dark red steel. The beams were larger than any we had seen before. The thought of getting them up and put together was daunt-ing at best. No one had any experience in constructing steel beams.

On that 32-degree day with the feel of possible snow in the air, it didn't seem that we could set these beams, much less build a building of this magnitude. This was a bigger task than any I'd faced before. Although I'd seen God work in miraculous ways over and over again through the years at Quentin Road, I couldn't imagine how in the world we could do this. My faith wavered.

I remembered the early days when we were fortunate anyone came in the door of our first location, a small storefront in Chicago. The years when all we did was sweat and work but nothing happened flooded back into my mind. All those difficult days ran together into a constant refrain: *It can't be done. It can't be done. It can't be done.*

3452 Fullerton Ave. Chicago – Storefront where it all began.

A cardinal lighted in a tree on the far side of the property. Its deep red color took my breath away. God was a Miracle Worker. How else could that brilliant color be explained? Considering the miracle of the cardinal made me think of other things God had done through the years: how one of our first members showed up at the door of our storefront in downtown Chicago (normally, he would have missed us at that hour); how Earl Livesay started contributing $50 a week so we could rent a bigger facility in the suburbs; how a drunken realtor paved the way for us to purchase our first piece of property. Recalling these miracles brought fresh courage. With God's wisdom and supernatural strength, we could put up these beams.

I prayed for confidence while directing the crane operator to pick up the first beam. For the first foot or two, it lifted perfectly.

We heaved a sigh of relief. Yes! This would all work out fine. We could set these beams ourselves. The building would get built on time. God would be glorified, and the church would grow.

Slowly the crane lifted the beam another five feet.

The beam bent.

Like a piece of cooked spaghetti.

The 8,000-lb piece of steel strained like it would thunderously break into two pieces. We stared in horror. Steel wasn't supposed to bend like that. The beam was designed to hold the incredible weight of the roof and the whole structure with ease. Instead, it looked like not even one beam could be lifted.

Twisted Beam.

My heart dropped in my chest. If that beam snapped, the workers could lose their lives. I quickly motioned for the operator to lower the beam. Someone could get seriously hurt if we didn't think of a way to get the beams up and set. And how was it going to be possible with one crane operator and a bunch of inexperienced steel workers?

The entire project might have to be scrapped. The building wouldn't get built. We wouldn't continue to grow. Our church would, in fact, crash and burn. The devil must be laughing, saying, *Look at Jim Scudder. He thinks God is going to help him with that huge piece of steel? No way. This isn't possible.*

At that moment, I could almost hear those who opposed God's work say, *Look at that crazy church. This trial will be too hard for them. They will fizzle and die.*

The dark powers of the universe centered on the beams as they sat useless on the concrete. They were too big. They couldn't be lifted. It felt impossible. There was no hope.

I have to be honest—I wanted to give up.

Hating Church

Like many kids who grow up in a preacher's family, I hated church. Actually, I probably hated the institution more than most kids hated it. (It is a pretty sad commentary on the state of the church today when you see how many young adults are leaving the church.)

Despising church didn't mean I hated Dad, a Methodist preacher for over 40 years. On the contrary, I had wonderful parents who loved me. (Honestly, all a kid needs is to be loved and cared for — to know that his parents are there for him no matter what.) They set boundaries for me. (These are good for a kid, too. If a child knows where the guardrails are, then he can be free within those limits and won't constantly be testing them.) My parents gave me a great start in life. I owe a huge debt to them I could never repay.

Dad was mistreated by some of his churches. They didn't realize what our family was going through for him to preach or the sacrifices Dad made for the people of the congregation. Even as a seven-year-old, I remember how much their oversight hurt.

I was born in Lexington, Kentucky, but we moved to different Kentucky towns

My parents, Isaac and Esther, with me and my sister, Pauline.

throughout Dad's ministry. During one of those moves, the parsonage had rats in it. Dad brought the matter to the church board and the board said they had gone through the house and hadn't seen any rodents. When Dad came home and told Mom the news, she wasn't happy. Neither were my siblings or myself. We had all seen the rats.

The varmints did finally leave. We spent the next four years in that location. I'm sure that church didn't mean to ignore our concern. They probably had the best of intentions. But that incident made an impression, strengthening my resolve to get out of church as soon as possible.

The stiffness; the formality; the solid, wood pews; the tiresome, white walls; and the deacons gathered outside smoking after the service contributed to the boredom. Even as a child, I recognized hypocrisy and hated it.

There was no reality in church. That was the one reason I hated religion the most. No life. Nothing to make it interesting. Nothing to keep me wanting to come back for another service.

So I sat in church week after week, like a prisoner marking imaginary X's on the walls for each service, planning how many more X's I would have to endure before I could get out of there and get on with my life.

Dad stayed at each church for four years because this was the way of the Methodists. Some preachers stay only two years at a time. Dad was one of the best preachers, so we got to stay four years in a town. Four years was like an eternity, because it simply signaled the start of another stint in a new town with a new church.

The *Going to Heaven Scale*

Though I sat in service after service, though I knew all the Beatitudes — when Jesus said blessed are the meek, blessed are the peacemakers, blessed are those who endure sitting on hard pews listening to messages — I missed the message from the Bible about salvation.

The way I saw it, going to Heaven was like the scale at the butcher shop when my dad bought minute steaks. These steaks go through a tenderizing machine. The butcher put the steaks on one side of the scale and a weight on the other. If the minute steaks were heavier, then the butcher took one of them off. Once the scale evened out, we would know how many pounds of meat to buy.

I gathered from attending church that going to Heaven must be like that. God would put my good deeds on a huge scale. He would put my bad deeds on the other side. If the good stuff outweighed the bad stuff, I could go to Heaven.

It was as simple (and as difficult) as that.

How could my good deeds ever outweigh my bad deeds? In my moments of honesty, the sheer number of bad things on the *Going to Heaven Scale* worried me. My conscience would prick me with some of my sins: Like the time my brother David and I turned off the electricity while a church service was going on. Dad was on the radio in that town so the power going off cut off the radio broadcast, too. My father was not happy with me, to say the least. He brought us into a meeting with the elders and paddled us in front of all of them. My dad didn't often spank us, but he did that day.

❧

What We Deserve

David and I deserved to be paddled that day because of our sin. God's grace is something no one deserves. In spite of our sin, God sent His Son to die for us. I discovered this truth many years later after much frustration and sorrow. I thought salvation was Jesus plus my works. I didn't know that it was Jesus only. Titus 3:5 says, "Not by works of righteousness which we have done, but according to his mercy he saved us, by the washing of regeneration, and renewing of the Holy Ghost."

Not by works. Only by His mercy.

What is the difference between grace and mercy?

Mercy is not being punished like we deserve. Grace is God giving to us something we don't deserve.

Grace is defined as unmerited favor. That's why I love the song "Amazing Grace" and am using the four stanzas throughout *Finish Strong*. The first verse says it all: "I once was lost but now am found, / Was blind but now I see."

No one could describe God's grace better than that.

❧

Victory in Grace

After we trust Christ as Savior, we need to learn to walk in God's grace; but as believers, we are incomplete, insufficient, unable, and incapable of living the Christian life on our own. As pastors, lay leaders, and members of a church, we don't measure up. But that's why Jesus came. To give us

His grace. To help us walk in it every day. Christ is complete, sufficient, and capable. Second Corinthians 12:9 says, "And he said unto me, My grace is sufficient for thee: for my strength is made perfect in weakness. Most gladly therefore will I rather glory in my infirmities, that the power of Christ may rest upon me."

Maybe as a pastor you want to know how to more fully communicate God's grace and also how to disciple believers in their walk with Christ. Perhaps you are a lay leader who wants to see your church grow in grace more than anything else. It could be that you are a faithful member who cares deeply for God's precious Church. Are you a believer who desires to discover practical help for everyday living? Whatever your situation, all of us want to finish strong.

Mike Ianniello, an elder in my son-in-law Neal's church, was diagnosed with terminal cancer in April. He had heard a missionary from Mexico mention that his one goal was to finish strong. Throughout the summer, Mike mentored his brother and sister-in-law through their church's discipleship program. When he was in the hospital, his daughter came into the room crying, having learned more bad news about her dad's diagnosis. He opened his arms and hugged her.

Mike whispered, "I'm not afraid. I want to finish strong."

By November of the same year, Mike had passed away. He left behind a legacy in that church and in his family that will never be taken away from him. He understood God's grace. He finished strong because of his God.

Do you have hope for your church to finish strong like Mike? Do you have a confident expectation that God will work everything out in your life for His glory? That God, who started a good work, will complete it? Throughout these pages, you will discover strategies that will help you and your church. You will find out some of the things that helped me after founding Quentin Road Bible Baptist Church. I share it all: the blessings, the trials, the good times, the bad. It is my deepest prayer that these stories will give pastors, leaders, members, and believers grace for the race.

Though I wanted to give up on the day the beam bent like a piece of cooked spaghetti, I knew deep within my soul God would carry us with that same grace. He would place the beams in the right place. Him and Him alone. In the same way, when you trust and walk in the grace God has given you, no matter what obstacle you face, He will enable you.

Finish Line Strategies

- Believe God will take care of you and the church. Ephesians 5:27 says, "That he might present it to himself a glorious church, not having spot, or wrinkle, or any such thing; but that it should be holy and without blemish."
- God will supply all your needs. Philippians 4:19 states, "But my God shall supply all your need according to his riches in glory by Christ Jesus."

Chapter 2
The Vicious, Spiritual Cycle

And if by grace, then is it no more of works: otherwise grace is no more grace. But if it be of works, then is it no more grace: otherwise work is no more work. Romans 11:6

A group of us boys found the water reservoir on the top of a small mountain in Morehead, Kentucky. It sure beat the swimming hole in the creek. We loved goofing off in the beautiful, pristine pool.

One morning, our family sat at the breakfast table eating country ham

Location of old reservoir tank in Morehead, KY.

and eggs. Dad was a great cook. I loved the salty, cured ham and the eggs scrambled in the same pan to soak up more of that wonderful flavor. Dad was reading the newspaper and came across a story about the reservoir.

"What's this in the paper about a group of boys swimming in the town's water reservoir?" he asked. "Do you know anything about this, James Allen? I hope they catch those boys, lock them up, and throw away the key. The whole town has to boil its water."

The eggs turned tasteless in my mouth. I shoved back my plate. I had to answer at some point or Dad would become even more suspicious.

At age eleven, I knew a thing or two about my name. If I was called "James," then all was well with the world. Whenever the name "James Allen" came out of Mom's or Dad's mouth, my life might as well be over.

"I don't really know anything about that, Dad."

Dad shook his head and raised the paper to continue reading. I started to sigh with relief and leave my chair when he cleared his throat.

"Son, you probably need to let your friends know about this article."

"No problem. I'll do it right away." I stood up.

"Aren't you going to finish your breakfast?"

"I'm not hungry anymore. I better get to school." I didn't like school any more than church; but at the moment, I had to get out of the kitchen. School was preferable to hanging around with my father reading an article by some nosy reporter.

We didn't swim in the reservoir anymore; and in about seven days, they lifted the boil order because the town's water supply had become clean again.

Another time, we discovered how to remove a window from the local college pool building and swim there. Somehow, we were never caught.

Ashland, Kentucky, was the first place I remember living. A man lived there who was wealthy but didn't drive his car. So Dad would drive this man's car with his family and our family; and we would go to St. Petersburg, Florida, together. I caught my first fish there at one or two years old. Little did anybody know that I'd be hooked on fishing for the rest of my life. Nothing against those who golf, but fishing is my second favorite thing to do after sharing the gospel. Remember, who did Jesus call when He was on the earth? That's right, fishermen. So fishing must be biblical.

My brother David and me in St. Petersburg, FL.

In Versailles, Kentucky, my younger brother David, then three years old, got out a gallon of green paint and two brushes. He went to the fence between our house and the neighbors' and handed one of the brushes to a three-year-old girl named Vicki. When Dad came out of the house, he found David and Vicki painting each other with green paint. Dad grabbed a bucket of turpentine and dragged my brother to the basement. I remember the screams that came out of there as he tried to get the paint off David.

Later, he told me, "James, I normally wouldn't be so hard on David, but a gallon of green paint? What was he thinking?"

We moved to Carrollton, Kentucky. My brother and I were playing at a friend's house. For some reason, I gave David a whole bottle of Tabasco sauce and told him to drink it. He did what any three-year-old boy would do: obey his four-year-old brother because of his brother's vast experience. David swallowed the whole bottle in two or three gulps. He started crying and screaming. It was horrible. I didn't know what to do. I called Mother and asked her what to do. She said to give him a stick of butter. I grabbed a stick of butter out of the refrigerator and shoved the whole thing down his throat. It's a wonder he didn't die. The butter stopped the pain, but I'm surprised David ever forgave me. Whenever we are around Tabasco sauce, David flinches.

I wrote before about the *Going to Heaven Scale.* Because I worried about having enough good deeds to outweigh my bad deeds, I couldn't know I was going to Heaven. I wasn't sure how I could stop doing bad deeds. The vicious, spiritual cycle exhausted me.

Imagine if you were told you were going to go on a trip to the moon. There are conditions to get there, but no one is exactly sure what those conditions are. At first, you are excited about the trip. You've always wanted to travel to space. But then you find out you don't know what you have to do to go on the trip or even if you really qualify to go.

In the same way, going to Heaven was unclear to me as a child. Since I couldn't know if I was even going, if I was qualified to go, or what it would really take to get there, everything about that destination felt nebulous.

Who would want to try to do something that had no guarantee of success? Definitely not a kid who liked to play tricks on the district superintendent of the Methodist church by replacing the contents of a Coke bottle with Tabasco sauce. You'd think I would have learned that this wasn't a good trick after torturing my brother, David. I guess I couldn't resist.

Dad and I knew the man loved Coke in those old-fashioned, glass bottles. We made sure he knew they were in the fridge, available whenever he wanted one of them. We thought he would likely get up in the middle of the night to open the fridge to drink one. Sure enough, at two in the morning, we heard the fridge open. We popped out of bed, snuck to the door, and cracked it open. There stood the superintendent, a medium-sized man with a balding head. He rummaged around the fridge for awhile and grabbed something. We heard him open the bottle. I had to hold myself against the wall to keep from laughing and ruining everything. He opened the bottle and downed the whole thing in one gulp.

The sounds that came from that man could not be transferred to the written page. He yelled, hollered, and pranced around the room like he was going to die. When he heard us laughing, he turned on the light. His poor face was blotchy and red. We wondered if we would have to take him to the emergency room. I couldn't help but wonder what would appear in the newspaper. "Local Preacher and Son Try to Kill District Superintendent with Tabasco Sauce" would be my guess at a headline.

This time it wouldn't just be me in trouble, but Dad too.

Fortunately, the man recovered and started to laugh at the joke himself. Well, maybe it was much later when he laughed about it. Or maybe I wrote that to make myself look a little better.

The bottom line was this: I understood that on my best day I wasn't good enough to enter God's perfect Heaven.

I knew I had sinned.

The more I tried to clean myself up for God, the dirtier I would get. The more I tried, the more I failed.

Even as a boy I knew this, and knew it well.

I wouldn't learn the true meaning of salvation for many years.

❧◉❧

Saved out of the Rubble

Had I understood salvation as a child, I would have rested securely in Christ's love for me. Instead, I was destined for Hell and not at all sure how to avoid what seemed unavoidable. That's how many people felt on September 11. It's especially etched in my memory because my daughter, son-in-law, and their children were on a plane traveling from Florida to

Illinois when the first plane hit the tower.

We all still remember that day and how we felt there wasn't much hope for America through the weeks following the terrorist attacks.

Genelle Guzman-McMillan was the last of four people caught in the debris of the Twin Towers to be found alive. After the planes hit the World Trade Center, Genelle descended a staircase from the 64th floor of the North Tower. Steel beams weakened to their breaking point. Solid concrete was pulverized.

Her body found an air pocket, although heavy concrete pillars pinned her right leg and pieces of wreckage pinned her head in place.

How she was alive no one would ever know. But she was.

Trapped and seriously injured for 27 hours, Genelle came to consciousness every once in awhile and prayed. In recent months, she had started attending church. The rubble was all around her and she didn't think anyone would find her.

Shortly after noon on September 12, she heard voices. She screamed as loud as she could, "I'm here! Hey, I'm right here!"

"Do you see the light?" a rescue worker responded,

Genelle couldn't see it. She took a piece of concrete and banged it against a broken stairway overhead—probably the same structure that had saved her life. The searchers found the noise. She wedged her hand through a crack in the wall, and felt someone grab it. Genelle heard a voice say, "I've got you."

"Oh God, thank you!" Genelle Guzman-McMillan said.

Twenty minutes later, Genelle was rescued out from the rubble.[i]

Genelle represents all of us in a sense. We are all buried under sin. We can't pay for that sin on our own. Romans 3:23 says, "For all have sinned, and come short of the glory of God." The words "come short" literally mean an archer missing the bullseye.

My grandson, Jamie, loves archery. When he was ten years old, he decided to save his money to buy a bow. He put up a sign with his goal and how much money he would have to earn each day to buy it. He found work in the house, garage, and even the neighborhood so he could earn money for his bow. At Christmas, he had earned half the money and the family, including myself (mainly because I'm a softie — but I'm glad to have a grandson who loves to work), gave him the rest of the money so he could buy a bow. He practiced every day so that he would get good enough to make a bullseye. One time, Jamie's sister, Amanda, went downstairs and saw that he was practicing on one of her stuffed bears, which she wasn't very happy about.

My grandson Jamie with his new compound bow.

With God, we are always missing the bullseye. As a matter of fact, we miss the entire target. That's why God gave the Law, so we could see where we fall short and know we need a Savior.

❧◦⌘◦❧

In the Boat

Recently my granddaughter, Amy, was privileged to go to Israel. She loved seeing the Galilee area where Jesus ministered. It is one of the most beautiful places in Israel. If you've ever seen a storm on the Sea of Gali-

My wife Linda and I with our granddaughter, Amy, in Israel.

lee, you will quickly realize why it is called a sea, not a lake. With the unique geographic position of the water with the hills all around it, the wind whips down and churns the sea. While out in a fishing boat, the disciples looked around for Jesus assuming He was awake, and they found Him asleep in the stern. Mark 4:37–40 says, "And there arose a great storm of wind, and the waves beat into the ship, so that it was now full. And he was in the hinder part of the ship, asleep on a pillow: and they awake him, and say unto him, Master, carest thou not that we perish? And he arose, and rebuked the wind, and said unto the sea, Peace, be still. And the wind ceased, and there was a great calm. And he said unto them, Why are ye so fearful? How is it that ye have no faith?"

If you were in the boat with the disciples, I promise you would think the problem was the storm. The disciples thought the problem was the storm. The waves lashed up the sides of the boat, and the wind blew so hard they thought they were going to be blown into the sea. The water poured into the vessel and filled it up. If we were in that boat, we'd be trying to figure out an exit strategy real fast.

But when Jesus woke up, He quickly identified the problem. He said, "Why are you so fearful? You have little faith."

The problem wasn't the storm. The trouble was the disciples' lack of faith.

Often as pastors, leaders, and members of our church, we might think our predicament is the opposition, the critical spirit that some people can have, or financial issues. But the real problem is our lack of faith and our failure to understand His grace. We have a big God who can do mighty miracles. I can't look back on my life without seeing His strong hand on every aspect of our church life. This doesn't mean the ministry is an easy stroll along a fishing pier. On the contrary, the ministry is one of the hardest jobs in the world. But our Lord has promised us that He will guide us, He will strengthen us, and He will help us.

Hope for Your Church

Churches are going through difficult times. Pastors, leaders, and members need to know from the Word of God how to fight the good fight of faith.

"I was caught like a deer in the headlights," the pastor explained to my friend, Pastor David Bauer, of Bible Related Ministries. "Neither I nor the board knew what to do with the loudly complaining couple in my office."[ii]

Trouble in a church can come unexpectedly, without warning, and at the most inopportune time. When a loud, accusing person addresses a pastor or board member, sometimes a pastor feels intimidated or unprepared to deal with the out-of-control person.

In another congregation, one of the main families lost their aunt to a heart attack while the uncle lay at death's door. Another family found out their oldest daughter was an alcoholic and a newly married couple almost got divorced, all in the same week.

One pastor in the inner city continues to love and help his congregation although people are leaving in drastic numbers due to the high crime levels. He is discouraged and wonders why God hasn't called him to an easier type of church. He has to pay precious money from the church budget for a high-tech security system so they aren't vandalized on a regular basis.

I've also recently heard of a critical church board which launched an all-out assault on their pastor and his family. Many new members had joined without being aware of what was going on in the congregation. Now they are grieving for their departed pastor and don't know what to do.

The life of a church isn't a sprint. It's a marathon. As a body of believers, we can use all the spiritual Gatorade we can get. That's the purpose of *Finish Strong*: to give you a sense of confident expectation that God wants to work in your church and in your life.

According to George Barna in the "State of the Church" Report, pastoring is not an easy job.

"The typical senior pastor works 55–60 hours per week, often working under high pressure and with limited resources at his disposal. Pastors are constantly on-call, often sacrifice time with family to tend to congregational crises, carry long-term debt from the cost of seminary, and generally receive below-average compensation for performing a difficult job. Trained in theology, they are expected to master leadership, politics, finance, management, psychology, and conflict resolution. Sometimes it seems miraculous that we have anyone left in the pastorate!"[iii]

Friend, do you feel like some of the pastors and their church members that I mentioned earlier?

You want to see your church finish strong, but you might wonder if that is possible. I want to share with you that all things are possible with our great God. As a child I didn't understand that. I thought it was impossible to go to Heaven. But God in His great mercy brought people into my life who shared the gospel with me.

Maybe right now you need to look back at your own salvation experience. When did you first understand what Jesus did for you? Who was instrumental in sharing that message? When we understand the need for the clear gospel and how to walk in the grace of God every day, we experience victory instead of discouragement. God labors through His people in the local church. He works in mighty ways greater than we could ever ask or think. The church is at a crisis point. There's no need to go through the vicious, spiritual cycle. There is hope for every person and for every church.

Finish Line Strategies

- God doesn't give us grace to put into our pockets. Rather, He gives us grace as we need it. As you minister to people, remember God will give you the grace you need. Maybe you don't know what to say to the person who hurt you, or to the disgruntled member who can't be pleased, or to the backsliding family member. God will give you the grace to know what to say and strength as you say it.

- Remember Jesus told us to speak the truth in love. I titled a sermon years ago, "Truthing It in Love." I know the grammar isn't perfect, but it makes a great point. When we speak the truth, we need to also share how much we love that person.

- You won't have strong friendships unless you spend time with your friends. In the same way, you won't have a strong relationship with Christ if you don't spend a lot of time with Him. As a preacher, lay leader, church member, or believer, I'm sure you already know this. And yet, how easy it is to not be as close to Him when life gets busy. What are some practical ways you can spend more time with the Lord? Can you put Bibles in every room so you can always pick one up and read it? Can you install a Bible app on your phone? Whatever your method, commit to spending more time learning about God's grace.

Chapter 3
Hope No Matter What

Be of good courage, and he shall strengthen your heart, all ye that hope in the LORD.
Psalm 31:24

That day the steel beam bent like cooked spaghetti, I needed to remember that the Christian life was a marathon. Instead, I felt like I was at Mile 25 and couldn't muster another step forward. I had hit the wall.

The workers and men from our church gathered around me. They had gone through so much for the Lord. They had suffered by coming out every evening and every Saturday to work. I knew we had to have a breakthrough. We needed help—the supernatural kind. My limited resources meant nothing. The only kind of help that mattered came from God.

God never runs out of strength. I knew this from long years in the ministry, being a pastor, starting a church, going to Bible college, and receiving God's call on my life. I knew God had done much for us in the past.

At that moment, I chose to trust He would continue the work He had started.

This decision wasn't based on my strength, because I knew I didn't have any. The workers around me didn't have any.

Everyone gathered around. I addressed the workers. "Men, I want all of you to get alone. Go to a place on this building site where you can be totally by yourself. I want you to pray like you've never prayed before. I want you to ask God to show us what we need to do to lift this beam."

The workers nodded. Their faces were drawn and serious. They walked to different parts of the concrete. My foreman, Pastor Paul Julian, and my son, Pastor Jim Scudder, went off separately to pray. The other supervisors and pastors went off to pray.

My job was to direct the lift —
but this was the time to ask
God for strength.

Then I was alone by the beams. They screamed as they reminded me of all my past failures.

All I could do was pray.

So that was what I did.

"Lord, I know You are in control. I know that the situation seems hopeless and there is no way we can get this huge beam up in the air. I know that through Your strength no situation is ever hopeless. You have proven that to me time and time again. So I am asking You for wisdom. I am asking You to show us what to do. You said in James 1:5, 'If any of you lack wisdom, let him ask of God, that giveth to all men liberally, and upbraideth not; and it shall be given him.'

"Lord, I lack wisdom right now. But You have promised in Your Word that You will give it to me when I ask. So we are asking right now. We are asking for You to show us what to do."

I knew He would answer.

But it sure felt hopeless.

The Road to Hope

Imagine how the followers of Jesus felt after He died. They felt more hopeless than I did when the beam bent. Here they had walked and talked with the Son of God for three years. They stayed with Him and camped out with Him like I did with my friends by the creek. They loved Him with everything they had.

Then the most terrible thing happened: Their friend was killed. In the most cruel way possible, crucifixion. Branded a liar, He died with common thieves. Most of the disciples ran for their lives. I hate to say it, but I probably would have been right there with them. If you were being totally honest, you would most likely have run with them as well.

But more than that, their Messiah was dead. What were they supposed to do now? How were they supposed to go on? You may have felt this feeling, too. I know I have—but never to this degree. Picture two of the disciples—not part of the twelve disciples that we hear about, but two others who weren't as well-known. They had followed Jesus as much as the others. They had loved Him as much as the others. But now their Savior was dead. Their Friend was gone. And they didn't know how to keep going.

Only a week before, life was wonderful. Their long-awaited Messiah rode into Jerusalem on a donkey, a fulfillment of an ancient prophecy. The crowds shouted, "Hosanna! Blessed is He who comes in the name of the Lord!" Everyone cheered and laughed for joy. The Jewish people would get out from under Roman oppression. They would be able to live peaceful lives now that the Romans would be kicked out of their land.

But now, their Messiah had been killed. Their hope was gone.

The two disciples talked about all of these things as they walked toward their hometown of Emmaus. They hardly noticed when a third man joined them. He asked what they were talking about and seemed genuinely concerned about their well-being. The disciples told him about what had happened, how their Messiah had died.

They were surprised when the third man told them of even more prophecies that Jesus had fulfilled. They listened carefully, finding their hearts strangely stirred. They had thought their souls were dead and hope was gone. Human hope is a fragile thing. When it withers, it is hard to resurrect. But now, somehow, there was something different.

Luke 24:28–33 tells us what happened next.

"And they drew nigh unto the village, whither they went: and he made as though he would have gone further. But they constrained him, saying, Abide with us: for it is toward evening, and the day is far spent. And he went in to tarry with them. And it came to pass, as he sat at meat with them, he took bread, and blessed it, and brake, and gave to them. And their eyes were opened, and they knew him; and he vanished out of their sight. And they said one to another, Did not our heart burn within us, while he talked with us by the way, and while he opened to us the scriptures? And they rose up the same hour, and returned to Jerusalem, and found the eleven gathered together, and them that were with them."

They had hope. Their Messiah was alive. Their perspective had changed forever. I knew that day when we needed to lift the steel beam that I needed hope most of all. And I already had it. Not the hope the world gives, where people say, "Oh, I hope that this will happen." But rather the biblical sense of hope. A confident expectation of good.

❧

The Revival

In spite of thinking that I couldn't be good enough to go to Heaven, one time when I was about eleven years old I decided to give it an honest try. Famous evangelist Ford Philpot came to our town to do a series of meetings. He stayed at our house. Mom cooked wonderful meals of roast chicken, homemade noodles, and mashed potatoes for him. (There are no cooks like Kentucky cooks. Mom's noodles were full of flavor. Dad was a great cook, too. My parents have both passed away; but my

Evangelist Ford Philpot.

mom's sister, Lucille, is still alive and she makes the same recipe. When I see Aunt Lucille, before I even say hello I want to ask her when she is planning to make noodles for me. Instead, I refrain from bad manners and say hello first. Then I ask her about when she plans to make her noodles.)

Ford was one of the great preachers of his time. When he preached at my dad's Methodist church, he could make Hell so real that I definitely did not want to go there.

I distinctly remember that I sat on the right side of the sanctuary, about three-quarters of the way back. I did not want to go to the place that burned forever and ever and where the worm died not. He said if you don't come forward, you may never have a chance again to go to Heaven.

While I doubt Evangelist Philpot meant that coming forward was the only way to go to Heaven, I knew I did not want to go to Hell. My friends would laugh at me if I went forward. It is tough being a preacher's kid because of the pressure to be perfect. But I didn't care. I came forward and kneeled at the altar. I cried, I wept, I begged for Christ to save me; but I didn't really understand what I was saying. I didn't recognize the fact of Jesus' death on the cross for my sins or His resurrection from the dead which proved my sins were paid. While I'm sure the evangelist said this information, that part of his message didn't reach into my brain.

Going home that night, I was glad I finally could go to Heaven. My father and I went out with Evangelist Philpot that night, but neither one of them asked me about my experience at the altar. That night, I got down on my knees to pray. I don't know why I did this as a child, but I always did. I kept doing this pretty much every night, even through high school. I told God I wanted to go to Heaven and live a perfect life; but by the next morning the more I tried to have good thoughts, the more bad thoughts came into my head. By the end of that day, I knew I couldn't go to Heaven, so I might as well live it up before I died and went to Hell.

Invitations at church services can be confusing to people. One preacher said to his congregation that they had to come forward to go to Heaven. He later said on the radio that people could get saved in their cars or at home. The truth is, we can get saved no matter where we are. There are some people who are so shy they would never come forward in a service, raise their hand, stand up, or do anything publicly to indicate they trusted Christ. Does this mean they aren't saved? Of course not. As long as they understand that Jesus Christ died for their sins and rose again and that they can't contribute one bit to their own salvation through their own works, they can know they are going to Heaven.

Unfortunately, I didn't understand this at that revival, and I didn't get saved that day.

I stopped trying. I continued to hate church; and I kept marking imaginary X's on the walls of the church building, awaiting the moment when I could get out and be on my own doing what I wanted to do. But since I was still young and in my parent's house, it would be years before I could stop attending.

✵

No Secret What God Can Do

I met Stuart Hamblen, the composer of the song, "It Is No Secret What God Can Do," during a camp meeting in Wilmore, Kentucky. Hamblen wrote the song after John Wayne asked him about the change he saw in his life.

"Did you get religion?" John Wayne asked.

"It is no secret what God can do in a man's life," Hamblen replied.

"That sounds like a song," John Wayne said, planting the idea in the composer's mind.

When I got saved, I found it is no secret what God can do in you and in your church. In fact, my opinion of the church drastically changed after my salvation.

Singer Stuart Hamblen.

As we see the crumbling world around us and the crazy things people are doing, we should remember God can do amazing things in a life, and that should give us hope. Do you question whether you can have a godly family and kids that turn out for the Lord Jesus Christ? Do you observe what is happening, the attacks on Christianity, the terrible crimes, the shootings? Do you see what is occurring in our churches where pastors are falling into sin, members are doing wrong things, and people aren't living in unity but are backbiting and hurting each other instead?

The sad state of the Body of Christ today doesn't have to frustrate you. Remember Romans 5:20 says, "Moreover the law entered, that the offence might abound. But where sin abounded, grace did much more abound."

Where there is sin, there is hardship, frustration, disunity, and no hope for the future. But in these hopeless places is exactly where God wants to work. In the darkest place, in the most difficult of times, He wants to work through His mighty Church. He wants to give you the same encouragement that He gave to me on that day when we had to figure out how to lift the beams.

Do you wish to learn about grace today? Do you want to discover more insights on how to keep your church and your life vibrant and alive? Are you facing some situations like the ones I described earlier? Perhaps you are facing circumstances that are even worse, or possibly not as bad. Know this: God wants to work through you and your church.

Trust Him to give you hope for the marathon of the Christian life. Take a moment to pray, "Lord, I don't know how You can move through what I'm going through, but I trust You. I trust Your power and Your strength, even when it feels hopeless."

Don't give up, fellow racer. Help is on the way. Hope in Him.

Finish Line Strategies

What do you do when you run out of hope as a pastor, as a member, or as a worker? Here are some practical things that have helped me when a situation looks bleak:

- Write down the worst thing that can happen. I know it sounds crazy, but it works. This is a tried-and-true tactic that I have used for years. Write what is really bothering you, the worst possible scenario. You might find out when you see the "worst thing" in black and white that, while it isn't a great outcome, God will help you handle it better than you think you can.

- Remember ultimately the worst thing that could happen to a believer is to die and go to Heaven. This gives you perspective when you're going through hard times.

- Do the hardest thing that you have to do in a situation first thing in the morning. Don't put it off. It will only get more difficult and more frustrating the longer you procrastinate.

- Pray. This is obvious, but sometimes we get so caught up in a situation we forget to regularly talk to God about it.

- Seek the counsel of other godly believers. Call a pastor you trust. Talk to him. Don't be afraid to say something because you think you know what that person is going to say. Instead, trust that he has wisdom. Talking it out will give you perspective and strength.

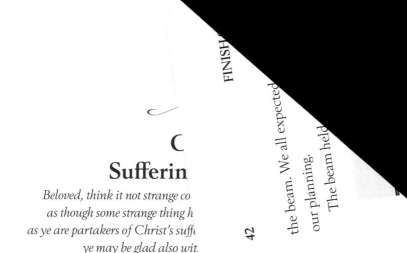

C

Sufferin

Beloved, think it not strange co
as though some strange thing h
as ye are partakers of Christ's suff
ye may be glad also wit

FINISH

the beam. We all expected
our planning.
The beam held

42

The cold wind whipped across　　　　　　　　　.. beams were just as large. The steel beams came in four sections each, for a total length of 120 feet. Assembled, they formed a V shape like the roof they would support. But I had great peace that we could get these lifted. Our group came back together from prayer. The workers studied the problem together. Since the beam was attached to the crane cable at the center and to two other points on either side, when it was lifted, the center cable would lose its tension because the peak was higher than the rest. The sheer weight of the steel meant the beam would twist as it lifted.

A church member had an idea: we could use several come-alongs at the center point of the crane's cable attachment to shorten the distance of the center point until the beam could be lifted completely vertical. Workers raced to the store to get more come-alongs.

After we had what we needed, we attached two come-alongs to the

The solution came from above — use come-alongs to shorten the center point!

center attachment point; and then with a deep breath and another prayer for continued guidance, I gave the order to lift the beam.

Our hearts were in our throats with fear. The crane slowly lifted

it to twist like cooked spaghetti in spite of all

steady.

A real miracle — 1st beam up and steady!

One of the workers cheered, but we were all afraid to applaud with him. We didn't want to celebrate too soon. We had a long way to get the beam to its proper position. For the next hour we lifted that beam, adjusting the come-alongs as it went up.

Finally, the beam was set. But it was still in an extremely dangerous position since it didn't have anything to attach to. We used steel cables and even more come-alongs attached from the ground to the beam to secure it before detaching the crane. Then we started with another beam, using the same procedure to lift it. Four hours later we had it in the right position, where we secured it to the first beam.

The two beams used their strength to support each other and held together in an amazing way. We all cheered. It was time for celebration. No more worries at that point. The beams had gotten up safely. We worried that it might take all winter to set the beams, but none of us cared. We knew that God had answered our prayer in a huge, miraculous way that still brings tears to my eyes when I think about it. God had come through. He had given us wisdom. He had given us His grace. He would help us finish strong.

Grace Revealed

During the 40th Anniversary celebration of Quentin Road Bible Baptist Church, my son, Pastor Jim Scudder, engineered and built a special display in the hallway of the church. The display was about Israel. It had a special scroll copied meticulously from the book of Isaiah. Jim did all of this as a surprise for me. He had to get the work done on the display when I was out of town. He had only a few days to get it on the wall, and worked feverishly to get it done. On the day of the 40th celebration, he brought me out to the hallway to show me the display. When I got there, I saw a huge sheet hanging on the wall. But then Jim took down the sheet. I saw the beautiful work he had done, the lovely stones from Jerusalem, the wonderful scroll, the artifacts from the land of Israel, and the mural of the Holy City. I wanted to leap for joy. I gave a little shout and went up to the wall to see it closer up. It was beautiful.

This is a small fraction of how I felt the day I learned about God' grace.

God revealed to me something of inestimable value. Except the difference is that my son wanted to keep the display a secret until the time it needed to be revealed. God wanted me to know about grace as soon as I was old enough to understand it.

Sadly, that didn't happen.

As you know from the last chapter, I went through my young years completely sure I was going straight to Hell, and there was nothing I could do to stop this terrible thing from happening.

During school, my teachers tried to help me, but I hated school even more than I hated church. And since I've already told you about how much I hated church, you can imagine how much I hated school. After one move, the school I was supposed to attend offered kindergarten; but at that time, it was optional. I didn't want to go to school one more day than

I absolutely had to, so I refused to go. This decision probably hurt me academically for the rest of my life. I didn't like anything that restricted me and kept me from fishing, hunting, and building forts in the woods.

I committed one of my earliest sins in first grade. I walked into the classroom and saw a trinket sitting on one of the kids' desks. It looked so cool sitting there, so shiny and pretty. I honestly don't remember what it was, but I knew one thing: I wanted it for myself. None of the kids was in the classroom, so I strolled over to the girl's desk and swiped the trinket into my pocket. I sauntered to my desk and sat down as all the kids flooded into the room after recess.

I secretly congratulated myself at my stealth and amazing ability to steal as everyone settled into their seats. Then the girl raised her hand. "Teacher," she said, "I had a trinket on my desk. It was brand new, and I can't find it. Someone must have stolen it."

My heart sped up. *Oh no, she noticed it was missing.* I forced myself to sit still so I wouldn't reveal I had the trinket.

The teacher got a stern look on her face. "Stand up and get in line. I want each of you to show me your pockets. I will not tolerate having a thief in this classroom."

The room got so quiet you could have heard an ant crawling along the baseboard. My hands felt cold and clammy as I slowly stood and got into the line. Now what was I going to do? Maybe I'd try to slip the trinket back on the girl's desk without her seeing it; but she sat there, her pigtails sticking out of her head with her hands folded on her desk. She would notice if I tried to do that.

Smarter than your average thief, my only option appeared before me: A chair stuck out into the aisle a little bit. I quickly bumped into the chair and fell onto the ground. I flipped the trinket out of my pocket as I fell.

"Oh, here is the trinket, Teacher. I got it." I picked it up and held it up to the teacher.

"Thank you, James," the teacher said, taking the item and giving it back to the little girl. I know the teacher was on to me, but she was probably glad that I returned it. I stopped my life of thievery at that moment. It wasn't worth the scary feeling in the pit of my stomach.

The only thing I steal now is pens — only I do it by accident. If someone wants me to sign something and they hand me a pen, I usually sign what that person wants me to sign; and then without thinking, I slip the pen into my pocket. When I get home, I find the pen and feel bad. But many times I don't see the person again and can't give it back.

Children (and adults, too) can know and understand that they are sinners. It is one of the great proofs that there is a God and that He designed and created us. He put in us an understanding of right and wrong from a young age. Psalm 69:5 states, "O God, thou knowest my foolishness; and my sins are not hid from thee." Our sins are not hidden from the Lord.

The Schoolmaster Taxi

Another time while walking to school, my friend said to me, "Let's play hooky today." This was very dangerous, since Mr. Brad Mutchler was the principal of Paducah Tilghman High School. He had been an All-Amer-

Bradford D. Mutchler

ican basketball player at Western Kentucky University and a member of their hall of fame. When he spoke, the entire school listened; we had such respect for him.[iv] (More on this story later.)

Once Mr. Mutchler called over the loud speaker, "James Allen Scudder, come to the office immediately." My heart rose into my throat. When I arrived at the office, he was holding my report card.

"James, your grades are terrible. What are you doing?"

I couldn't answer. I was too terrified.

"You aren't studying. You will

start studying and bring your grades up."

Trembling, I made my way out of his office and determined immediately to give up watching *Bonanza* on Sunday evenings and start studying. I did a little better after that, but my grades were never too great. Still, I respected Mr. Mutchler so much. He passed away at age 90 in 2004; but if I ever had another chance to meet him, I promise you that my knees would tremble.

Schools could paddle their students then. The teachers would take the kids out into the hallway, and I could hear the whistle of the paddle and the thump as students got in trouble. I was determined to try to be a good student when I heard those sounds.

(Now back to my story...) For some reason, the day my friend suggested playing hooky, I went along with it. We snuck out the end door of the school and went to a small, neighborhood grocery store about two blocks away. We called a taxi from the store.

We waited outside the store, ready to jump in the taxi the moment it arrived. Soon enough, there came the taxi. We sprinted to the back of the vehicle, opened the door, and slid inside. There were only two seats in the back. A woman occupied one of the seats. We took a closer look, and almost fainted. She was one of our teachers, a former Miss Kentucky. She looked over at us, and her brow furrowed. "Where are you two boys going?" she asked.

Definitely one of the smarter boys among my friends, I quickly said, "We're going to school."

"To school? It's only two blocks away."

I'm sure that teacher was thinking we had to be some of the laziest kids she'd ever known, but that day I had to go to school. Otherwise, the teacher would alert the truant officer.

The Bible uses the term for truant officer when it speaks about the Law. Galatians 3:24 states, "Wherefore the law was our schoolmaster to bring us unto Christ, that we might be justified by faith."

The Law alerts us to the severity of our sins and shows us our need for a Savior. The knowledge of my sins weighed heavily on my heart, even as a young boy. I knew the Ten Commandments and other parts of the Bible. I knew about good things I should be doing. But I didn't realize that the Law was given so I would know of my need for a Savior.

At Paducah Tilghman, I attended high school with nine merit finalists. I still hated this school, but it was a better school than some of the others I had attended. I applied for the Key Club, but couldn't make it in because of my grades. That was a huge disappointment to me.

But on the bright side, I had a debate teacher who was a wonderful help during my high school years. I also had a teacher who had us all read a passage and then vote for who did the best job. The students voted for someone else, but then the teacher said something I will never forget: "You voted for the wrong person. James Scudder has the best voice."

Paducah Sun Democrat, January 24th, 1963.

TILGHMAN DEBATE WINNERS—Top students of debate at Tilghman took second place at the Daviess County invitational debate tournament Jan. 19. Robert L. Flowers, right, took the trophy for being the "best debator of the tournament." All in all it was a very successful venture for the local school. Shown from left to right are Richard Burrill, James Scudder, Harley Jones and Robert Flowers.

You could have knocked me over with a ruler. I was stunned she thought that. Teachers should never underestimate the effect they can have in a young person's life. That teacher will never know how much of an encouragement she was to me and how often I remember her support.

As a pastor, are you a help to others like the teacher who encouraged me? As a lay leader, do you take the time to encourage your pastor? One of the best ways to get through difficult times is to encourage others. Maybe you don't feel like encouraging others. Instead, you wish others would encourage you. May I plead with you to remember that when you give others a kind word, your own spirits will be lifted?

Belinda had a family which constantly criticized her when she was growing up. She was a straight-"A" student, lettered in two sports, and earned a full scholarship. In spite of this, her mom and dad never gave her a word of encouragement. They felt if they ever told her she was doing well, she would become complacent and stop doing so well. Belinda determined she would not be that kind of person. She started attending church during college and helping out in the AWANA programs. She was put with the junior high girls; and she quickly saw that if any age needed encouragement, it was that age. She started to write short notes of encouragement to the girls. The junior high girls started to invite their friends to AWANA and soon the group had to move to a bigger room. All the girls would gather around Belinda every week for their dose of encouragement.

Belinda didn't let the fact that her parents never encouraged her keep her from encouraging others. We need to do the same thing. When we take time to think about others and what they are going through, we will feel better knowing we are making a difference in their lives.

❦

Are You an Encourager?

Missionaries Robert and Mary Moffat labored in Bechuanaland (now called Botswana) for ten years. They couldn't report a single person trusting Christ. The mission directors began to question the wisdom of them continuing to work in this country. But the couple didn't want to leave the work. They knew God was with them and they would soon see people come to the Lord. They kept going on in spite of great hardship.

One day, Mary received a letter from a dear friend in England saying she wanted to send them a gift. What did they think they needed? Mary wrote that she would most like a communion set because she was sure they would need it soon, although no one had yet trusted Christ.

Soon, a group of six converts united to form the first Christian church in that land. The communion set from England was delayed in the mail, but on the very day before the first commemoration of the Lord's Supper in Bechuanaland, the set arrived.[v]

Robert and Mary Moffat's daughter eventually married David Livingstone, the famous missionary to Africa.

Sometimes you have to keep going even when the way seems bleak. There might not be much encouragement from the situation you are facing. You might feel like Robert and Mary Moffat. Or maybe you were fortunate like I was and had a teacher who told you that you had something special to contribute.

How do you keep going even when you feel like quitting? How do you hang in there when you'd rather stop?

Only one person can give you true encouragement: the Lord Jesus Christ. He is the One who called you to the church you are in. He is the One who called you to the situation you are facing.

Kentucky's Lincoln

A young Midwestern lawyer suffered from such deep depression that his friends thought it best to keep all knives and razors out of his reach. He questioned his life's calling and the prudence of even attempting to follow it through. During this time he wrote, "I am now the most miserable man living. Whether I shall ever be better, I cannot tell. I awfully forebode I shall not." Somehow, Abraham Lincoln received the encouragement he needed. He led the nation through one of the roughest times in history with great courage and devotion.[vi]

The encouragement you need might not be right in front of you. It might be a little way down the road. It might take time for you to see the fruit of what you are doing. But I want to encourage you most of all, don't quit.

Throughout the years, I've encouraged my people with the saying, "After the testing comes the blessing."

I don't use this saying in a trite way. I'm not even going to say, "Come on, get over how you are feeling."

You will feel discouraged. This is a normal part of ministry. God allows testing to come into our lives, helps us get through that testing, and then blesses us for getting through it.

The blessing may not come until Heaven, but what a wonderful thing that will be. The Apostle Peter is one of my favorite disciples. In my book, *Beyond Failure*, I go in depth about Peter and all that he went through in his life. I love Peter because he was an impulsive follower of Jesus. He constantly had what I call foot-in-mouth disease, where he would say whatever came to his mind. But at the end of his life when he wrote 1 and 2 Peter, he had a lot to say about trials. He writes, "Beloved, think it not strange concerning the fiery trial which is to try you, as though some strange thing happened unto you: But rejoice, inasmuch as ye are partakers of Christ's sufferings; that, when his glory shall be revealed, ye may be glad also with exceeding joy." 1 Peter 4:12–13

It's not easy to rejoice when trials come and things get hard; but when we do, God reveals His glory through us.

Is the fiery trial you are in overwhelming you? Do you wonder how much more frustration you have to go through before you experience victory in your Christian life? Dear friend, I encourage you to rejoice even in the middle of what you are facing. This has been difficult for me to learn in my own Christian life, but it is an important principle. When we learn how to give thanks even when things are difficult, we discover a Heavenly vantage point. Our hard times may never make sense on this earth; but we can rest fully, knowing that one day we will understand.

Are you suffering? Surely you are. Everyone who is involved in ministry suffers. You suffer for a purpose. Ask God to give you encouragement as you go through hard times. And also ask God to reveal His glory through your circumstances.

> **Finish Line Strategies**
> - Where are you at in your place of suffering? Take a moment to write down the top two things that you are facing right now.
> - Remember that our great God will be with you in your deepest suffering. You may not feel like it now; but eventually, you'll look back at the things you wrote down and see how God has taken you through them. I promise you this is true. God specializes in making the impossible possible.

Chapter 5
Detours Are Good

Seemeth it but a small thing unto you, that the God of Israel hath separated you from the congregation of Israel, to bring you near to himself to do the service of the tabernacle of the LORD, and to stand before the congregation to minister unto them?
Numbers 16:9

The houses cost $50 each. While walking home from my summer job at Bob's Dairy Queen, I saw the houses for $50. The owner wanted them torn down because they weren't livable. I decided to buy one at 16 years old.

Bob's Dairy Queen — Paducah, KY.

On the lawn, I put out signs that said, "Hardwood Floors $300," "Cabinets $100," "Fixtures $50," and so on. Over the next few weeks, people came and took out the hardwood floors, cabinets, fixtures, and other things, paying me for each item. Soon, I had made a whole lot of money. When a local restaurant called "The Chef's Hat" became available, I went to the owner and inquired about the price. He sold me the restaurant for $5,000. One lady would bring in 25 lemon meringue pies every morning, and I would sell out before noon. Since we sold a lot of eggs and hash browns, I bought large, oblong plates and put toast at either end so that the breakfast special really looked like the customer was getting something for their money. It was great fun running the restaurant.

One day, I got a call from a state agent who asked me if I planned on paying sales tax. I didn't even know what that was. He said, "Did you know you are the youngest restaurant owner in the state of Kentucky?" I didn't know that, either. I'd already sold the restaurant by the time I had talked to him, so he said not to worry about the sales tax.

I never thought of the work I was doing as work at all. I actually thought of it as tons of fun. Making money made every drop of sweat worth it. I would also go for summers to my brother-in-law's farm in Oklahoma. He would let me drive a huge tractor across the field for 12 hours at a time. We would fuel the tractor in the field and keep the tractor going every day, all day long during harvest. It was one of the best times in my life. Even though Oklahoma was hot in the summer and it was hard work, I enjoyed doing it. I loved that my brother-in-law trusted me enough to allow me to run the tractor. I truly looked up to him and respected him. He and my sister, Pauline, were great influences in my life.

I bought three plots of land and put a road into the woods so they could be accessed. A gravel company needed the lots for storage, so they bought them from me. With the profit from that sale, I was able to purchase some land that had many feet of shoreline on Kentucky Lake. We built a cabin there. Eventually the governor of Kentucky, Julian Carroll, bought the cabin from us. With that profit, Mom and Dad were able to retire to Florida.

Now it was time to go to college, and I decided to actually start studying. No one was more surprised than I was to get "A's." Actually, I probably liked college because I only had to go to school for a short time each day, and could even skip classes as long as I knew the material for the test. After

Scudder Is Elected By Circle K Group

James Scudder, 170 Fairview Ave., is the new governor of Circle K Clubs of Kentucky and Tennessee.

He was elected Saturday afternoon.

Winners of various offices were not announced until the group held the final session of its two-day convention here.

Scudder, 19, a sophomore at Paducah Junior College, is the son of the Rev. and Mrs. I. J. Scudder. The father is pastor of Lone Oak Methodist Church.

Scudder is a native of Ashland. He has been a resident of Paducah for six years, coinciding with the time his father transferred to the Paducah district of the Methodist Church.

Other officers elected were James Barnett, Pikeville Junior College, treasurer, and Bob Pruitt, University of Tennessee, secretary. Jesse Jones, Paducah, was elected an international trustee and Danny Kreutzer, Paducah, was the winner of a speech contest.

More than 100 young men attended the two-day session. They heard U.S. Sen. John S.

Cooper speak about Viet Nam and heard addresses from various leading officials of the Kentucky-Tennessee district of Kiwanis, the sponsoring group for Circle K.

Front Page
Paducah Sun Democrat.

attending junior college for two years, I began attending the University of Kentucky. I loved their basketball team and still do to this day. We would go to games and shout ourselves hoarse cheering. I enjoyed learning about political science the most, deciding to make my career in politics. I became involved with our Circle K and was elected as Kentucky-Tennessee Circle K governor in 1966–1967. During that time, I got acquainted with Senator John Sherman Cooper, who came to speak at one of our rallies; and I was able to spend the entire day with him.

Thank you letter from me to US Senator John S. Cooper.

May 11 1966

```
Senator John Sherman Cooper
U.S.Senate Office Building
Washington, D.C.

Dear Senator Cooper:

    I was very happy to receive your nice letter.  Our Circle K Club
wishes me to express our deep gratitude for your visit with us, and
for the wonderful talk you brought to the convention.  It was most
timely and everyone was delighted with it.

    The convention was very successful, at least for me, as I was honor-
ed by being elected governor of the Kentucky-Tennessee District.

    If there is anything I can do to help you in your campaign I will
be glad to do it.


                    Sincerely,



                    Jim Scudder
```

My friend, Jesse Jones, ran for International Trustee of Circle K while I was the Kentucky-Tennessee Governor. We drove to Dallas, Texas, for the convention. I planned to help him get elected. Jesse was one of the most studious people I'd ever met. Unfortunately, he lost the race. On the way home, I could tell Jesse was down, so I said I would buy him the biggest steak in Texas to cheer him up. We stopped at a restaurant and ordered the largest steak on the menu, a 32-ounce porterhouse. They brought out our salads, and we ate them quickly. We were starving and really looking forward to a real Texas steak. But it was taking forever. After an hour, the waitress came out and apologized. She said she didn't know what was wrong, but they couldn't get the steak cooked. She asked us if we wanted to come see the steak. We agreed and came back to the kitchen. A massive steak sat on the grill. It had bubbles coming out of it. They had cooked it for a long time, but it just wouldn't cook through. Probably no one had ordered that huge steak for a long time, and it had marinated for too long. We went back to our seats. They didn't charge us for the salad. As we left, Jesse said, "I can't get elected. I can't even order a steak in Texas."

The next year, I ran for International Trustee and got elected.[vii] Poor Jesse.

Kiwanis Circle K International Trustees in Chicago, IL.

We Need a Preacher

My roommate Charlie Saladino and I had determined we would never pledge to join the fraternity. Because of my involvement in Circle K and him being the student body president, the fraternity invited us to join.

When Charlie told me we didn't have to pledge, I said, "That's great. And we'll get pledges to torment next year." Sad how the human mind works.

Circle K provided an office and a secretary for me in the student union campus. One day, the Methodist district superintendent (fortunately, this wasn't the one who drank the Tabasco sauce) came to see me in my office.

He asked something that really surprised me.

"I would like for you to be the preacher of a church."

My jaw dropped, "Preach at a church? I promise you don't want me to do that."

"I want you to do more than preach at a church. I want you to be the preacher at a church."

I didn't know what to say. Did this man know how I was living? I could promise him that there was no way I could take a job like that. I wasn't living right. To put it bluntly, I was living like the devil himself. On top of everything, I hated church and had decided never to go to church when I was in college.

The one time I had broken that promise, I regretted it for months. Feeling guilty about never attending church, I went once on a Sunday on campus, and the visiting preacher talked about being a good student. I wanted

nothing to do with that message, so I never went back.

I had known the district superintendent for many years. He knew my great-grandfather had started a college in College Hill, Kentucky. He wanted me to take the church in this picturesque town.

"You would be a perfect fit because of your name," he said. Then he mentioned the salary. It was a pretty good number.

"You would only need to preach three times a week, and there is a parsonage you could live in. There's a garden out there with fully grown vegetables ready to harvest."

So against my better judgment, I

accepted the offer and started preaching.

Nothing is worse than preaching when you are not saved.

Little did I know I'd agreed to something that would change the course of my life.

Detours

What kind of detours has God brought into your life? Has He brought an alternative route like the one when I was asked to preach? Have they been good detours for you? Or have they turned out badly? I've been surprised as I went through life how many times a detour turned out to be far more than I ever dreamed possible.

Sometimes when my wife Linda and I are driving, we'll see a detour sign. The road is closed for construction. We have to alter our course and figure out another way to get to our destination. But what if you chose to take a detour and then when you got around the situation, you found another detour? A path you didn't know about.

One morning, a man named Balaam rode his donkey to visit the King of Moab. Understand that Balaam was not a good man to start out with. He was much like me the day I sat in my office at the university: he was set on going his own way in his own time. He was going to visit the king because the king wanted to use him to curse Israel. Balaam was known as a sort of sorcerer who had special powers, so the King of Moab wanted to use his power to make Israel suffer. But Balaam wasn't an all-bad guy. He did believe in the God of Israel as the only true God. He just didn't want to do anything to help God or His people—to the point that he was willing to curse them.

Imagine Balaam as he rides to his destination. Maybe it is in the spring, when even the desert has some green on it. A perfect day to take a drive out into the country. (My daughter, Julie, lives in Ohio in a very hilly area. She would definitely prefer to drive a car in the country than ride a donkey.) But cars hadn't been invented yet, so Balaam is stuck on his donkey. They travel to a place where a stone wall is on the side of the road.

The donkey stops. Balaam almost falls off, but in the nick of time grabs hold of the donkey's mane. Unable to go forward, Balaam kicks the donkey. The donkey doesn't move. He slaps the donkey. Nothing.

Balaam strikes the donkey, but the stubborn animal won't go forward. He strikes harder; and the donkey leans against the wall, pushing Balaam's foot against it.

"Ouch! You dumb animal!" says the exasperated Balaam. "That hurts!"

Looks like his trip is about over. But that can't be possible. It is almost like the donkey has been stopped by something. Its eyes are big like it has seen a ghost.

Because it has.

A spirit.

An angel.

A divine detour. Much like the one my life was about to take. Let's look at what happens next. Numbers 22:26–35 says,

"And the angel of the LORD went further, and stood in a narrow place, where was no way to turn either to the right hand or to the left. And when the donkey saw the angel of the LORD, she fell down under Balaam: and Balaam's anger was kindled, and he smote the donkey with a staff. And the LORD opened the mouth of the donkey, and she said unto Balaam, What have I done unto thee, that thou hast smitten me these three times? And Balaam said unto the donkey, Because thou hast mocked me: I would there were a sword in mine hand, for now would I kill thee. And the ass said unto Balaam, Am not I thine donkey, upon which thou hast ridden ever since I was thine unto this day? was I ever wont to do so unto thee? And he said, Nay. Then the LORD opened the eyes of Balaam, and he saw the angel of the LORD standing in the way, and his sword drawn in his hand: and he bowed down his head, and fell flat on his face. And the angel of the LORD said unto him, Wherefore hast thou smitten thine donkey these three times? behold, I went out to withstand thee, because thy way is perverse before me: And the donkey saw me, and turned from me these three times: unless she had turned from me, surely now also I had slain thee, and saved her alive. And Balaam said unto the angel of the LORD, I have sinned; for I knew not that thou stoodest in the way against me: now therefore, if it displease thee, I will get me back again. And the angel of the LORD said unto Balaam, Go with the men: but only the word that I shall speak unto thee, that thou shalt speak. So Balaam went with the princes of Balak."

Think about Balaam's surprise when the donkey talked to him. This is one of the most humorous stories in the Bible. (Anyone who tells you that a person shouldn't laugh when they are in church hasn't read the Bible. The Bible is full of humor. Jesus used humor. Think of Him saying that it is hard for a rich person to go to Heaven and comparing this to a camel going through the eye of a needle. [Now this isn't to say that a rich person can't go to Heaven, just that sometimes their riches might keep them from seeing the truth.] Picture a camel trying to get through the eye of a needle. Wouldn't you laugh if you saw a camel doing that? I know I would.)

But here is Balaam trying to go forward, and the donkey is talking to him and saying she won't go. Eventually Balaam realizes the problem and decides to do what God says. If Balaam hadn't had this detour, then there was no way that he would have been able to do the right thing. The circumstances in his life caused him to look at his life differently. Detours can do the same thing for you and for your church.

Your Personal Detour

Has God placed a detour in the path of your church? Maybe there is disunity right now, and some members are grumbling about the pastor. Believe it or not, this is common in churches. A church functions so much better when there is unity. Disunity definitely can keep people from hearing about the gospel, and that is sad. Maybe some people are saying the church isn't as friendly as it used to be, or people are posting on Facebook and other places bad things about the church. They are like Balaam. They believe in the God of the Bible, but have little use for Him in their own lives. They want their own way, and are even willing to curse the people of the church.

Balaam saw the truth because of divine intervention. God might be trying to reach those people in your congregation who are saying bad things about your church, but maybe they don't want to respond. They want to block God from being able to make a difference in their lives. The sad thing is, they can be especially hurtful to newer attendees of your church.

The truth about detours is this: they can be helpful. While some people may not respond positively to them, a detour for your church is always positive.

It may not seem positive. Like the day we tried to lift the steel beams and they bent like spaghetti. It can feel completely hopeless when a detour arrives.

And yet, those detours are often there to show your church a great truth. If you can stick it out and do what's right, you will see your congregation unified as a result of the detour. You will see great growth in your church in spite of the people who leave.

The Apostle Peter writes in 1 Peter 1:7, "That the trial of your faith, being much more precious than of gold that perisheth, though it be tried with fire, might be found unto praise and honour and glory at the appearing of Jesus Christ."

The detours of your faith mean God is still at work in your life. He will not stop working in your life. He will not stop helping you. He loves His Church. I want to encourage you to keep going. During my detours, God showed me His greatest power.

Have you allowed the detours to discourage you? Are you tempted to give up because of all the hard times that you've gone through? Maybe the backbiting in the church is reaching epic proportions, or someone who isn't the pastor wants to control the church. Perhaps you have family members who don't understand why you want to keep attending church. Do you need to remember detours can be made into good? Whatever the case, know this. God has allowed the trials you are going through, and He will help you get through them.

Just as He helped me in ways I never thought possible.

Finish Line Strategies

Here are some ways to be an encouragement to others when you are facing tough times:

- Pick up the phone and call someone who has helped you in the past. Let that person know that he or she was an encouragement to you and you appreciate them.
- Write a quick note or email to someone who is going through a difficult time.
- Witness to someone. This is a surefire way to get yourself excited again. It is one of the best pick-me-ups out there.
- My son, Jim, buys small items like balloons, plants, flowers, and more to give to people he visits in the nursing home. This is always an encouragement to them and to him as well.
- My daughter-in-law, Karen, is always thoughtful to others. She loves to help people and work behind the scenes to organize things in a wonderful way. She also speaks and ministers to women, and gives her all in everything she does. My granddaughters, Amy and Erica, both attend Dayspring Bible College, and they have the same kind of compassionate hearts. Being thoughtful on an ongoing basis means it is a part of your life. You will never know the good that it does for other people to be thoughtful towards them.
- From the pulpit, mention someone in the church who has been an encouragement and blessing to you.

- Don't be afraid to be honest about your feelings with the people you trust in your church. When they see you hurting, they will better know how to pray for you and encourage you. If you put up a front to them that you never get down, then don't be surprised when they don't encourage you.

- Don't take anything people say too seriously after you have preached. When you've given your all in the pulpit, you are often vulnerable and can take comments differently than people intended. I'm pretty sure that some people are wired to say hurtful things right after a preacher preaches. It is probably Satan's prime way to discourage a pastor for the next week. Pray before every handshake. This helps me a lot.

Chapter 6
The Light

For by grace are ye saved through faith; and that not of yourselves: it is the gift of God: Not of works, lest any man should boast. Ephesians 2:8–9

The day after the first beams were in place, I figured it would take all winter to get the rest of them set up. But the first two beams joined together helped the process of getting the other beams up. The next day we were able to get the rest of the beams up, and the crane operator ended up charging us for one day of work. He hadn't known how to help us the day before.

I love deals like that. I love a good deal, period. When my kids were younger, I was always looking for deals so we could all go out to eat on a budget. I found one place that had a huge salad bar and a cheap lunch special, so we would often go there. My kids still talk to this day about the fun we had together during those lunches.

But the best deal of my life came soon after I began preaching at the Methodist church as I attended the University of Kentucky. Oh, it didn't seem like a good deal at the time. In fact, it seemed like a pretty rotten agreement at first.

That's because when I got in the pulpit that first Sunday, I looked over the congregation and realized the UK Dean of Men, who had been the preacher a few years before me, attended that church.

That's right.

The Dean of Men.

The district superintendent had told me that the church was far enough away from the University of Kentucky that no one in the church would possibly know my current lifestyle.

He could report to the whole university that I was a preacher. Somehow I preached that first message. Actually, I opened my book of sermons and read the first one out loud. No one minded. They actually seemed to love it. My sermon was only fifteen minutes long; so that meant our church dismissed before the Baptists, and we could get to the restaurants first.

At least I was popular and didn't really have to study to make that happen. I continued to preach at that church, and kept living the way I wanted during the week; though I carefully avoided the Dean of Men when I was on campus.

In spite of my best efforts, one Sunday three guys showed up to hear me preach. Word must have been getting around campus that I was a preacher. By then I was getting pretty good at reading the sermons. I would even add my own thoughts once in awhile.

But that Sunday, I couldn't figure out why my three friends kept their heads down. They didn't make eye contact with me once during the service. Now after over 40 years of preaching, I can only imagine what they must have thought of my efforts; but at that time, ignorance was bliss. After the service, they came up and shook my hand, carefully avoiding saying anything about the message.

It must have been bad, I thought. *I must have preached a really bad message.* Even though I had hoped they were only praying during my preaching, I now knew from their downcast eyes that they thought the preaching had been pretty bad.

"Why don't you come up to the campus tonight? We have some people coming who we'd like for you to talk to," one of my friends asked.

"Sure. I'd be happy to," I said.

That night I went up to the dorms and met some men from Campus Crusade for Christ. They wasted no time. They quickly opened their Bibles and started to tell me about going to Heaven.

I tried to stop them. "Hey, I know all about this church stuff. In fact, I hated church as a child. I've decided that it isn't even worth it to try to go to Heaven."

"Then why are you preaching?"

I didn't want to answer them, since it sounded bad that I only did it for the salary and the parsonage.

They opened their Bibles and showed me that God's Word said I was a sinner. As you already know, I had come to realize this before. I'd discovered this on the day I came forward. I had found out that no matter what, I couldn't stop myself from sinning. I definitely couldn't earn Heaven on my own. I couldn't be perfect. They showed me some verses I hadn't heard before that said the same thing.

"Romans 3:23 states, 'For all have sinned, and come short of the glory of God.'

"Romans 3:10 says, 'As it is written, There is none righteous, no, not one.'"

Okay, I was all good with this. I got it, I thought. (This was the reason I hated church.)

I didn't realize it, but they had more bad news for me. (This was getting depressing. I wondered why in the world I had bothered to come back to the campus.)

"Romans 6:23a says, 'For the wages of sin is death.'"

Death. That's why my friends had asked me over? To tell me I was going to die? I sure didn't want to die. I didn't want to go to the place the evangelist had said was hotter than hot.

Then they showed me that Heaven is perfect and not one sin can go there.

So I told them about my efforts as a child to live without sin. They shook their heads knowingly. They seemed to understand. But if they did comprehend my despair, how were they so full of joy?

❧

Glorious News

The Campus Crusaders turned in their Bibles to the last part of Romans 6:23 and asked me to read out loud. I took a Bible, looked at the print, and prepared to read, not knowing that the following words would be the biggest detour of my life:

"...But the gift of God is eternal life through Jesus Christ our Lord."

"What is the gift of God?" I asked. They turned to another verse. (These guys really knew their Bibles. I was shocked. I didn't know college students could actually get excited about what I thought was the most boring book in the world.)

They showed me John 3:16, which states, "For God so loved the world, that he gave his only begotten Son, that whosoever believeth in him should not perish, but have everlasting life."

What did this mean about God loving the world and sending His Son to die? I knew Jesus was a good man. I knew He was the Son of God (My father was a Methodist who believed the Bible and understood Jesus was the Son of God.), but was there more to it?

A shiver of excitement jolted up and down my spine as I studied the verse. Did it say that whoever believed in Jesus would have eternal life? How could I not have seen this in the Bible before? I couldn't tear my eyes off the passage. I read it over and over. Then the men turned another few pages and had me read aloud again.

I read, "For by grace are ye saved through faith; and that not of yourselves: it is the gift of God." Ephesians 2:8

And then came the clincher, the verse that I'm sure God put in the Bible just for me and for anyone from Missouri, the show-me state: "Not of works, lest any man should boast." Ephesians 2:9

"Not of works." Could that really be written in the Bible? The words leaped off the page. This didn't seem possible. There was no way the text actually said "not of works." This was the reason my efforts at being perfect had failed so miserably, why I couldn't make it to Heaven on my own merit.

My own efforts were like the first steel beam that bent like a piece of cooked spaghetti. Going to Heaven wasn't dependent on me at all. Rather, it was dependent on Christ dying for my sins on the cross and rising again from the dead. The *Going to Heaven Scale* didn't exist. My good deeds could never outweigh my bad deeds.

I read the verse again. Did it really say "not of works"? Could that be possible? It explained so much: Going to Heaven is a gift. That is the reason Jesus came to the earth. He lived a perfect life and then died for the sins of mankind.

I needed to believe this. It was so simple.

I looked around at my friends' faces, "Why hasn't anyone told me this before?"

There wasn't really an answer to the question. (While the people in my childhood church experience meant well, either they hadn't known the gospel, or if they knew the gospel, they didn't know it well enough to share it with anyone.)

"Would you like to accept the gift of eternal life?" they asked.

I might be from the sticks of the country and not know as much as I should, but I wasn't dumb enough to turn down a free gift. Right then and there I accepted Jesus as my Savior. I understood that it wasn't anything I did that got me to Heaven. Instead, it was what Christ did on the cross for me. It was His payment for my sin that got me to Heaven. I couldn't pay for my own sin, but Jesus could.

That night when I got back to the parsonage, it was like the bedsheets didn't touch me. I almost floated on air. The next morning, I drove to class; and when I got to the room, I saw a friend. I couldn't wait to tell her the news. I raced up to her, "I got saved last night!"

She frowned. "Saved? I didn't know you were lost."

Didn't everyone want to know about how to go to Heaven? Wasn't everyone as frustrated as I had been about trying my best to work my way to Heaven? I told all my friends in the best way I knew how (which wasn't very good, but I was sincere and excited—a potent combination) that they could go to Heaven, too. I showed them John 3:16 and Ephesians 2:8–9. I found other guys on campus—Ed Sutton, Rance Darity, and Bill Adams—who understood about salvation as well. We all started sharing our faith with everyone we knew.

My fraternity thought about kicking me out. They said I'd gone too radical, that I needed to tone down my faith a little. They didn't like it that I was witnessing to everyone I knew on campus. I hadn't been around Christians that long yet, and didn't know you weren't supposed to get excited.

The fraternity decided not to kick me out. "He'll get over it," they said.

I haven't gotten over it.

Over 40 years later, if anything, I've only gotten worse.

❦

On Fire

Enthusiasm has been defined as "energy that boils over and runs down the side of the pot." One of the keys to the New Testament Church was they never lacked for enthusiasm. The Apostle Paul writes in Romans 12:11, "Not slothful in business; fervent in spirit; serving the Lord." We are to be fervent and enthusiastic when we serve the Lord. A great, enthusiastic spirit will help a church like nothing else. When people are excited for the Lord, they can't do enough to make sure that the gospel is given to as many people as possible. As a preacher, you almost wouldn't have to motivate your church if your people witnessed to others like they should. Their enthusiasm would be carried by your fervor, and the two would work together to do great things.

Many pastors have lost their enthusiasm. And I'm not saying I blame them. I personally know how hard it is to endure people not serving the Lord, backbiting, criticism, low turn-out for projects, and more. I don't want to portray that it is easy to be a part of a church, that it is easy to be a pastor, that it is always easy to serve the Lord.

But I do want to mention that I am so blessed with the congregation at Quentin Road. Unlike many churches where 20% of the people do 80% of the work, we have the exact opposite. The whole church does all of the work. Still, there are times when the work is daunting.

All of the work won't be easy. The key is, don't let the hardship of the task keep you from your initial enthusiasm to serve the Lord. I often recall those first days after I trusted Christ and how excited I was about knowing I was going to Heaven. This helps me to continue being excited more than 40 years later.

❦

My Plane Almost Hit Me

Charles Lindbergh delivered mail via airplane before he became famous for his solo, trans-Atlantic flight. He encountered fog in September 1926 while flying the mail run from St. Louis to Chicago. He tried to drop a flare to illuminate a farmer's field so he could land, but the flare malfunctioned. So he continued towards Chicago. For a half hour he circled the area of the Peoria airport, searching in vain in the fog. He eventually banked the plane southwest away from the city to attempt once again to land in a field. At 8:20pm in the dark, the engine cut out. Lindbergh followed the emergency procedure to switch to the reserve fuel tank, and the engine sputtered back to life. He found the problem with the malfunctioning flare and dropped it so he could see to land, but it disappeared into the mist. Using the little remaining fuel, he climbed to five thousand feet altitude. His engine died again. He unbuckled his safety belt and rolled out the right side of the De Haviland biplane open cockpit. After a few seconds, he pulled the ripcord on his parachute. Floating down under canopy, the sound of passing air switched to the approaching whine of his 400-horsepower plane engine. Somehow without his weight in the plane, a little more fuel had trickled into the engine and it coughed back to life. Now the plane flew in circles near Lindbergh and the parachute, its left wing down. The first pass was a mere 100 yards away. Again and again the plane buzzed towards him, descending with him. Five more times, it came around. The ground was less than 1,000 feet below as Lindbergh sank into the fog bank. He held his feet together, guarded his face with his hands, and waited. The plane roared towards him again, and then passed by him one final time before crashing near a farmhouse. Lindbergh braced for impact, plowed through corn tassels, and landed safely on the ground. He had almost been hit by his own plane six times. In spite of this and other experiences like it, the pilot still had enthusiasm for flying.[viii]

Eternal salvation is the gift God gave us when we believed in Jesus, and we should be thankful for it. But some people should get on their knees and ask for an extra dose of enthusiasm. There is nothing more exciting than when you look at what Christ did for you.

The first cell phone was called a brick. That's because it really looked like one at eight inches high, one and a half inches wide, four inches deep, and weighing two and a half pounds. Martin Cooper is a former vice president at Motorola who is called the father of the cell phone. The Motorola DynaTAC weighed the same as about ten iPhones.

The phone battery lasted about twenty minutes, but that was okay. The phone was so heavy a person could only hold it for about twenty minutes. It was a crucial time in cell phone history, and technology had been moving at an accelerated rate. At that time, we got a phone service plan that charged us five cents for every fifteen seconds. We learned to talk fast.

There was a decision between having phones where you are confined to your car and having a phone you could take with you anywhere. Most companies were leaning towards putting money into car phones because the technology just wasn't there for a cell phone. Cooper decided they had to take the phone everywhere; and they feverishly worked on making the phone out of thousands of little parts, inventing new devices and a new antenna. Soon after that, a call placed by Cooper in 1973 changed the world forever.[ix]

That kind of fervor to create the first cell phone is the kind of excitement we should have for the things of God. We need to be innovative and always look ahead to how we can improve things in our churches.

Maybe you are in a church of 25 people and you wonder how in the world you can be innovative. You are barely bringing in enough money to pay your bills, much less the pastor's salary. And yet, are there some things that you could be doing that would change the face of your ministry if you were a little inventive?

My mother Esther and Linda's mother Mary at an early Mother-Daughter Banquet.

Early on in our ministry, we began doing a Mother-Daughter Banquet. But we didn't do it the ordinary way that churches usually do it, with paper tablecloths and fake flowers on every table. (We didn't go out of budget, either.) Instead, we asked each lady to be the hostess at a table. She was in charge of setting the table with her china, glasses, and silverware. She was also responsible for the centerpiece. We also did all of our own food; so we knew it would taste really good at a fraction of the cost of having it catered. You would not

Over 1,000 mothers and daughters at one of our latest banquets.

believe how incredible the event turned out. The tables were beautifully set; the food was absolutely delicious; and every table was filled. We've continued to do this through the years, and now we have over 1,000 ladies who come to our banquet. We did this event very successfully on a low budget when we were a small church. The whole secret is that every lady in the church had the chance to contribute something unique.

Some churches that are in more rural areas have had successful ladies' banquets, too. Sometimes the ladies decorate the tables with the nice plasticware that looks like fine china. They might decorate their tables more casually, but it still turns out to be a wonderful occasion with many people trusting Christ.

These kinds of events are prime opportunities for sharing the gospel. A friend of mine went to an evangelistic seminar where the speaker encouraged the attendees to make sure that the gospel was shared at every major event of the church, including Christmas and Easter. Since my friend loves the gospel, he was puzzled that this should even be stated. In his church the gospel is given all the time, and especially at every major event like Christmas and Easter. (It is more likely that unsaved people will be at those services than at any others.) And what is the purpose of an event if the gospel isn't given and an opportunity to trust Christ isn't given?

Churches need to realize that events are not done because they need to be done. All the hard work, all the dedication, all the people giving of their talents works together so the stage is set perfectly for the gospel to be given. The gospel is the power of God unto salvation. If it is not given, then there is no power.

As a pastor, one of your primary responsibilities is to share the gospel at these events and make it as clear as possible so that everyone who is in the room can understand it. Spend some time learning how to give the gospel in an effective manner, and you will be amazed by the number of people who trust Christ as a result. Be the main person who gives the gospel at events, even ladies' gatherings. The pastor should be a gospel professional. (And let me mention one sure-fire way to not have a problem speaking at a women's event—just tell some jokes about men.)

Another of your responsibilities as a pastor is to train and teach your people that the reason you have events is for the gospel's sake. Everything that is done at your church has to have a central focus and that focus should be the gospel. Share from the pulpit how important it is when you are preparing for events. Explain the reason your church does what it does. If your congregation starts to make the connection that everything they do is for souls, you won't be able to stop them from working. They will give everything they have to work for the gospel's sake and for lost souls.

While the previous paragraphs were written primarily for the pastor, I want to also give some practical ways every person can have enthusiasm in the church. Be open to new ministry opportunities in your church. Maybe a new ministry started and you are hesitant about helping out because you don't know if you are qualified. Go for it. You might be surprised how God can use you in this new opportunity. This might seem like a crazy idea; but walk up and down the aisle of Sam's Club or Costco, looking for ideas that will help your church. Always be open to new ideas and things that would make your church more effective in ministry.

Be aware of potential ministries. Don't be closed-minded to the idea of doing something in your church outside the box. Be open-minded about ways you can help others and minister to them with the gospel. Here's an example: Since I always hated school, when I started a school I was always sensitive to the kids who were frustrated by learning. When I heard about a dyslexia tutoring program, I arranged for some of our teachers to see the program and get training. What resulted has been an amazing dyslexia tutoring program that teaches kids to read and write, and it also reprograms their brains. They are also introduced to Christian teachers who love the Lord. Through the dyslexia program, we have found ways to reach the special needs community that we never would have considered if I wasn't sensitive to the fact that school was difficult for me.

✦

Your First Love

If you ever feel discouraged in the ministry, I encourage you to go back to your first love. That love should be the gospel. How did you get saved? You got saved by hearing the gospel.

Revelation 2:4 says, "Nevertheless I have somewhat against thee, because thou hast left thy first love."

Our love should be for the gospel and for others hearing the gospel. Sometimes we can look at the world around us and think it is hopeless. Every time you turn on the news, it seems like there has been another shooting. Drugs are rampant. Alcoholism is an epidemic. Kids have to go through metal detectors at school because they might be carrying guns.

Our churches are full of Christians who are half-hearted about serving the Lord. They have lost their excitement and their joy. Sometimes as leaders, we can get discouraged in seeing all of this; and yet, I have a simple cure for all of these sad and difficult things: the gospel—I once was lost but now am found.

All I need to do to get perspective on this life is to remember what it was like before I knew Jesus Christ. I remember the attitude I had—how I hated church. How I'd never read my Bible. How when the Sunday School teacher asked me what my favorite verses were (every Sunday School teacher seems to delight in doing this to pastor's kids), I would say, "Jesus wept." When the teacher would look surprised at my obvious lack of Bible knowledge, I would quickly add, "But the verse shows emotion."

Second Corinthians 4:4 states, "In whom the god of this world hath blinded the minds of them which believe not, lest the light of the glorious gospel of Christ, who is the image of God, should shine unto them."

The worse the world gets, the worse that even the Church gets. I know this: the god of this world (the devil) is working to blind lost people from the light of the gospel. The devil didn't care that I went to church as a child. He delighted in that happening because he knew I would only hear part of the Bible, but not the gospel. (This is why it's not easy to have a Philadelphia church [a church of brotherly love] in a Laodicean Age [the time of people's rights].)

Consider your own salvation experience. (If you haven't yet trusted Christ, I encourage you to do so right now. Christ died for your sins and rose again. If you have already trusted Christ, then why don't you take a moment and thank God for the gift of His Son. Ask God to help you tell others about the greatest news in the universe.)

The gospel can't be hidden if we choose to tell others about it. Our churches will come alive when we share the gospel. Our people will get excited and tell others, and many will get saved. Our schools will change. Our world will change. Not because of us. Because of the gospel.

Going Home to Share the News

Part of growing in Christ is that you can't wait to share the news of your salvation with family and friends. This was true of me. I returned home and found my mother in the kitchen. She smiled when I told her the news, "James, I've known this for many years. I got saved at a revival many years ago."

She showed me her Scofield Study Bible that she read from every day.

I raced to the study to tell my dad. He sat at his desk. His name was Isaac James Scudder, and many people called him I.J. I was so glad to see him.

My parents around the time I trusted Christ.

"Dad, I got saved."

"You got what?" he asked.

"I got saved. I know for sure I am going to Heaven."

He slowly put his hands on the desk, "Son, no man can know for sure he is going to Heaven."

The words shattered my spirit.

What? My own dad didn't know he was going to Heaven? How was this possible? How had he preached for 40 years and not known he was saved?

Tears came to my eyes. I sat down in a chair across from his desk. "But I do know for sure, Dad. Let me show you what the Bible says." I opened the Bible to 1 John 5:13, "These things have I written unto you that believe on the name of the Son of God; that ye may know that ye have eternal life, and that ye may believe on the name of the Son of God."

"Dad, it says right here in the Word of God that you can know."

But no matter how much I shared my heart and the Scriptures as best I knew how, Dad didn't want to listen. Finally, I gave up. I was so discouraged. Here was a man I admired more than any other person, and he didn't know for sure he was going to Heaven.

Everyone needed to know. I didn't understand it then, but it was the beginning of a journey. A journey to tell the world about the greatest news in the world.

Maybe you have struggled with giving the gospel clearly. Perhaps you haven't understood as I did that going to Heaven is a free gift. Or perhaps by reading my story you've realized how easy it is to mess up the gospel when you give it. It is so important that we don't confuse the Good News. Romans 1:16 says, "For I am not ashamed of the gospel of Christ: for it is the power of God unto salvation to every one that believeth; to the Jew first, and also to the Greek." The word "power" in this verse is the word *dunamis* from the Greek. It is where we get the word "dynamite."

The power of God is the dynamite of God, causing explosive action in people's souls. The gospel itself brings people to understand crucial truth. That's why it is so important we make it clear and why I am so passionate about making it as simple as the Bible does.

God loves us, but He hates our sin. Sin separates us from a holy God.

We can't go to Heaven with our sin on us. Sin has been paid for by death. Not just any death, but the death of the Son of God. He lived a perfect life and died for our sins. He rose again the third day, proving that He was God. The only way to Heaven and to a relationship with God is through Jesus Christ. Simple belief is all that is required to go to Heaven; not cleaning up your life first, like I had always been taught. Not trying so hard to be perfect. None of that—only Jesus Christ and Him crucified.

This knowledge purified me like nothing else. Knowing that Jesus had come and died for me made me want to live for Him like nothing else—not for salvation, but because of salvation.

I knew God didn't want me to hide this light from the world. He wanted everyone to know.

Finish Line Strategies

- Take some time to brainstorm about different ministries your church could start. How about a ministry to the homeless by providing meals? Maybe a reading and writing tutoring program. Perhaps your church could make pizzas and people could come and eat them before Wednesday night church as we do. That way people can come straight from work to youth programs and midweek prayer meeting. There are so many ways that your church can reach out. Don't be stopped by not having enough people or a large building. (Once, we took our staff on the church bus to a restaurant where they could grill their own steaks. It was a few-hours drive, so we used the time to brainstorm ideas for the church.) No matter the size of your church, you can have an effective ministry every day. God has equipped your church uniquely to bless your community spiritually.

- How can you cultivate a spirit of enthusiasm in your church? How can you get more volunteers to help with church ministries? One of the ways is to show enthusiasm yourself. If you aren't excited, then for sure the people around you aren't going to be. The other is to present the needs to the congregation. Let them know what is going on in the ministry and how they can help. If no one responds right away, don't be discouraged. Sometimes it takes people a little while to decide to help. Keep going. Be enthusiastic about God's work, and your enthusiasm will motivate others.

- Share specifically with people in your church about what is going on with your ministries. Let them know that their prayers and support are making a difference. Be open with people, and share your heart with them. A good leader is always encouraging the people around him to keep going. Give this to people whether or not they encourage you back.

- Take the time to thank people for all they are doing. Be genuine in your thanks. Let them know you appreciate them and love them. It takes time for people to support the church and their pastor, but it will happen.

Chapter 7
Why a Clear Gospel?

But if our gospel be hid, it is hid to them that are lost: In whom the god of this world hath blinded the minds of them which believe not, lest the light of the glorious gospel of Christ, who is the image of God, should shine unto them.
2 Corinthians 4:3–4

In the break room at Brinks, a job I worked during college, I talked to a man named Eddie. I showed him in the Bible how Jesus Christ died for his sins and rose again, and how not one work could get him to Heaven. It was Jesus Christ and Jesus Christ only. I showed him John 3:16, and we read it together.

"Eddie," I said, "do you understand that Jesus died for your sins on the cross?"

"Yes, I do," he said. "I know He died for me on the cross."

"Do you understand that Christ's death paid the penalty for your sins?"

"Yes, I do."

"Then if you were to die right now, where would you go?"

"I'd go to Hell."

Eddie didn't understand the gospel. He understood a part, but not all of it. I opened my Bible so I could share more with my friend. I thought back to that moment in the dorm room when the Bible was opened to me and verses like Ephesians 2:8–9 were shared. When I realized that Jesus paid for all my sins and rose again from the grave, my perspective on church and the Bible was changed forever. (Eddie eventually got it. More on that story in the next chapter.)

The gospel makes the difference between night and day. Between darkness and light. Between complete, utter boredom and thrilling excitement about the things of God.

The gospel was what had been missing for me all those years. The gospel was what had been hidden from me. Not intentionally, but because the adults in my life didn't know it themselves. (Or if they did know it, they didn't understand it enough to share it with me.)

That is a tragedy beyond words. If my former church experience is what millions of people experience every week, then of course people are leaving the church in record numbers. There is no power. No life. No reason to keep attending.

Enter the gospel, and everything changes.

❧⌘❧

Some Barriers to a Clear Gospel

I want to use this chapter to explain some of the other aspects of giving the gospel. There are well-meaning people who might be saved; but when they give the gospel, they give it in a polluted way. Some of the things I'm going to cover might be precious to you. Maybe they were even used when you heard the gospel for the first time. I don't want to offend people by this, but I want everyone to understand the importance of a clear gospel. Since I was confused about the gospel as I grew up, I don't want anyone else to go through that same misery. 1 Corinthians 14:8–9 says, "For if the trumpet give an uncertain sound, who shall prepare himself to the battle? So likewise ye, except ye utter by the tongue words easy to be understood, how shall it be known what is spoken? for ye shall speak into the air."

We need to make the gospel clear with words that are easy to understand. I care so deeply about this that if you cut me, I'd bleed the gospel. This is why I love and care about Dr. Art Rorheim so much. He is the co-founder of AWANA Clubs International and has won thousands, if not hundreds of thousands, to Christ. I met him many years ago when our church was in the Palatine area, and have been blessed by his friendship. He serves on the board of Dayspring Bible College and Seminary and means so much to me. He has devoted his life to the clear gospel message as well. I admire him so much for that.

I'd like to share with you an interview I did with Dr. Art Rorheim where he explains why giving the gospel clearly is so important.

Art Rorheim (AR); Jim Scudder (JS)

JS — Tell us about the beginning of AWANA.

AR — God so wonderfully uses ordinary people to have a part in His work. We are very honored. We printed our first book in 1950, and that was the official beginning of the AWANA program.

JS — When I was on your board for seven years, we knew AWANA was going to get big, but I don't think we believed it would keep growing so rapidly that it would be in every country in the world.

Dr. Art Rorheim — Founder of AWANA Clubs, Int'l.

AR — I look back at those starting years, and I realize that I really wasn't adequate for the job. I was not a trained person. I didn't have that ability. I knew God had to do something marvelous in me because I knew nothing about putting together an organization with all the needs of a staff, fundraising, and developing a program. If I had known back then what was going to happen, I would have run away. I would have been scared.

JS — You know, Art, that's true. The amazing thing is we both started out almost in the same place, not knowing each other. We both started out within about two blocks of each other on Fullerton Avenue.

AR — We did, very close.

JS — I met Lance Latham before I met you, and I remember the first thing he did was make sure that I had a clear gospel. That's the heart of AWANA. Your heart is to have a clear message so that everybody can understand it. You pretty much have always stood against this trend called Lordship Salvation. Why would you be against that?

AR — Well, because we know that salvation has no strings attached to it. I mean, God does not say, "I'll give you My salvation on the basis that you'll do this or that for Me," because we have nothing to give. We're dead in trespasses and sins. A dead man cannot give anything until he gets life. Once you get saved, you get life, and then you can give Him everything. But as far as being part of salvation, as an attachment to that, of course not, because we're dead in trespasses and sins. We can't do it.

JS — That's correct. They'll say, "Well, they believe it's by grace, but if you don't show works...." That's like saying you can get on an airplane and it's free, but you pay to get off. Salvation starts free and it ends free. Now we all should serve, of course—that's logical—but everybody doesn't. I tell people that the Corinthians didn't. They were pretty messed up, but they were still saved. If anybody has any questions, they need to read I Corinthians chapter 5, showing that a man had committed the most horrible sin; but he was still saved, although he was not going to be rewarded for his life's works at all.

AR—God also judges them and takes the lives of some of these Corinthians.

JS—He doesn't let people live in sin. Someone asked, "Does that mean you can live as you please?" Not really, because God will chasten you, and even take you home to Heaven early. Paul's biggest fear was being a castaway, put on a shelf. Not losing his salvation. That's been your fear, hasn't it? It's been my fear.

AR—He says, "Lest that when I have preached to others, I should be a castaway," or "disapproved" is what he's really referring to here.

JS—I believe in America we have one million AWANA kids per week. Around the world, what would you think? About five million or so?

AR—Well, it could be. But you know the one joy we have, because of the time around the world, is that every moment of the day there's an AWANA club in action. Isn't that a thrill? All around the world, there's one in action.

JS—The world is basically 24,000 miles in circumference, and we have 24 hours in a day. That's interesting, isn't it? I used to pray for the churches that were going to have church at 10:00 or 11:00. But now when I pray on Saturday night, I say, "Now, Lord, we know that all over the world there are churches meeting right now, and every hour." It's important we pray like that.

AR—Yesterday I was on a plane, and I talked to this fellow about the Lord; and I said to him, "Do you realize that there are only two kinds of people on this plane? There are those who are going to Heaven and those who are going to Hell." I must constantly realize the awfulness of Hell. I often use this illustration: Suppose you were standing at the Niagara Falls, and there was a group of one hundred blind people standing there with their walkers and canes. They've been told that they're heading to a park for a beautiful concert. I stand there and I see them going over the falls to their doom. I stand there, and I don't push them in; but I am as guilty as if I had pushed them in if I don't respond. I've got to respond, saying, "Stop! You've got the wrong message! That is not the right message!" And I give them the right message. That's what life is all about. People have the wrong message, and we have to stop them in their tracks and give them the right message of the gospel. When we realize that they're Hell-bound and we don't respond to them, God says we'll have blood on our hands.

JS— You've got quite a story when you were young about Toccoa Falls. Would you share that? Our readers will get a real blessing out of hearing what could have happened in your life and didn't happen, but was used to get you going.

AR— Well, I was just a typical, little, live, wild, young fellow.

JS— No, Art, you were not typical! There was nothing typical about you. You were a little bit wilder than the average person!

AR— I used to sing with a wonderful group, the boys called the Whiteshirt Brigade. My mentor, Lance Latham, was such a tremendous pianist, and loved the Lord. To travel with him was the most wonderful thing, because he was about the Lord all the time. We had this date at Toccoa Falls, a Christian...college. We got up to the top of the falls; it was very tall. It's as high as Niagara Falls. A couple of us, very daring, said, "Let's get an exciting-looking picture, and see how far we can walk out to the end of the falls." We walked out to within about four feet of the end of the falls. When we got out to the end, I said to this buddy,

Young Art foolishly posing at the top of Toccoa Falls.

"Let's make it dramatic. Why don't you get on the top of my shoulders?" And we stood at the end of the falls. Just the slightest little slip, and there would have been nothing to grab onto. I look at that and I thought, "Wow! God's angels were there to protect me!" This was before I was involved in AWANA, and I'm sure the devil was there ready to push me over. Two weeks later, the president of the school came to preach at our church. He said, "We had a tragedy at the falls last week. A fellow went over the falls. It took us two days to find his body wedged under a rock." I shuddered. I said, "God, thank You for taking care of the most foolish man in the world." Because my whole ministry for God would have been gone right there if God had not wonderfully spared me.

JS — See, Art, I don't think most of our readers would think you were typical. You used to go and climb up chimneys in Chicago so you could study and be alone. Sometimes you climbed up three or four stories without ropes. I don't know how you could do that.

AR — You know today, peer pressure is what ruins most kids. The peer pressures were different down there in those days. The peer pressure we had was what we call "skitching automobiles." You talk about that [today], and they don't know what you're talking about. Cars back then had a spare tire on the back with small bumpers on each side. The real "cool" thing was to be able to slip in at a stop light and slip onto that car and see how far you could travel. And they didn't know you were on there. The more miles you traveled, the cooler you were. Then my dad found out about this and he said, "Son, please, this is dangerous. Please don't do that."

I said, "Dad, you're a killjoy. You don't understand. You spoil all my fun." Then God had to do something to wake me up. My best friend and I used to walk to school together, and a big trailer truck came along. We decided to get behind that trailer truck in between a car. As the trailer truck started, I don't know what happened, but my little friend got his foot caught in the wheel of that truck. And he went around with the truck. And I ran up and got the truck stopped. Boy, there were ambulances all over the place. They got him to the hospital, and his leg had to be amputated; and that night he died. I want to tell you, it took that to wake me up. It was serious enough. Worse than that was, as I look back at it, I was just a nominal Christian. I really hadn't witnessed to this kid about the Lord.

That I regret. The one tragedy was bad, but the other was worse. God hadn't really gotten all of my heart yet, to really be the witness I should have been at that time.

JS— I remember, Art, I had a dear friend who claimed to be a Christian, but he wasn't serving Christ. He went away to college, and he hopped on a train; and he got knocked off the train and lost both legs at the hip. My dad called me into his office; and he said, "Son, sit down." He said, "Your friend, Jimmy, has lost both legs in a train accident." He never lost consciousness—that's hard to imagine. That shook me up so bad that I could hardly do anything for a long time. He did trust Christ, and—it's hard to believe—he became a preacher. I went and picked him up with my arms once, and carried him out to the car to take him with me to preach. That guy would have never served the Lord if that hadn't happened. We have experiences in our lives, and sometimes God has to wake us up. In your case, being a preacher for many years, you weren't typical. You were way worse than typical. It took something like that to get your attention. Maybe some of the people reading this book are like you. Maybe they're the kind that everybody thinks will never serve the Lord. Maybe those are the best kind, because if they do serve the Lord, they're going to do something for God.

AR— We have to remind everybody that God's favorite people are ordinary people, and we can prove that because He made so many of us.

Even in my daily life, I realize the people that slip through me every day. I'm more conscious of that in my latter years than I've ever been that if God opens that crack a little bit, I've got to speak up. Without question. I wish that were true my whole life, but it's far more effective in the latter years of my life.

JS— God has given you a certain ability and a power. I was with you with a funeral director. I thought, *There's no way*. She'd been witnessed to by every preacher on this earth. You started asking her if she were to die right now, where she would go. And this lady got saved. Then she says this most haunting question that still haunts me, "Why hasn't any other preacher ever told me that?" So Art, AWANA, and *Victory In Grace* all have one goal, and that's to make a clear gospel presentation. The power is in how clear the message is. There's no power in any preacher. I know preachers a lot more powerful than [me], but they don't get the souls saved because their message is muddy and unclear. I want to encourage all the readers to be as clear on the gospel as possible. Pretend that you're talking to a young child. God says unless we become as children, we cannot enter the Kingdom of Heaven. In other words, the gospel is simple. Make it clear, and explain to them what the gospel really is. That's what AWANA has done. Art, it's been great having you on this interview, and we appreciate you so much.

AR — It's great, Jim, that you and I have been real partners together in this clear message of the gospel. I feel that we are like brothers in this all these years.

I hope you enjoyed that interview with my dear friend, Dr. Art Rorheim. He is 95 at the time of this printing, and is still going strong for the sake of the gospel. In the next chapter, we'll look at some ways to avoid giving an unclear gospel.

Finish Line Strategies

- Think of some of the phrases you've heard when someone was giving the gospel. How do those phrases line up with what the Bible teaches about salvation?

- Consider doing a mini-series in your church on the clear gospel and how to give it.

- Give opportunities for your people to witness and share the gospel. Bring your teenagers to pass out tracts at public places. Do fair evangelism with your people. Make sharing the gospel an important part of your life personally, and other people will catch your enthusiasm and do the same thing.

Chapter 8
Avoiding an Unclear Message

The Spirit of the Lord is upon me, because he hath anointed me to preach the gospel to the poor; he hath sent me to heal the brokenhearted, to preach deliverance to the captives, and recovering of sight to the blind, to set at liberty them that are bruised. To preach the acceptable year of the Lord. Luke 4:18-19

After a meeting where another leader gave the gospel, I took the opportunity to talk to two children who were about ten years old.

"Are you saved?" I asked the first one, named Katrina.

She nodded.

"What does 'saved' mean?" I asked.

"It means I took Jesus into my heart, and He is right here." She pointed to her heart.

"If you went out and did something wrong, would you still go to Heaven?"

Katrina shook her head no.

I shared the clear gospel with her, explaining from Scripture what it means to be saved and to understand Christ died for her sins and rose again. She could not do one good work to save herself. Going to Heaven was a matter of Jesus plus nothing.

Jesus in Your Pump?

Many people use this phrase, "Take Jesus into your heart to get saved." If you ask them what is getting them to Heaven, they might say, "I took Jesus into my heart." I had one child say he was worried that if he got a heart transplant, then he wouldn't be saved. (We recently had a young man in our church, Andrew Collison, who did receive a heart transplant. He wasn't worried that the surgeons would take Jesus out of his body along with his heart.) The words "take Jesus into your heart" have become a catch phrase. We've added this phrase into the salvation message, and it causes confusion.

I don't want to hurt people who have used this phrase to give the gospel. I also don't want to disrespect your experience if someone said this phrase to you when you heard the gospel. The phrase isn't in the Bible. When we witness, we use verses in the Bible to give the gospel.

First of all, what does the Bible mean when it uses the word "heart"? In Jeremiah 17:9, it states, "The heart is deceitful above all things, and desperately wicked: who can know it?" The word "heart" here is from the Hebrew word, *leb*, and it means "feelings, the will, and the intellect." So when we say the heart is deceitful, we mean that our will and intellect are deceitful, not our literal, actual heart that pumps blood in our body.

When people hear that they should take Jesus into their hearts, they get confused: Children might think this means their actual heart that pumps blood, and this will really confuse them. Older people may think it means that they need to ask Jesus to come into their lives or into their minds so that they can get saved.

We don't ask Jesus to do anything in order to be saved. We believe in what Jesus already did in order to be saved.

The Bible says over and over again that people believed and were saved in order to go to Heaven. It doesn't say they asked Jesus to come into their hearts to get saved. Let's look at a few examples.

John 20:31 states, "But these are written, that ye might believe that Jesus is the Christ, the Son of God; and that believing ye might have life through his name."

Acts 15:11 says, "But we believe that through the grace of the Lord Jesus Christ we shall be saved, even as they."

Acts 4:4 explains, "Howbeit many of them which heard the word believed; and the number of the men was about five thousand."

The key is that people believed in the death, burial, and resurrection of Christ. They believed it wasn't their own good works that saved them, but rather Christ's work on the cross that saved them.

There is one verse in the Bible that says Christ dwells in our hearts by faith. Let's look at it together. Ephesians 3:17 says, "That Christ may dwell in your hearts by faith; that ye, being rooted and grounded in love."

What is faith? Hebrews 11:1 says it "is the substance of things hoped for, the evidence of things not seen." Faith is belief, pure and simple. Christ dwells in our innermost being by faith. Right now, Christ is at the right hand of the Father. Who actually indwells us? The Holy Spirit.

Ephesians 1:13 says, "In whom ye also trusted, after that ye heard the word of truth, the gospel of your salvation: in whom also after that ye believed, ye were sealed with that holy Spirit of promise."

We are sealed with the Holy Spirit after we trust Christ as Savior. We don't ask the Holy Spirit to come into our innermost being; this happens automatically the moment we trust Christ.

Make a Commitment

There are some people who say salvation is a free gift; but when they give the invitation, they say we have to make a commitment to Christ in order to be saved. This goes along with my earlier point of making Jesus Lord. Salvation is not by our works. We do not receive salvation because we make a commitment in order to get saved. We receive salvation because of what Christ already did.

Galatians 2:16 says, "Knowing that a man is not justified by the works of the law, but by the faith of Jesus Christ, even we have believed in Jesus Christ, that we might be justified by the faith of Christ, and not by the works of the law: for by the works of the law shall no flesh be justified."

We are justified (declared righteous) because of Jesus Christ's payment on the cross for our sins. We are not justified by making a commitment to Christ, but rather by His commitment to us.

Turn from All Sin

Still others say that you have to turn from all sin to be saved. They say the word "repent" means to turn from sin. They interpret a verse like the following to mean they have to stop sinning in order to be saved:

"Repent ye therefore, and be converted, that your sins may be blotted

out, when the times of refreshing shall come from the presence of the
Lord;" Acts 3:19.

The word "repent" here is from the Greek word *metanoeo*. It means "to
think differently." This is different from our modern, English definition,
"to be sorry for sin." You once thought good works got you to Heaven; now
you think differently. You understand your good works do nothing to get
you to Heaven. Instead, you only trust in the payment Christ made for
you on the cross. You once thought salvation was by works, and now you
know salvation is by grace.

If we had to turn from all sin in order to be saved, how would we ever
get saved? How many sins would we have to turn away from? How many
sins would we have to remember in order to be sorry for all of them?
This process could take months, even years, and even then we might not
remember every sin.

In saying this, I don't mean to say that sin isn't serious. Sin was so serious that in the Old Testament, the people had to bring lambs and goats
to be sacrificed so that God could look on them. These sacrifices covered
their sins, but didn't take them away.

Hebrews 10:4 says, "For it is not possible that the blood of bulls and of
goats should take away sins."

When John the Baptist saw Jesus, He said amazing words. John 1:29
says, "The next day John seeth Jesus coming unto him, and saith, Behold
the Lamb of God, which taketh away the sin of the world."

The Lamb of God would take away the sin of the world. The earlier
sacrifices of animals were *kipporahs*, or coverings for sin.

Salvation is dependent on Christ, not us. It isn't about us turning from
sin to be saved. Rather, it is believing on the sacrifice Christ already made
for our sins. The only requirement for salvation is belief.

If preachers, teachers, and laypeople made sure to give the gospel
clearly, they would be amazed at the number of people who would trust
Christ. When I was in India and preaching to thousands, I had some of the
other preachers ask me why so many people trusted Christ when I spoke.
I told them that it wasn't because of me; it was because I strove to make

the gospel as easy to understand as possible. I made a clear distinction between salvation and service, and I didn't use terms that were confusing or hard to understand.

In other words, I simply shared what the Bible said about salvation, not man's opinions or made-up sayings.

※

Grace Grafted

Everything we have we owe to the grace of God, because we're unworthy of His favor. I love my grandchildren very dearly. I can still remember when my first granddaughter Amy was born. I was going through some real struggles at the church. I was discouraged because a good member had suddenly left. But when that little baby was born, I held her and forgot my worries. I felt the same way when her sister, Erica, was born. That was grace. But that was nothing compared to the Son of God taking on human flesh. That was really grace.

The question was asked at a conference, "What makes Christianity different from all the other religions of the world?" Some argued that Christianity is unique in teaching God became a man, but someone made the objection that other religions teach similar doctrines. Others suggested the resurrection. No, it was argued; other faiths believe the dead rise again. The discussion grew heated. C.S. Lewis, a strong defender of the Christian faith, came in late, sat down, and asked what the ruckus was about. When he learned what they were debating, he stood up and said, "The uniqueness of Christianity lies in only one thing—it's grace."

So what is grace? Some say grace is undeserved kindness. Others would declare grace is everything for nothing for those who don't deserve anything. These are good definitions; but G.W. Knight sums it up best: "When a person works an eight-hour day and receives a fair day's pay for his time, that is a wage. When a person competes with an opponent and receives a trophy for his performance, that is a prize. When a person receives appropriate recognition for his long service or high achievements, that is an award. But when a person is not capable of earning a wage, can win no prize, and deserves no award—yet receives such a gift anyway—that is a good picture of God's unmerited favor. This is what we mean when we talk about the grace of God."

An atheist once said, "If there's really a God, may He prove Himself by striking me dead!" Nothing happened. He said, "See, there's no God." A wise Christian told him, "No, that only proves grace because God could strike you any time."

God would be just for striking any of us. We fail to measure up to His standard of holiness. It is only in His grace that we are spared from immediate judgment. Everyone knows there is a day of judgment coming. On the one hand, some people with no spiritual backbone would rather "air-condition" Hell than tell others the truth about this place of judgment. On the other hand, some are so busy debating doctrinal truths that they won't share the truth with others. Hell is a real place, and people who die without Christ are going there!

A certain Jim Scudder was living in Arkansas deep in the Bible Belt, but he could not be convinced of the reality of God's judgment and his need for Christ. He told his wife, "I'll never be saved until God points me out directly from one of those TV preachers." While watching our program, *Victory In Grace*, he heard me say, talking about myself, "If God can save an old, stinking sinner like Jim Scudder, He can save anybody." He was so surprised he fell out of the bed and trusted Christ on the spot.

God's grace is not willing that any should perish. Some people ask, "Well, why would a loving God send people to Hell?" God doesn't send people to Hell; they go there of their own free will. If they trust anything besides His grace to get to Heaven, they cannot be saved.

A prominent Christian leader teaches salvation by grace; but also believes a Christian must have fruit present in his life, otherwise he was never saved in the first place. He believes by making the gospel "hard" enough, we might see more reality in salvation. In reality, he is adding works to the gospel. Like oil and water, grace and works don't mix.

When I was growing up, absolutely no one would ever have thought I would become a preacher someday. On one of my broadcasts, I asked the audience if anyone from Paducah, Kentucky (my hometown), would write me. One woman wrote and said, "... After 15 years, you might really be saved." God saves everybody. He likes to save bad people. By the way, that includes all of us. And He doesn't wait for us to reform ourselves before He extends His grace. (Aren't you grateful for that?) He doesn't wait for us to have a certain amount of spiritual fruit in our lives in order for us to stay saved. He will discipline us when we don't serve Him, but He will never take our salvation away.

Some might ask, "Do you believe in 'easy believism'?" No, I believe you get saved by believing. You don't have to believe "hard." You don't have to believe "easy." You simply believe. Easy believism is the preaching of a watered-down gospel. When a child is told, "Take Jesus into your heart," he's going to do what you tell him to do. *But he won't understand what he did.* The heart of the gospel involves understanding Jesus died and shed His blood on the cross for you. You must trust Him and Him alone, not your good works. Only then are you saved.

If you plant an acorn today, it won't become a mighty oak tree tomorrow. But that's what many people expect of a new Christian. They expect that he will immediately start serving and immediately lose his desire to sin. When one becomes saved, he may *not* automatically serve. He might not even know how to serve. This is where discipleship comes in. The Holy Spirit works within the new believer to reveal the way of God to him. Over a period of time, the acorn splits the ground and a seedling sprouts up.

Christians don't grow immediately for perhaps the same reason an acorn doesn't instantly mature into an oak. If the acorn doesn't first send its roots deep within the soil, the tree will be uprooted in a storm. In the same manner, a Christian must first establish a deep root in Christ before he can mature spiritually; otherwise the storms of religious opposition, trials, and suffering will uproot him. To add to all of the outside pressure, the new Christian must fight a daily battle against his flesh. This means he has the ability to fall into sin. But even though he falls, he will never be able to destroy the work God has begun in his life. He can never escape his new family ties.

My son, Jim, is my son, whether he wants to be or not. He can't some-how change his birth and be born into a different family. What's done is done. Jesus said we must "be born again" to enter the Kingdom of God (John 3:3b). We receive the new birth by faith in Christ. After we're born again, it's impossible to be "unborn." When Jimmy was one year old, I came into his room and found the goldfish bowl upside-down, with the goldfish flopping around.

"Jim, did you mess with the goldfish?"

"No, Daddy." At one, he knew how to lie as all of us do.

If we understand we are saved, never again to be lost, this ought to create within us a desire to serve the Lord. The lives we live should be a melody of praise to our Savior.

Have you ever transfixed yourself listening to the melodies of the eagle, the penguin, the peacock, the pelican, the flamingo, and the vul-ture? These birds don't make any melody. It's the smallest birds which make the sweetest music. In the same way, it's the small Christians—those who say, "I know I'm nothing. I know Jesus saved me by the grace of God, and I don't deserve it at all"—these make the sweetest melody to God.

❧◦❧

Make Jesus Lord of Your Life to Be Saved

Many Bible teachers today love to throw in "make Jesus Lord of your life" when they give the gospel presentation. They might say Jesus Christ paid for a person's sins on the cross; but at the end they say in order for someone to be saved, the person has to make Jesus Lord of his or her life.

Just like we answered the question of whether or not we should ask Jesus to come into our hearts with the question, do we have to do anything but believe to be saved? the same question applies when we talk about making Jesus Lord of our lives to be saved. The answer is, of course not. Then why would we say a person has to do this? Why would we put this burden on someone who doesn't know Jesus Christ yet? I've been saved for over 40 years, and I've never made Jesus completely Lord of my life. Sure, I've tried. I've done my best to live for Christ. But I can't possibly make Jesus Lord of every aspect of my life.

Besides, the truth is Jesus already is the Lord. I don't make Him Lord of anything. He is already the God of the universe, the Creator of the heavens and the earth. He is all-powerful, all-knowing, and everywhere-present.

If we had to make Jesus Lord in order to be saved, then that means we would be adding works to our salvation message. We would be muddying up the waters of the clear gospel. It saddens me so much when people do this. Galatians 2:21 says, "I do not frustrate the grace of God: for if righteousness come by the law, then Christ is dead in vain."

Salvation is a gift. No works are required. After you are saved, you should strive to obey Jesus as the Master of your life. But this is only because you are saved, not in order to be saved. It was because this message was unclear through the years that I hated anything to do with the church and the Bible. We have to make the gospel as clear as we can so as many people as possible will hear and understand it.

Grace, Grace

Grace is an attribute of God. It's part of who He is, just as our traits make us who we are. God always acts out of His character. He gives us the grace we need when we need it.

While grace is freely given, we must avoid the temptation to abuse it. When we choose to sin willfully under the cover of grace, we are making a mockery of the cross and the sacrifice that was made there for our sins. A.W. Tozer wrote: "Sin is never a thing to be proud of. No act is wise that ignores future consequences, and sin always does. Sin always sees only today, or at most, tomorrow. Never the day after tomorrow, next month, or next year." Sin doesn't look to the future, but grace does. Sin only provides for our imprisonment; grace provides for our freedom.

Grace Gifted

Rather than judging us according to what we deserve, God has shown us His grace. We live by this grace. I want to ask you one question: are you committed to grace? If Calvary doesn't melt and break your heart, nothing else will.

When I talked to my co-worker, Eddie, about salvation, I was tempted to be frustrated with his response. He understood that Jesus died for his sins, but didn't seem to further accept he could go to Heaven based on that belief.

So I started again. "Eddie, do you understand Jesus Christ paid for all your sins?"

"Yes," he said.

"Do you believe that your good works can help you get to Heaven?"

"No," he said.

"Eddie, if you were to die right now, where would you go?"

"Hell."

Did Eddie not understand a word I was saying? I showed him John 5:24 which states, "Verily, verily, I say unto you, He that heareth my word, and believeth on him that sent me, hath everlasting life, and shall not come into condemnation; but is passed from death unto life."

"Do you believe on Jesus Christ?"

"Yes."

"Do you believe He paid for your sins on the cross?"

"Yes."

"If you were to die today, where would you go?"

"Hell."

I shook my head. Obviously, Eddie didn't understand Christ had truly paid for all of his sins. I showed him Titus 3:5, which says, "Not by works of righteousness which we have done, but according to his mercy he saved us, by the washing of regeneration, and renewing of the Holy Ghost."

I opened the Bible to 1 John 5:13, "These things have I written unto you that believe on the name of the Son of God; that ye may know that ye have eternal life, and that ye may believe on the name of the Son of God."

Eddie could *know* he had eternal life. He didn't have to hope or wonder if he was good enough. I asked God to help me make the gospel as clear as possible so Eddie could understand it.

I read 1 John 5:13 to Eddie several times, going back through the questions I'd been asking. Suddenly, he said, "I get it. I know I have eternal life."

"Do you believe Christ died for your sins and rose again?" I asked.

"Yes, I do," Eddie said.

"Do you understand that going to Heaven isn't about your good works but about what Christ did?"

"Yes, I do," Eddie said.

"If you were to die today, where would you go?" I clenched my hands waiting for his answer.

"I'd go to Heaven," Eddie smiled. "I know I'd go to Heaven."

Finish Line Strategies

- Take our Personal Evangelism course. Learn more at **www.dbc.edu**

- Always have tracts with you. We distribute millions of tracts through our television and radio broadcast. Visit **www.victoryingrace.org** for more information.

- Pray for opportunities to witness and then take those opportunities. Philippians 1:18–20 says, "What then? notwithstanding, every way, whether in pretence, or in truth, Christ is preached; and I therein do rejoice, yea, and will rejoice. For I know that this shall turn to my salvation through your prayer, and the supply of the Spirit of Jesus Christ, According to my earnest expectation and my hope, that in nothing I shall be ashamed, but that with all boldness, as always, so now also Christ shall be magnified in my body, whether it be by life, or by death."

- Make sure your community knows of your willingness to help out as a church. Our church is a polling place, a graduating place for most of our local, public junior high and high schools, a learning place about dyslexia for local teachers, and more.

- Support worldwide missions. Share the importance of missions with your people. Support national pastors and missionaries who are really doing a work for the Lord. Bring your people on mission trips so they can see for themselves the importance of missions.

- Have you thought about what it was like before you knew Christ as Savior? Have you considered the fact that you are saved because someone chose to share with you the Good News?

- Think of five people you know who don't know about the gospel. Find a way for them to hear the gospel. Pick up the phone and invite them to a church where you know the clear gospel will be given. Send them an email. Use the old-fashioned mail service and write a letter.

Chapter 9
Can You Call God Off?

And I give unto them eternal life; and they shall never perish,
neither shall any man pluck them out of my hand. John 10:28

While I was driving down the freeway, I picked up a hitchhiker and witnessed to him about Christ. I shared with him that he could know for sure he was going to Heaven. He trusted Jesus as his Savior right then and there. Then I told him he had the Holy Spirit living inside of him. I showed him Ephesians 4:30 which states, "And grieve not the holy Spirit of God, whereby ye are sealed unto the day of redemption."

I took him by our trailer, which had a little enclosed porch. He met my wife, and we had a meal together. I learned his name was Gary.

"Gary, where do you live?" I asked him.

"The University of Miami," he answered. He was living outside the campus on the streets, but he was able to make it by using the campus showers and stealing money from people.

"I'm on the run from the police," he said.

My jaw about hit the table. "Really? What did you do?"

"I'm AWOL from the army and also I murdered my father."

Here I'd brought this man home, and he'd met my wife. What had I been thinking? "You should turn yourself in," I said.

His face hardened. He glared at me, looking like a caged animal. "I could never turn myself in," he said.

Can You Live Any Way You Want and Still Go to Heaven?

A girl started attending a church in a small town. She got excited when she learned salvation was a free gift. She went home to tell her family, and they questioned her.

"Are you saying that you can live any way you want and still go to Heaven?... You mean you can commit murder and still go to Heaven?... You can do any terrible thing and still go to Heaven?"

The parents refused to let the girl go back to church because they didn't understand salvation. They didn't understand we don't get cleaned up in order to get saved; we get saved so God can clean us up. It is a process we go through once we become God's children. Of course, God doesn't want His children to murder or commit a terrible sin. He wants us to live holy lives. But can we live any way we want? The Bible says God will chasten and discipline us when we are on this earth because we are His children; so in the literal sense, we can't live any way we want. There are consequences for our actions here on earth and then a lack of rewards in Heaven.

Once we are born into God's family, we become God's children, just like when children are born into our own families. After birth, we can't have our children become unborn, no matter what sin they commit. The same goes for God. He will never kick you out of the family you were born into. He will never lose you.

Some people teach that while God can't lose you, you can lose God. They say there is a point where you can fall away from God once you have trusted Him as your Savior.

Suppose I took my two kids to the mall when they were younger and returned with only my daughter Julie. My wife Linda would ask where Jim was.

"I don't know," I would answer.

"What do you mean, you don't know? He's our son. You better go and get him right now," she would say. "In fact, I'm getting in the car right now and going back to the mall."

"But Linda, it's not my fault. I didn't lose Jim. He lost me."

Do you see the ridiculousness of that? God can't lose us. He is the One holding onto us. He is the One sustaining us. He sent His Son to die for our sins—all sins: past, present, and future.

Romans 5:8 states, "But God commendeth his love toward us, in that, while we were yet sinners, Christ died for us."

Romans 5:6 says, "For when we were yet without strength, in due time Christ died for the ungodly."

First Corinthians 15:3–4 is a great set of verses, "For I delivered unto you first of all that which I also received, how that Christ died for our sins according to the scriptures; And that he was buried, and that he rose again the third day according to the scriptures."

Christ died for you. He rose again for you. He died for your sins. All you need to do is believe. Can you live any way you want and still go to Heaven? Hang onto your hat, because we're going to be doing some flying through the Bible.

⁂

The Relationship

Many believers don't understand the difference between a relationship and fellowship. It is possible to be in a relationship with God but not in fellowship with Him. Picture this: When you were a child and you threw a fit because your mother wouldn't give you something you wanted, does that mean she could cause you to become unborn from your family? Of course not. If she was a good mother, she would make sure you received discipline for your actions, but you couldn't become unborn from the family. You wouldn't be in fellowship with your mother (i.e., she is happy with you) but you would still be in relationship (a part of the family).

Christians can commit any sin that a non-Christian can commit. They shouldn't. They should stay in fellowship with God, but they have the ability to sin. God has a remedy for this. In 1 John 1:9 it says, "If we confess our sins, he is faithful and just to forgive us our sins, and to cleanse us from all unrighteousness." Some call this verse the Christian bar of soap.

This is a verse for fellowship. How do we stay in fellowship with Christ? By confessing our sins and by living and walking in the Spirit of God. The moment you trusted Christ as your Savior, you were indwelt by the Holy Spirit. If you lean on Him and walk with Him, then you will live in fellowship with Christ.

Our churches across the country are full of people who are used to

"Christianity Lite." Many preachers don't really delve into the Word of God. They don't preach verse by verse in the Bible, and often the gospel isn't given. In addition, salvation and service are woefully confused to the point that people think they have to clean up their lives perfectly to get saved; or once they are saved, they can't have confidence and assurance in their salvation. As a result, they don't live victorious lives, but they are bogged down and frustrated.

❧

Can You Call God Off?

The hitchhiker's mouth tightened and his eyes hardened. I had just told a murderer he should turn himself in. I couldn't believe I'd taken him home to meet my wife.

Still, I had to tell him to do the right thing.

"Gary, you are not going to be happy unless you turn yourself in."

"No way. I'm getting out of here." Gary opened the door and was gone.

About a week later, I got a call from Gary.

He had a question I would never forget. "Can you call God off?"

"What are you talking about?" I had no idea what he was saying at first.

"I'm miserable. I know the Holy Spirit is living inside me and I can no longer steal. I can't knock people [on] the head and steal money. I'm starving to death."

Here was someone who realized that the Holy Spirit was inside of him. Though he had lived a bad life, he understood the influence and conviction of the Holy Spirit. "Gary, you are going to have to turn yourself in. It is the only way you are going to be happy."

Gary hung up. I thought I would never hear from him again.

He called me the next day. "I'll turn myself in if you will feed me a meal. Don't forget that I'm starving to death because I can't steal anymore."

I really didn't think about the potential danger this situation could have been for us since I was a young, brash college student. We had very little money, but we went over to the Miami campus and picked him up. We took him to a restaurant close to Florida Bible College, and he ordered a meal. Linda and I sat there and watched him while he was eating because we didn't have enough money to order food for ourselves. He enjoyed every bite. Then he said, "Will you buy me a second meal?"

Linda and I put together every penny we had. I knew we wouldn't have enough money for a tip. I've always believed that if a person can afford to eat out, he can afford to tip; but I told the waiter that we were trying to help this boy out, and we were really sorry but couldn't afford it. The waiter brought him a second meal. Gary wolfed it down.

I didn't know what police station to take Gary to. I didn't want them to be too rough on him, so I decided to take him to Opa-locka, where I had owned a restaurant called Chicken Town USA. I figured the Opa-locka Police Department would be bet-ter than Miami.

"I have a young man who claims to have killed his father and is AWOL from the army. All I ask is for you to treat him gently because he has trusted Christ as his Savior." They looked at me like I was crazy, but I kept explaining. They looked up Gary's name.

Chicken Town Restaurant I owned with my friend, Ed.

"Yes, this man is wanted." I went out with the police officers, and they arrested Gary.

The judge eventually ruled Gary insane and put him in a mental health institution, saying he was mentally unsound because he kept talk-ing about how he had trusted Christ as his Savior. Linda and I would go to visit him. It was quite an experience. Gary was really smart and was always studying his Bible. He had read through the Bible at least twice. Gary started studying Greek. He told me about a psychiatrist who had trusted Christ since he had witnessed to him. I went over and talked to the psychiatrist because I didn't believe it could be true.

"Sir, Gary told me that you have accepted Christ."

The psychiatrist looked at me with tears in his eyes and said, "Yes, I have."

Gary was quite a witness, even in the mental health ward.

We eventually lost contact with him, but his story is such a good example of what happens once you trust Christ. God can take the worst criminal and make him whole.

I'll never forget Gary or his question, "Can you call God off?"

Finish Line Strategies

- Consider some ways that your church could reach out to people like my friend, Gary. Now I'm not saying you should get together with murderers, but I am asking you to think about people you could reach out to that you normally wouldn't consider.

Chapter 10
Eternal Insecurity

Verily, verily, I say unto you, He that heareth my word, and believeth on him that sent me, hath everlasting life, and shall not come into condemnation; but is passed from death unto life. John 5:24

Larry was never much of a religious person. He went to church occasionally; but for the most part, he wanted nothing to do with the Lord. After many years addicted to alcohol and his fourth DUI, he decided to come back to visit his family before he went to jail for the latest offense. Jim Boyce, the head of our addictions ministry, took Larry out to breakfast when he heard he was in town. Over pancakes and bacon, Jim shared the clear, simple gospel with Larry. Although Larry had heard the gospel before, he had never really listened. He accepted Christ that day, much to the amazement of his relatives. He is going back to jail determined to share the gospel with the other inmates.

Many denominations teach parts of the gospel, but they don't make it easy to understand. Other churches teach that you can get saved, but then you have to have a bunch of works to keep your salvation. This was how I was taught as a child in the Methodist denomination. (Understand that I love Methodists. I love people from any church background. I love people with no religious background. As I'm sharing about my experience in church, I don't want you to think I don't appreciate the people—my Sunday School teachers, the deacons, or my parents. All of them tried to teach me what was right; but for the most part, they didn't understand the gospel. Most of them taught me there was no way to know for sure you were going to Heaven. Dad used to tell me never to believe the Baptists because they believed in that dangerous doctrine of eternal security.)

This is ironic now because, of course, you know I'm a Baptist. Some people think if you teach the doctrine of eternal security, then people will go out and live as they please, thinking they can go to Heaven no matter what. I believe exactly the opposite. When people realize they are kept by the blood of Christ and they can absolutely know for sure they are going to Heaven, this knowledge keeps them serving—not out of guilt, but out of love. And when a person serves out of love, they can't do enough for the person they love.

What if I told my wife, "When I get home, everything needs to be perfect. If it isn't, I'll divorce you. Dinner needs to be on the table cooked to my specifications. The house needs to be perfectly clean, and I'll be doing a white-glove inspection to make sure it is."

Do you think Linda would enjoy getting the house perfectly clean out of guilt? I doubt she would want to do any work on the house if I had this attitude. (By the way, she is already a perfect housekeeper — this is only an illustration.)

What if I told her instead, "Honey, no matter what, I will still love you."

Which way would make Linda want to do things for me? (If any of you husbands think the first way, then maybe you ought to rethink your marriage!) The truth is we do way more out of love than we do out of guilt.

When we teach eternal security from our pulpits, it frees people up to serve the Lord. They will see the reason they are doing it, and they will realize they could never do enough to repay the One who has done so much for them.

It is a whole other dynamic when you teach what the Bible says about Jesus saving us and keeping us. It is one of the keys to having an effective church that will cross the finish line and hear the Lord say, "Well done, thou good and faithful servant."

When I was a Methodist, I was like the chicken that swallowed the yo-yo and laid the same egg 18 times. Saved. Lost. Saved. Lost. Saved. Lost. I could leave God at home, go live as I pleased, and then pick Him up later. This was a false doctrine, and it caused me no end of frustration.

You don't raise your children and say to them every morning, "Now kids, make sure you don't sin today; because if you do, I'm going to kick you out of my family." I imagine kids raised in this kind of environment would be very insecure and frustrated at life.

So many people don't understand that when we teach the doctrine of eternal security, it inspires people to work for God. That's because they aren't working *for* their salvation but *because of* their salvation.

❦

One Doctrine

The doctrine of eternal security is not separate from salvation. Those who think they are saved now but can lose their salvation later have one of two problems: either they are trusting to some degree in their works to save them, or they don't understand that once they trust Christ as Savior, their eternal destiny is not in their hands but in the hands of Christ.

John 6:37 states, "All that the Father giveth me shall come to me; and him that cometh to me I will in no wise cast out." What do you think this verse means? It says that we will not be cast out once we trust in the Lord Jesus for our salvation.

Some might say, "God might not cast me out, but I could go of my own will and choice." Let's look further in John 6:39. "And this is the Father's will which hath sent me, that of all which he hath given me I should lose nothing, but should raise it up again at the last day."

What do you think "lose nothing" means? God saves you forever.

When Christ died on the cross, all of our sins were future. He died for all of them. Philippians 3:9 says, "And be found in him, not having mine own righteousness, which is of the law, but that which is through the faith of Christ, the righteousness which is of God by faith."

❦

Are Works Necessary?

When we trust Christ, we should walk in Christ. We should do the right thing. We should be like Gary and understand that the Holy Spirit inside us convicts us of sin. But not all believers walk in Christ. I like to use the following verses for those who don't get the concept that salvation is eternal:

"For other foundation can no man lay than that is laid, which is Jesus Christ. Now if any man build upon this foundation gold, silver, precious stones, wood, hay, stubble; Every man's work shall be made manifest: for the day shall declare it, because it shall be revealed by fire; and the fire shall try every man's work of what sort it is. If any man's work abide which he hath built thereupon, he shall receive a reward. If any man's work shall be burned, he shall suffer loss: but he himself shall be saved; yet so as by fire." 1 Corinthians 3:11–15

When believers appear before Christ, we will be judged, but not about whether we are going to Heaven or Hell. That was decided the moment we trusted Christ. Instead, it will be about whether we have done works for Christ that will last or works for ourselves that will not last. The works we do for Christ are compared to gold, silver, and precious stones. The works we do for ourselves are compared to wood, hay, and stubble. The fire talked about in these verses isn't the fire of Hell, but rather a purifying fire at the Judgment Seat of Christ. The works that will last will be rewarded when we stand before Christ. We will wish we had done more for the Lord Jesus Christ at that moment. We will understand the souls we could have won and the things we were supposed to do. This is for service, not for salvation.

Just don't miss the last verse: "If any man's work shall be burned, he shall suffer loss: but he himself shall be saved; yet so as by fire."

"He himself shall be saved." If you don't live for Christ, you will suffer loss at the Judgment Seat of Christ; but you will go to Heaven.

Salvation isn't about what we do, but about what Christ did.

The Two Natures

When we trust Christ as Savior, we receive a divine nature. This nature is diametrically opposed to the nature we were born with. These natures are at war with each other. When we yield to our new nature, then we will not walk in the flesh. But when we do what the nature we are born with wants us to do, then we will not walk in the Spirit.

Colossians 2:6 says, "As ye have therefore received Christ Jesus the

Lord, so walk ye in him." The Apostle Paul, who was probably the greatest man to walk on this earth after the Lord Jesus, understood the battle of the two natures. Look at Romans 7:14–25.

"For we know that the law is spiritual: but I am carnal, sold under sin. For that which I do I allow not: for what I would, that do I not; but what I hate, that do I. If then I do that which I would not, I consent unto the law that it is good. Now then it is no more I that do it, but sin that dwelleth in me. For I know that in me (that is, in my flesh,) dwelleth no good thing: for to will is present with me; but how to perform that which is good I find not. For the good that I would I do not: but the evil which I would not, that I do. Now if I do that I would not, it is no more I that do it, but sin that dwelleth in me. I find then a law, that, when I would do good, evil is present with me. For I delight in the law of God after the inward man: But I see another law in my members, warring against the law of my mind, and bringing me into captivity to the law of sin which is in my members. O wretched man that I am! who shall deliver me from the body of this death? I thank God through Jesus Christ our Lord. So then with the mind I myself serve the law of God; but with the flesh the law of sin."

Paul understood that he had to walk in the Spirit to have true victory. He had a new nature, the Holy Spirit, inside him who would help him to do right. He understood that his old nature was always ready to do wrong. If he followed his old nature, then he would sin. If he allowed his new nature to lead, he would walk in the power of the Holy Spirit.

My Last Movie

Soon after I trusted Christ, my friend, Rance, and I took two girls from Asbury College to a movie. This movie probably wouldn't even be rated PG now. But as we were sitting there, a scene came on that I knew wasn't right. I looked at Rance and told him that I was leaving.

The girl followed me out of the theater. "What are you doing?" she asked.

"I just got saved. This movie doesn't glorify Christ."

The Holy Spirit had convicted me of sin. Although I hadn't had any real Bible teaching at that time, I knew enough about my new faith to know this. The conviction of the Holy Spirit taught me to stay away from sin and to serve God fully.

Needless to say, my date wasn't happy. Neither was Rance's girlfriend, but we left anyway. Since they didn't want to walk 20 miles home, they came with us.

Maybe as you've read this chapter, you've thought of someone with whom you could share these verses. Perhaps you need to do a sermon series about the security of the believer. You will be so amazed by how people want to serve the Lord when they know they are eternally secure. Perhaps this has strengthened your resolve to give the gospel. That is my prayer. There is no greater joy that I could have than to know you are sharing the good news about Jesus Christ with all who will listen.

For now and all eternity, Larry couldn't be happier that someone took the time to share the gospel with him.

Finish Line Strategies

- We started a program for the addicted in our community several years ago. It has been a huge blessing to the people torn up by terrible addictions. Their families are also ministered to and their children. We have it every Friday night no matter what. We have seen hundreds of people come to Christ. Maybe you could start something like this in your church. One of our sister churches in Milwaukee with Pastor Dan Reehoff as pastor has an addictions program; but since they rent a building, the times they can meet are more limited. The program has still been successful, with many trusting Christ, coming to church, and getting their lives turned around.

- Start a prison ministry. Many jails and prisons will allow you to go in and do Bible studies with the inmates. We also have juveniles from the county jail come most Sundays.

Chapter 11
Called to Serve

But the God of all grace, who hath called us unto his eternal glory by Christ Jesus,
after that ye have suffered a while, make you perfect, stablish, strengthen, settle you.
1 Peter 5:10

Rance nudged me while we sat in the audience at the Circle K International Convention. I was supposed to speak to all the delegates in about an hour. I looked over at Rance. He said, "Jim, you should give the gospel when you speak."

"What are you talking about? I can't give the gospel to this huge group of people. Besides, that isn't what they want me to speak about."

"The Apostle Paul would do it," Rance said.

Now Rance had thrown down the gauntlet. If the Apostle Paul would do it, then of course I should have the courage to give the gospel. When I got up to speak, I just went ahead and gave the gospel. I'm not even sure what I said. I had no training. But I was so excited about the Lord that the words just spilled out of my mouth. I'll never forget the leaders of Circle K. Their jaws dropped all the way to the floor when I gave the gospel instead of my speech. Afterwards, the entire convention gave me a standing ovation.

Now I could go into politics and use the opportunities that came to give the gospel. A slam dunk.

Since I was International Trustee of Circle K, I had spent the day with John Sherman Cooper, who was on the Warren Commission. I only had a few months left of my senior year, so I figured all was well with the direction of my life.

Feeling sure of my calling and my future, I continued to preach at the church an hour away from UK. Bill, Rance, and Ed (another friend from college) came to the church too, and we would often go to the home of a dear couple named Bill and Jo Norris.

Bill and Jo Norris — Jo prayed me into the ministry.

Jo was probably the best cook in the world. She would make country ham, grits, biscuits, and gravy. (I was skinny back then and could eat whatever I wanted.) As poor, starving college students, we loved her cooking. Sitting around her table, we'd sometimes watch her hold up a perfectly baked biscuit and say, "This biscuit isn't up to my usual standards. It just doesn't taste that good."

We'd stare at her in disbelief. The biscuits absolutely melted in your mouth. They tasted so good with that farm-fresh butter and homemade, blackberry jelly. (It makes my mouth water to think about it. Except now I can't eat biscuits. It's a sad life at times.)

After lunch, we'd all go to the living room and pray. I wish I could explain to you exactly what that room felt like when Jo prayed. This dear woman didn't have a lot in the way of earthly possessions. Her furniture was worn, her carpet threadbare. She was beset with health problems. One time the doctors did surgery on her stomach. They found so much cancer that they didn't close her back up, thinking she was soon going to die.

But she didn't die after a day or two, so they went in and sewed her back up. Jo was the first woman to receive an artificial valve, so she was a medical miracle. She never got angry about anything. She was always so sweet, but also knew how to speak the truth.

She could pray like no other person. It was like the angels stopped to listen, like God was sitting right with us in the room.

After we prayed on that Sunday afternoon, Jo looked me in the eye. I can still picture her dear face and graying curls. Her mouth was turned up a little in the corner like she was about to smile. "James, you are going to be a preacher."

Fortunately, I was already kneeling so I couldn't fall over. Me, a preacher? There was no way I could ever be a preacher. That was ridiculous. At the time, I was still very carnal.

"Jo, you know I'm supposed to be a politician. That's my calling."

Her reply was calm. "You are supposed to be a preacher." Her eyes twinkled. "James, you'd make a good preacher. Stop resisting your real calling."

Didn't Jo know how much I had hated church as a child? Even though I was continuing to preach at the little Methodist church, that wasn't my career choice. Didn't Jo understand the extreme need for me to go into politics?

But she wouldn't stop saying it. "Jo, I'm not going to be a preacher," I would answer over and over. I didn't want to go through what my father had gone through all those years. I didn't want to make only a small salary. I wanted to do great things with my life, and I perceived preaching to be a small thing.

If only I knew the truth of what I know today. But back in those days, I didn't know.

I only knew one thing: I wanted to be a politician.

Considering the Call

Sometimes we wait for a phone call with more anticipation than we wait for God's call on our lives. Cell phones make it easy to place calls to people. In fact, there are almost no times in our lives when we are out of range of a cell phone. (Except for my daughter Julie. She lives in a rural area of Ohio where cell phones don't always have the best service. Of course, it doesn't help that she forgets to carry her phone half the time. So between her going in and out of service and not having her phone, if I ever do get a hold of her, it is a miracle!)

For most of us, we can get a call at any time. And most of the time we answer the phone. We might not answer if it is a political call, or a telemarketer, or someone we really don't want to talk to; but when the phone rings, we answer.

Sometimes when God is calling our churches, we aren't willing to answer the call. I've shared with you part of my story about my initial struggle to answer God's call on my life. But now I want to consider what it means to answer the call.

God calls His Church to be a hospital for the spiritually sick and hurting, not a museum for stuffed and starched Christians. He wants His Church to be a place where people can find out about the gospel first and foremost.

When sick people come to the hospital, are they looking for a doctor to tell them, "You are totally fine as you are. You don't need any medicine or surgery. Just go and have fun in your life"? Of course not. Sick people want to find out what is wrong and how to fix it.

Lately, I've found out that I have a bulging disc in my neck. It causes me a lot of pain in my arm. (It's my casting arm, so it affects my fishing.) I've tried lots of different things to help my arm feel better. When the doctor recommended the test for my neck, I didn't tell him, "I don't want to know what's wrong with my arm, so don't do this test." I was at the doctor so he could help me.

All around us people are spiritually sick. They are lost without Christ. They don't need a church patting them on the head and telling them that they are fine. They need The Great Physician. They need Jesus Christ. They need to understand He died and paid for their sins on the cross. If we don't tell them, then who will?

Norman was raised in a strong, Christian home. He trusted Christ when he was eight years old. When he was thirteen, he started hanging out with a group of unsaved people who drank. So he drank, too. Six months later, he started smoking. He went to various churches, but continued to drink. For the next 26 years, he never had a sober year. He married, had two children, and then divorced. Then he married again. His alcoholism was getting worse, though there would be periods when he was sober.

Not long ago, he owned a real estate company with sixteen

employees and $50 million a year in annual business. He was living large by the world's standards, but had also been warned that his alcohol and drug use were a problem to his work. His employees told him that if he fell back into this problem, they would have to remove his shares per their partnership agreement.

When Norman received a bonus for a particularly good year, he decided that he deserved to celebrate.

Twelve days later, he woke up in a hotel room following a huge binge of alcohol and cocaine abuse. He was immediately removed from ownership of his company and lost everything.

Norman entered a Christian rehabilitation center for 28 days, and found it a good start to his recovery; but when he came out of rehab, he had no support system and nowhere to turn.

Then Norman learned about our addictions program on Friday nights. The faith-based program taught him that the only way to stay sober and have restoration is through a personal relationship with Jesus Christ. He started attending all services of the church; and found such great hope and encouragement, he could hardly believe it.

While Norman still faces many challenges, sobriety has become a way of life for him. His relationship with his children, which had been severely tested, has been restored. He constantly shares his story how God and his church family gave him the strength he needed to recover and be restored.

An addictions ministry is one way that your church can be a spiritual hospital in your community. There are many other ways it can serve the community as well. We do a foster kids' Christmas party every year. We do all kinds of things for the community because our church wants to help people in any emotional or spiritual state.

Every Friday night our addictions program meets. It has changed hundreds of lives.

The Great Physician

Jesus gave us the greatest example of love and care for those around Him. In fact, He was regularly criticized for caring for the tax collectors, the hurting, the poor, and others who needed Him. Luke 5:27–32 says,

"And after these things he went forth, and saw a publican, named Levi, sitting at the receipt of custom: and he said unto him, Follow me. And he left all, rose up, and followed him. And Levi made him a great feast in his own house: and there was a great company of publicans and of others that sat down with them. But their scribes and Pharisees murmured against his disciples, saying, Why do ye eat and drink with publicans and sinners? And Jesus answering said unto them, They that are whole need not a physician; but they that are sick. I came not to call the righteous, but sinners to repentance."

In John 5:5–9, a man was helpless by a small pool, unable to go into it by himself.

"And a certain man was there, which had an infirmity thirty and eight years. When Jesus saw him lie, and knew that he had been now a long time in that case, he saith unto him, Wilt thou be made whole? The impotent man answered him, Sir, I have no man, when the water is troubled, to put me into the pool: but while I am coming, another steppeth down before me. Jesus saith unto him, Rise, take up thy bed, and walk. And immediately the man was made whole, and took up his bed, and walked: and on the same day was the sabbath."

The man was helpless like the spiritually dead people around us. He was unable to move without help. He couldn't do anything until Jesus healed him. That is the way it is with the communities around us. They aren't able to do anything spiritually unless we go to them, meet their needs, and give of ourselves as churches. This is the call to the church, and we must heed it.

Into the Water

One afternoon I found myself restless at the parsonage. My friends had already gone back to school. I was supposed to be studying because it was only a few months until the end of the semester, but I couldn't study. I couldn't do anything. I paced my living room and finally decided to go for a drive. That's when I came to the edge of a stream. There had been rain so I couldn't drive anymore, but somehow I knew I had to get across the stream. I took off my shoes and socks and stepped into the icy water.

When I look back to that moment, I think of Naaman, the great captain of the King of Syria's army, who understood affliction well. He knew he needed a change of direction because his current course wasn't getting him anywhere. His strength as a mighty captain stood in stark contrast to his weakness — leprosy — a disease that caused him to be an outcast among his own people and family. I've met lepers in India, and so I know firsthand how this disease disfigures. While leprosy can be cured today, in many cultures the disease still makes one a *pariah*.

When Elisha told Naaman to wash in the Jordan River seven times, Naaman reacted as we all sometimes react. Second Kings 5:11–12 says, "But Naaman was wroth, and went away, and said, Behold, I thought, He will surely come out to me, and stand, and call on the name of the Lord his God, and strike his hand over the place, and recover the leper. Are not Abana and Pharpar, rivers of Damascus, better than all the waters of Israel? may I not wash in them, and be clean? So he turned and went away in a rage." Why would Naaman bathe in the small Jordan River? He hadn't come all the way to Israel to take a bath in a muddy swamp, but to get healed. And to add insult to injury, the rivers of Syria were much bigger and more well-known than the Jordan River. Did no one understand that a high-ranking captain doesn't wade into a puddle like a common citizen, like a servant?

Do you respond like this sometimes? When faced with the truth about God's calling in your life, instead of turning gratefully to the answer, do you want to run the other direction? Before I crossed the stream, I felt like Naaman. Who was God to change my destiny? Who was He to alter my best-laid plans? The uncharted territory on the other side was filled with risk. I was comfortable with my life as it was. I didn't know if I could give up politics. I wasn't sure I wanted to follow God fully when my own plans stretched out in front of me.

I love it that a servant of Naaman's came up to him and spoke some sense into the man. Second Kings 5:13–14 continues, "And his servants came near, and spake unto him, and said, My father, if the prophet had bid thee do some great thing, wouldest thou not have done it? how much rather then, when he saith to thee, Wash, and be clean? Then went he down, and dipped himself seven times in Jordan, according to the saying of the man of God: and his flesh came again like unto the flesh of a little child, and he was clean."

That servant had guts! He knew he could very well lose his life for telling his master to listen to the servant of God. But his love for Naaman overcame his fear. What he said shows how smart he was in dealing with his master: "If the prophet had asked you to do a big thing, then wouldn't you have done it gladly? All He asked you to do was wash and be clean."

The Bible doesn't record what Naaman said. Naaman was a man of action. He dipped into the water seven times and experienced healing.

God may be speaking to you through someone like your brother or sister or my dear friend, Jo. Maybe He is speaking through the snotty-nosed, junior high kid who cuts your lawn. Or the pastor of the tiny church on the corner.

God doesn't ask you to do a difficult thing like climb Mt. Everest with a Bible balanced on your head, or pray hundreds of times an hour for the next 49 years.

His request is simple: He's asking you to dip your toes into the water, to cross the stream.

That's what I did that day. I stepped into the water. I reached the other side. I climbed over some rocks to the shore.

That's when I saw him.

An African-American man on his knees, his clothing worn, eyes closed. I stood quietly, not wanting to disturb his prayer, and feeling the first real calm since Jo told me I needed to preach.

The man looked up. "Are you the preacher I've been praying for?" he said.

Tears came to my eyes. I glanced down at my feet. I stood on holy ground.

My answer came quickly.

"Yes, I am." No hesitation.

The *I Am*, the Living Water, reached out to simple, ordinary me. I couldn't refuse anymore. He filled my longing with His peace.

"God, I'm not much," I prayed, "But what I have is Yours."

God wants to do the same with you and with your church. He is calling you to His service. He is calling your church to reach out in ways that are greater than you could ever think possible.

He wants to change your course. He wants you to cross the stream. You are called to serve.

Will you answer with a yes?

Finish Line Strategies

How does your church answer the call to be a spiritual hospital? I mentioned earlier about ways to help your community as a church and congregation. Here are some practical ways that you can help those in your community who are hurting.

- Identify areas of the population around you that need the most help. Figure out what is being done to help those people in the community. Most likely there isn't much being done to help them.

- Talk to those who run the behavioral health meetings in your town or city. Talk to social services.

- Most likely there are people who struggle with addictions who are in your own congregation. Get to know them. Love them. Invite them to your home. Don't be offended if at first, they don't want to open up to you. Many people who are at the end of their ropes don't want to be around people who have their lives totally together. They feel those people don't understand their pain or what they are going through. But persevere, and you will find your life is richer as a result.

- For more information on starting a ministry to the addicted, contact us at **www.qrbbc.org**, and we'll be happy to help you out.

Section 2

'Twas grace that taught my heart to fear,
And grace my fears relieved;
How precious did that grace appear
The hour I first believed.

Chapter 12
Faith in a Big God

But without faith it is impossible to please him: for he that cometh to God must believe that he is, and that he is a rewarder of them that diligently seek him. Hebrews 11:6

As a kid, I couldn't wait for school to get out for the summer. Sitting at my desk in September, I'd dream of going down to Kentucky Lake, camping out in a tent, pulling fish out of the creek, and roasting the filets over an open fire. I resisted the urge to drum my fingers across my desk as my teacher explained another math problem. Would June ever come?

I could only think of camping and fishing when I was this age.

Waiting for the concrete trucks to come to our new, 40-acre property in Hawthorn Woods, I felt the same. It seemed like if it rained on the West Coast, the concrete supplier didn't want to pour our concrete in

The day of the concrete miracle.

Hawthorn Woods. Inclement weather kept the trucks from coming day after day and week after week.

We had to pour the concrete. Soon. Or we would get even farther behind schedule. Since our workers were members of our church, Saturday was a logical choice to have the trucks come. The problem? The weekend called for rain. Lots of it.

The concrete supplier told me in no uncertain terms how much extra

money I'd have to pay if concrete trucks came to our property and had to turn back due to bad weather because they couldn't pour.

The other side of this problem didn't look much better. If the weather held out while they poured the 15,000 square feet of concrete but it rained afterwards, workers would have to come and chip out the pad, which would cost a fortune.

We had no extra money to run the risk.

And yet, if we didn't progress, we wouldn't be able to start school in the fall.

The forecast didn't look good. The weathermen called for rain.

We'd waited so long to get to this part of the project.

Throughout the summer, Quentin Road met in a public school gymnasium after we bought the 40 acres. These few months were our only time to get our first building on the 40 acres built. We had a Christian school to open in September. Talk about pressure. It was intense.

This was a time to remember the second verse of "Amazing Grace." Grace teaches us how to fear because we learn that we have no hope without Jesus Christ. That same grace teaches we have no need to fear because of our wonderful Savior.

All the setbacks had cost us big time. We couldn't delay anymore.

"We need to pour 15,000 square feet of concrete," I said to the supplier.

"Sir," the boss' voice got louder, "you understand how much money you would have to pay if this goes wrong?"

I hated to go ahead and pour with all these odds against us, but I knew we had no choice. "In spite of the forecast, we have to pour today."

We had to have faith like never before.

Construction had to continue so we could open school on time.

God delights in the faith of His children. Hebrews says without faith it is impossible to please God. What is faith exactly then? Faith is *pistis* in the Greek, and it means "assurance or belief." Faith is belief that God will do what He says He will do. Faith isn't complicated. It is simple—believe God. Though Hell tries to stop you, though the legions of evil try to march against you, though carnal Christians hate you, though the world doesn't understand—believe God. Choose faith.

Abraham had faith. Hebrews 11:8–10 states,

"By faith Abraham, when he was called to go out into a place which he should after receive for an inheritance, obeyed; and he went out, not knowing whither he went. By faith he sojourned in the land of promise, as in a strange country, dwelling in tabernacles with Isaac and Jacob, the heirs with him of the same promise: For he looked for a city which hath foundations, whose builder and maker is God."

Abraham was told to move. The problem was he didn't know the destination. Can you imagine coming home to your family and saying, "Okay everyone, let's start packing."

"Where are we going, Daddy?" one of the kids would ask.

"I don't know, son. We're just moving."

Your wife's eyes might look like they are going to pop out of her head. "You're kidding. We're going to move right now?"

"Right now."

If this happened in your home, I'm sure you can only imagine what would happen. Yet we have Abraham who was willing to have faith and obey God.

Are you willing to obey God and have faith, even when the odds are against you?

Do You Have Faith?

You might say, "Listen, I appreciate all you are saying about faith; but honestly, I don't have that kind of faith. I'm just a layman in a church."

Or maybe you are the pastor of a small church or a pastor who has been through really difficult times. Could it be that you keep trying to be faithful in your church, but it seems like your church is falling apart no matter what you do?

How do you have the faith you need to have when you are at your wit's end? How do you have the faith you need when you feel weak and help-less?

The truth is, faith isn't about us or how good we are. Faith isn't about how accomplished we are or what we have done in our lives.

Faith is belief in a great God.

Faith isn't dependent on you.

This attribute is dependent on Him.

Gideon is a great example of faith. He was just an ordinary guy when the Lord gave him a big job.

Judges 6:11–17 tells us more:

"And there came an angel of the LORD, and sat under an oak which was in Ophrah, that pertained unto Joash the Abiezrite: and his son Gideon threshed wheat by the winepress, to hide it from the Midianites. And the angel of the LORD appeared unto him, and said unto him, The LORD is with thee, thou mighty man of valour. And Gideon said unto him, Oh my Lord, if the LORD be with us, why then is all this befallen us? and where be all his miracles which our fathers told us of, saying, Did not the LORD bring us up from Egypt? but now the LORD hath forsaken us, and delivered us into the hands of the Midianites. And the LORD looked upon him, and said, Go in this thy might, and thou shalt save Israel from the hand of the Midianites: have not I sent thee? And he said unto him, Oh my Lord, wherewith shall I save Israel? behold, my family is poor in Manasseh, and I am the least in my father's house. And the LORD said unto him, Surely I will be with thee, and thou shalt smite the Midianites as one man. And he said unto him, If now I have found grace in thy sight, then shew me a sign that thou talkest with me."

Gideon had a conversation with the God of Israel and asked Him for a sign. He said he was poor in his father's house, and his tribe was the small-est tribe.

In other words, Gideon was like you and me. He knew that he was weak. He knew he couldn't do the task that he had been given to do.

He was at a good starting point.

Why would I say that? Because until we are at the place where we understand that we are nothing and God is everything, we aren't going to be utilized of God. We aren't going to be used by God in our churches, in our homes, or in our lives.

Faith believes God. Gideon believed God. Through God's strength, he was able to do great things and help Israel. Although he considered himself poor before God, he was actually rich in faith. And that's all he needed.

Matthew 17:20 states, "And Jesus said unto them, Because of your unbelief: for verily I say unto you, If ye have faith as a grain of mustard seed, ye shall say unto this mountain, Remove hence to yonder place; and it shall remove; and nothing shall be impossible unto you." Jesus said that if we have faith as a mustard seed, then we can actually move mountains. I've never seen a mountain moved by my faith, but I have seen plenty of miracles that God has done. They might as well have been mountains in my life.

You always have to have faith. Hebrews 11:6 states that faith is necessary to please God. "But without faith it is impossible to please him: for he that cometh to God must believe that he is, and that he is a rewarder of them that diligently seek him."

People have said to me, "I've cried out to God, but He doesn't hear me." God hears you when you cry out to Him. You know this by faith.

Someone might say, "I really want this new Cadillac, and I've been praying for it for a long time."

God doesn't work that way. God isn't going to give that Cadillac to you unless He thinks you can use it to bring Him glory.

Those early years taught me about faith. I grew up in a home where my dad received a salary. My wife grew up in a home where her dad worked at National Cash Register. He received several patents from his time there. He was a very smart man. Both of us had never been in such a position where we literally had to depend on God each and every moment.

It is not a matter of what you have. It is a matter of having faith in God.

In our church, we used to bring many of the ladies and their children from the mission in Chicago. Often, many of them were happier than we were, even though we have so much more.

Poor believers and rich believers can have the same amount of faith.

The other day I took my sixteen-foot Carolina skiff out to the water. I enjoyed the same beauty that all the other bigger boats were experiencing, but without the taxes or the headache that those other boats bring their owners. We can all enjoy the same beauty, no matter what our circumstances or our wealth.

Faith is like that. It is a great equalizer of believers.

∽◦◦∽

Do You Believe God?

Dear friend, are you feeling a tug at your heart right now? You know God is powerful. You want to believe Him and His promises, but are you focusing instead on yourself and your perceived inadequacies?

As I considered the ramifications of having faith in God on the day I said to go ahead and pour the concrete, my thoughts went back to the time after I'd crossed the stream and answered God's call to preach. Faith was an extremely important factor in the decisions that were made in the following days and weeks after that call.

Filled with an overwhelming desire to go to Bible college, I didn't know where I was going to go or anything about Bible college; but I knew that God wanted me to do this.

I didn't care anymore about graduating from the University of Kentucky, though it was my senior year. I went home and told my parents about the call that I had received. They suggested that I go to Asbury Theological Seminary. I had a lot of family who had attended there, including my mom and dad. My Aunt Jane had a restaurant in the town by the college. My uncle had delivered ice cream there for years and had a scholarship program set up for family members, so I could have gone there for free.

In spite of the encouragement to attend Asbury, I didn't feel the Lord was leading me there. Rance, Ed, Bill, and I continued to get together to pray. We ordered free booklets from *Radio Bible Class* with M.R. DeHaan. One would be about angels, another about eternal security, another about the end times. We would study these books together and get so excited. That's why I continue to send our free resources—books, CD's, and tracts—to people who call and write our television program, *Victory In Grace*. It is sort of a payback to *Radio Bible Class* for being so generous and helpful at the beginning of my walk with the Lord.

We sent away for Bible college information. We would receive stacks of catalogs; and during our Bible studies and prayer meetings, we would read them and pray about them. Then we got a catalog from Florida Bible College. This was a smaller school. There was something about the catalog that drew me in. It wasn't that it was beautiful and full of glossy, full-color pictures, but because of the emphasis on the gospel.

Every day I thanked God for sending His Son to die for me. I knew God loved me. I wanted to live for the Lord Jesus Christ. Before my salvation, I had missed the crucial link between salvation and service because I had been taught in my childhood about Christianity.

I'm sure you realize by now that the gospel was

Florida Bible College's first campus was shared with the Florida Bible Church.

precious to me like a wonderful, priceless treasure. In my deepest soul, I knew we needed to go to a school that was centered on the gospel.

One night when we were praying, I said, "Lord, I know where we are going to Bible college. I know where we are going."

Bill Adams, a scholarship baseball and basketball athlete at UK, looked over at me and tapped my arm. "Where? Where are we going?"

He couldn't wait for the prayer to end. I finished the prayer and smiled, knowing deep peace: "Florida Bible College."

Your Next Step of Faith

Perhaps you are in the same place of needing to have faith like I was that day we decided to go to Florida Bible College (Because of the failure of two presidents, the school has closed, but I couldn't have received a better education.), or it could be you are a little further along and have been a Christian for many years; but God is calling you to step out in faith yet again. That's why we started Dayspring Bible College and Seminary.

Perhaps you've answered the call. You've crossed the stream. You've decided to follow the Lord, or you've renewed your desire to follow the Lord wherever He leads. Maybe you are like Abraham, absolutely ready to move and do God's will at a moment's notice. Or perhaps you are more like Gideon, more hesitant at first, but willing. What will you do now? Will you take the next step? Maybe you are a business person who realizes you need to make church more of a priority in your life. Perhaps you are a pastor who has been struggling with some issues in your life, and you know it's time to get them right. It could be that your boss has been frustrating you and you haven't been acting in a kind way towards him. Maybe your church is going through some situations with finances, and you don't know where to turn. Taking a stand is frightening, but you know you should.

Know this: Whatever your situation, wherever you are, God is with you. He will not fail you. He will keep you safe. He will guide you as you take the next step of faith.

Finish Line Strategies

Here are some ways you can develop a stronger faith:

- Faith isn't centered on you but on Christ. You may feel you have weak faith, but it doesn't matter how weak your faith is. God is who your faith needs to be placed in — not in yourself.

- Meditate on Scripture on a regular basis. Sometimes the world uses the term "meditate" to mean some weird, Eastern, religious thing. All I mean is the biblical term "meditate," which means to think and remember. Pick one or more of the following promises in the next section, write them down on a card, and put the card somewhere you can read it over and over. Or better yet, memorize one of them.

Promise: "I will never leave thee, nor forsake thee." Hebrews 13:5c

Promise: "So that we may boldly say, The Lord is my helper, and I will not fear what man shall do unto me." Hebrews 13:6

Promise: "And he said, The LORD is my rock, and my fortress, and my deliverer; The God of my rock; in him will I trust: he is my shield, and the horn of my salvation, my high tower, and my refuge, my saviour; thou savest me from violence." 2 Samuel 22:2–4

Promise: "For thou art my rock and my fortress; therefore for thy name's sake lead me, and guide me." Psalm 31:3

Promise: "He only is my rock and my salvation: he is my defence; I shall not be moved." Psalm 62:6

Chapter 13
A Passion for Souls

The fruit of the righteous is a tree of life; and he that winneth souls is wise.
Proverbs 11:30

The workers stared at me. "We're going to go ahead and pour the concrete?" they asked incredulously. With confidence not in myself but in a great God, I said, "Yes."

The men prepped the work site to prepare for the foundation to be poured. We all tried to ignore the humidity in the

A real miracle at Quentin Road.

Someone took a picture of that amazing day and added these words...

OH, YE OF LITTLE FAITH!

air, the occasional claps of thunder, the lightning coming every few minutes. No rain had come on our property yet. Our hearts were in our throats. And yet, an incredible peace was over me. God was in control. He already had this situation all handled.

Have you ever been at a place where things are out of your own control? Well, congratulations, you are at a place where God can truly use you. It is during those times when we realize that we can do nothing and God can do everything that we fully begin to trust the Father.

Far too often people stop doing what God has told them to do too soon.

They accept Christ as Savior; they decide to serve the Lord Jesus; and they go through a few trials that discourage them a little bit, but they make it through them. But then when something big comes, something that is really discouraging and frustrating, they want to quit. God wants them to reach out in faith, but they don't want to step out of their comfort zone.

Sometimes this happens to churches. They have had great things happen in the past. Many souls have trusted Christ. They've made a difference in the community. They've done what God has called them to do. But then opposition comes, and they want to stop having faith.

We've built seven buildings; and during the construction of every one of them, I've had someone come to me at the point of no return in the project and say, "I knew God wasn't in this." These are times when as a leader in the church, you have to find your encouragement in the Lord and try to pick yourself up. The same person will come to you after the project is complete and say, "I always knew God was in this." Be ready for it. While most of the time people are behind you, there are always one or two who have to say something negative.

Perhaps the church needs to take a big step like build a new building or start a ministry that will reach out to people. Maybe at first everyone was gung ho about the idea and couldn't wait to do it. Everyone had faith and trusted God to do it.

But now a few people are questioning the decision. Other people are talking amongst themselves, saying they think the church shouldn't go in that direction.

Let me encourage you right now. Once you have determined what God wants you to do, whether it is in your personal life or in the life of your church, know God will accomplish it. You have to remain willing, even during the hard times that are sure to come.

⁂

Seek Counsel

Throughout the years, one of the things that has always helped me was seeking counsel from other spiritually strong believers. Proverbs 11:14 states, "Where no counsel is, the people fall: but in the multitude of counselors there is safety." When you are discouraged and feel like you can't make it anymore, pick up the phone. Call someone that you trust who is spiritually mature. Ask their advice. (That day with the concrete, I asked many knowledgeable people their advice before I made the decision to pour. Throughout the years, I would say that has been one of the main reasons that I've made it at all—seeking counsel from wise people in the Lord.) If your church is at a place where a decision needs to be made, seek counsel from a pastor of a church you trust. If you personally need to make an important decision, don't make the decision in a vacuum. Talk to your pastor or to other godly leaders about what you should do. If you are a pastor, seek the advice of other pastors. If you are a leader or layperson, go to your pastor. If your counselors are godly, then you will come away stronger in faith.

When people come to a crisis in their life, they are often encouraged to go to a counselor. While this might help some people, this isn't the counseling I'm writing about. What I mean is learning to seek the advice and thoughts of spiritual people on a regular basis.

The Miracle

The first concrete truck turned into the driveway at our Hawthorn Woods location (now Lake Zurich). The truck's windshield wipers were on, and water poured off the hood of the truck. But there was no rain on our own property. More trucks arrived in the same condition.

One driver got out of the truck and said fervently, "It's raining all around this property, and it's not raining here! I can't believe it!" It rained 360 degrees around the 40 acres.

Another driver fell to his knees. "This will make a believer out of an atheist!"

The concrete got poured without one drop of rain falling on our property. Some trucks had to stop by the side of the road on the way because the rain poured down so hard. No one could believe that it wasn't raining on our property. Everyone was so excited to see God at work.

When God does a miracle, He makes it obvious and open for all to see.

All of our church people who observed this miracle still talk about it to this day. It was one of the banner moments in our church history.

One of the workers who smoothed the concrete said, "Pastor, we could use a little rain right now to set the concrete." Almost as soon as the words were out of his mouth, it gently rained for a few minutes, giving us the exact amount of water we needed.

How do I explain what happened? I can't. There is no way I could ever explain this miracle. It was one of those amazing times when you see the hand of God like never before. The truck drivers praised God. The workers praised God. Our church people praised God. I praised God. We were on schedule. We could continue building the building. God was so good.

Our new building taking shape.

When God Doesn't Answer the Way You Want

I shared earlier about the difference between smart faith and stupid faith. There are people who procrastinate to get something done; and then when they get into a really difficult predicament, they pray and ask God for a miracle. That's stupid faith.

If I had prayed not to have rain for a church picnic, it might have still rained. I've prayed for good weather for many events, and we've still had rain. God might not always answer our prayers the way we want, but He will protect His Church. At the same time, He wants us to have smart faith. He wants us to think through the choices we make in our lives. He wants us to seek the godly counsel of other believers. He wants us to make decisions that are wise. Proverbs 6:22 states, "When thou goest, it shall lead thee; when thou sleepest, it shall keep thee; and when thou awakest, it shall talk with thee."

God loves to answer our prayers. He will do miracles. If the rain had come during the pouring of the concrete and we had to chip it out, He would have shown us how to do it. He is a good God and always answers. Part of spiritual maturity is discovering how to have the faith no matter what answer God gives.

Visit to Florida Bible College

Ed, Bill, Rance, and I loaded up our Volkswagen to take a trip to Miami, Florida. Bill Adams was one of the top baseball players at UK. The university said Ed Sutton was either the smartest man who ever lived, or the dumbest—they didn't know which—and all of us were going to check out Florida Bible College.

When we crossed the state line into Florida, Rance called his mom and told her where he was.

"You're in Florida?" she asked in disbelief.

"Yes, Mom. I'm going to go to Bible college."

"What?" His mother's voice carried through the telephone.

The poor woman didn't know what to think. But none of us cared about anything except getting to Florida Bible College and checking out what was there.

When we arrived, we learned that the college was operating out of a church. We were used to the big university with sports programs, laboratories, and a student union. We weren't prepared for the school to be small. (The college had about 600 students, and that was small to us.) After touring the college, we stopped to eat at a restaurant.

"Guys, I don't think this is where God wants us to go. It isn't that big of a school. God must have told me wrong. He meant we should go to Miami Bible College. That school is bigger," I said. Throughout the whole process of figuring out where God was leading us, I had the most faith about where we were supposed to go. But here I was the first to not have faith when the school didn't measure up to what I thought it should be. As we left the restaurant, I got violently ill. The guys didn't know what to do with me; so they went to a motel close to the restaurant and the school, checked in, left me in the room, and went to the college to take some classes.

The food poisoning was some of the worst I've ever had. I couldn't get out of bed for two days. The guys all went back to FBC and loved it. They attended some of the classes, and started to realize all that they could learn about the Bible. They would come back to the mo-tel and say, "Jim, you are going to love this school. It is wonderful. We are learning so much. It is what we've been praying for."

But I hardly heard them, I was so sick. The next night, I felt a little less sick; and the guys persuaded me to go with them to a meeting called Youth Ranch, where I would get to hear the president of the college, Dr. A. Ray Stanford, speak.

Dr. A. Ray Stanford.

As Dr. Stanford spoke, I listened like I'd never listened before. As he explained the gospel, I knew that this was the school we'd been looking for. I knew the gospel, but hadn't heard it so clearly until that night. Then Dr.

Stanford did the Heaven illustration (originally given by R.A. Torrey), with his wallet. This illustration made the gospel so clear and so easy to understand. I determined that I would learn how to give that visual aid; and by God's grace, I would use it every time I preached. I never wanted there to be a time when I didn't give the gospel in the

Dr. Stanford taught me how to make the gospel clear and simple.

clearest way possible. I wanted everyone to understand the greatest news in the entire world.

Do you feel this passionate about the gospel? If not, take a moment to confess this to God. Start anew with a fresh desire to tell everyone how they can go to Heaven.

Is there an area of your life where you've tended to have stupid faith? You haven't sought the advice of spiritually mature people about this matter? You haven't sought God's advice on what to do? Or maybe there is an area in your church's life where you need to raise your faith IQ. Whatever the case, think about some areas where you plan to have more faith in our great God. Shore up these areas and strengthen them by faith. Keep a strong passion for lost and dying souls.

God will help you in every area of your life and ministry.

Finish Line Strategies

- Turn to **Appendix A** to see the illustration I use with my wallet to give the gospel. Study it. Memorize the verses, and soon you will be able to use it to share the greatest news in all the world.

- Write down the following verses about the importance of the gospel: Acts 20:24; Romans 1:16; Romans 10:15; Galatians 1:16.

Chapter 14
Operation What's Next

But if our gospel be hid, it is hid to them that are lost: In whom the god of this world
hath blinded the minds of them which believe not, lest the light of the glorious gospel
of Christ, who is the image of God, should shine unto them.
2 Corinthians 4:3–4

One afternoon while driving with my brother in Miami Beach, I saw two men putting a body into the trunk of a car. (This was Miami, after all.) Horrified, I pulled off the road to see if I could help. David jumped from the passenger's side to the driver's side and drove away, leaving me to deal with the mess. This was long before cell phones. A police officer soon stopped. I told him what happened. They brought me to the police station and promised me witness protection if I would testify, only I couldn't tell anyone what had happened. They had already arrested the perpetrators and wanted the crime to go to trial.

At the time, all of us guys were living in a house not too far from the campus. Bill Adams had prayed God would show him He loved him more by giving him more trials. (Yes, we were young and stupid at that time.) It wasn't long after that Bill suffered a back injury. He kept telling me that someone was following him, and he wasn't sure what was going on. I could neither tell him what had happened nor tell him that someone really had been following me, plus guarding the apartment.

"Bill, you're delusional. Why would someone follow you?" I'd say.

During Christmas break, I went home to Paducah to see my parents, but Bill couldn't go because of his injury.

Bill was sure someone was watching the house, and something terrible was going to happen to him. He began to wish that he hadn't prayed for God to give him trials. (When I got back to Miami, he told me he had slept with a knife beside the bed.) Someone had broken into the house and stolen some radio equipment that we had on the first floor. He said he knew he was right. Someone had been watching him.

Poor Bill. I couldn't tell him about the murder. Soon after that, another eyewitness who had actually seen the murder testified at the trial. I didn't have to testify after all. I could then tell Bill what had happened. Someone had been keeping an eye on our house. (The theft of the radio equipment remained a mystery.)

Part of having strong faith is being aware of the opportunities God has placed in your path. Ann loved to bowl every Thursday. One of her teammates named Nancy asked to talk to her at the end of their game. They talked for a few minutes. Ann then left the bowling alley, but felt like she should have talked longer. Throughout the next two days, Ann kept thinking of Nancy. At eight o'clock on Saturday night, Ann decided to call Nancy and invite her to church the next morning. Nancy said she would love to go to church.

The next day, Ann brought Nancy to church. After church, the two ladies went out for a bite to eat and then over to Nancy's house to talk. Nancy told Ann of some health challenges she was facing; and then said, "Ann, I sure hope I'm good enough to go to Heaven."

Ann didn't hesitate. "Nancy, it isn't being good that will get you to Heaven. It is what Jesus did on the cross for you. He died to take away your sins. Do you believe that He did this for you?"

The two talked for awhile, and Nancy made it clear that she now understood the gospel. The next morning, Ann received a call from Nancy's son. The night before, Nancy went to her son's home for dinner, and then drove home. In the morning, her kidneys failed and she passed away.

Have you ever had someone on your mind like Nancy? Do you need to call and extend an invitation for lunch so you can share the gospel with them? Why don't you do that right now? Look back over your list of people for whom you have a burden, and call them today.

❦

Sharing the Gospel

There was nothing my college friends loved better than to share the gospel. We'd go into a fast-food restaurant and witness to everyone there. We had seen an accident and had stopped to pass out tracts to people as they came by.

I came upon an accident of a couple of Florida Bible College girls. We called the ambulance; and right as they were bringing the girls to the hospital, one girl opened her eyes and shared the gospel with the paramedics.

Still another time, I shared the gospel on the beach, and witnessed to a man who trusted Christ. He then told me he was a Jesuit priest, and invited me to his school so I could address the students. One of my friends went to the school and witnessed in five classrooms before the nuns kicked him out.

❧

A Passion for Souls

Do you have a passion for souls? I don't care if you are the pastor or if you are a worker in your church—your job is to share the gospel. Mark 16:15 isn't limited to pastors: "And he said unto them, Go ye into all the world, and preach the gospel to every creature." I believe that in a strong church, the pastor is always witnessing to the lost. He always shares the gospel from the pulpit. At events, he is always sharing the gospel. When he does this, other people will also start to share the good news of salvation. The excitement in your church will grow greater than you could ever imagine.

The four of us determined that we wouldn't look at a girl unless she was godly and the woman God wanted for us as a wife. Not too long after I arrived at the campus, I met Linda Sue Hannah, a beautiful girl with a wonderful smile. After we got married, we settled into a trailer, went to school, and worked.

Our daughter, Julie, was born in November of 1969. We then decided to live in Paducah, Kentucky, for the summer, so we sold the chicken restaurant in Opa-locka. While we were there, I went to the local Methodist churches to see if they would financially support us; and to my surprise, they had me take over five churches. I would preach at two on Sunday morning, another two Sunday night, and another on Wednesday night.

Rubin Moyer loaned us a place where we could meet for Youth Ranch, similar to the one that I'd gone to on my first visit to Florida. We would sing songs and have a Bible study with the teenagers. Of course, when there are teens involved, there is usually food in- volved. We had events like a 100-

Early Youth Ranch.

Foot Banana Split Night and food relays. A man named Paul Washer at- tended Youth Ranch and trusted Christ. He offered to let us use his real ranch with horses and cows to meet with our group of kids.

The first week, we came to set up the meeting and saw cars parked up and down the street. Linda and I wondered what in the world was going on. When we got there, we found hundreds of kids who had come for Ranch. So many kids trusted Christ that night. It was amazing.

I led a city-wide revival in Paducah; and though I still didn't know much about public speaking, we had hundreds come out to hear the gos- pel. The local paper ran a big story about the revival. Linda and I were so excited to see God working; but we also knew after the summer ended it was time to go back and finish college. We asked some friends, Ray and Diana Dukes, to come and take over the Ranch ministry. They kept it going, and eventually started a church in that location. We then traveled back to Florida to finish up Bible college.

Back to Florida

We arrived for the Fall Semester; and a few months later, the due date of our next child was fast approaching. We had to have $600 before we could go to the Cedars of Lebanon Hospital to have the baby. This was definitely out of our budget, so I got a job working at Brinks as a night watchman. It was a great job because I was able to study in the evenings. We knew God would provide the funds we needed, but I am definitely one who believes in paying my bills. As poor college students who had to work full-time and were trying to raise a family, we had some pretty lean times financially. We were able to save up the $600, but I still didn't know how we would pay for the rest.

I was working at Brinks when I got the call Linda needed to go to the hospital. I had to leave the place unguarded for a little while. Fortunately, no robberies took place. Our son, Jim Jr., was born on December 23, 1970.

We took him home on Christmas Day in a stocking we still use as a decoration to this day. We couldn't have been happier. We didn't have much, but we had each other and a beautiful family.

The way it worked out with Linda at the hospital, she didn't have to stay there the full two days, so they only charged her for one day. A few weeks

My wife Linda and Julie's first glimpse at this strange newcomer.

later, we got what we thought was a bill. When we opened it, there was a $40 refund check inside. They never charged us another dime, but gave us money back.

Julie's reaction to the baby was quite different than ours. I'll never forget her looking in the bassinet and seeing her little brother in there. Even at thirteen months old, she knew her glory days as the only child were over.

◈

Paying Your Bills

The principles I learned in financial management when I was growing up and in college have stood me in good stead throughout the years. (My father was very open with me about the finances in our home. A Methodist preacher doesn't make that much money, so he had to find ways to make our money stretch. Also, while a church providing a parsonage for a pastor might be a good idea for the short term, it also means that many pastors have no retirement income or anywhere to live once they retire from the church. Sometimes pastors are so tied down they can hardly do the work of the ministry. They have to constantly think about their lack of money and how they are going to pay their bills. Fortunately, I have a church that truly cares for me and takes care of us financially.) But in the early years, we had little and had to find ways to make that money stretch.

❧

Burden for Dad's Salvation

My parents retired to Florida and bought a small home there. Then Dad was diagnosed with Hodgkin's Disease. He didn't have long to live. Since realizing Dad didn't know for sure he was going to Heaven, I had a heavy burden for his salvation. I would plead with him to trust Christ, but he had been raised to think that going to Heaven was part Christ and part works. This was deeply ingrained in him, and he didn't want to really look at what the Bible said.

My heart broke for Dad's soul on a daily basis. He was always so good to me. He would buy our kids anything they wanted. He loved to play practical jokes on people. He loved life and I wanted him to be in Heaven with me. I prayed for him over and over again. I so wanted him to trust Christ. But now, as his days were truly numbered, it seemed like there wasn't much hope. For the moment, Dad didn't want to listen.

Who are you praying for?

As you're reading this, are you thinking of someone you've prayed for? Have you prayed for many months or years that that person would trust Christ? James 5:16 says, "Confess your faults one to another, and pray one for another, that ye may be healed. The effectual fervent prayer of a righteous man availeth much." This isn't talking about physical healing (though it could mean that) but spiritual healing. Your prayers avail much. Your prayers are important. First Thessalonians 5:17 states, "Pray without ceasing." Your prayers are heard by God. He will answer them in ways that you will never imagine. You may not know in this life how your prayers are answered; but I can promise you, God hears your prayers. I had to trust this promise, though I sure was tempted not to. As part of Operation What's Next, I chose to trust God with Dad's future.

❧

Dad, Please Trust Christ

One night, I stood by the side of Dad's hospital bed. I so wanted him to trust Christ as his Savior, but he didn't want to listen. I couldn't contain my emotion. I'm not recommending that you say to your parent what I said to him—remember, I was young and not always the smartest college student—but I looked him in the eye and said, "Dad, you're going to Hell."

My brother, David, was with me as we walked to the elevator. I cried all the way to the main floor and all the way back to my home. I couldn't stand the thought that my dad wasn't going to trust Christ, but it was his decision.

In the middle of the night, Dad couldn't stand it anymore. He called Florida Bible College and asked them to send someone over to the hospital. The college sent over Herb Paynter, and he shared the gospel with my dad. He trusted Christ as his Savior.

For the next two years, Dad gave out tracts and shared the gospel with anyone who would listen. (Some in the family have said that the last two years of his life were Dad's happiest years.) On the day he died, I had people tell me that in the previous week, Dad had been going up and down the hospital hallways witnessing to people.

I'll never forget the moment he died. I held him in my arms as he died. The nurses told us to leave. I said, "The angels are coming to take my dad home to Heaven."

My dad was so happy during his final years after his salvation.

Then I got out my wallet and shared the gospel with the nurses.

It was what Dad would have wanted.

Finish Line Strategies

- When sharing the gospel, be sure to explain when you trusted Christ and the circumstances that led to that decision. This will become one of your most powerful tools in having people be open to the message.

- Do you ever worry that maybe it isn't the right time to share the gospel? Remember Paul's admonition to Timothy. Second Timothy 4:2 says, "Preach the word; be instant in season, out of season; reprove, rebuke, exhort with all longsuffering and doctrine." Be ready anytime to give the gospel.

- It is your job to give the gospel. It is the Holy Spirit's job to convict the person about the truth of the message. When you do your job, the Holy Spirit will do His. Don't get discouraged if the person doesn't accept Christ right then—you planted a seed.

Chapter 15
More Precious Than Gold

That the trial of your faith, being much more precious than of gold that perisheth,
though it be tried with fire, might be found unto praise and honour and glory
at the appearing of Jesus Christ. 1 Peter 1:7

Pearle Wait manufactured and peddled his cough syrups house to house. In 1895, he bought the patent for a gelatin product. After tinkering around in the kitchen, he combined the gelatin with fruit flavoring. His wife named the new product Jell-O. Pearle hoped to become rich from the new product, but sales were slow.

High school dropout Frank Woodward bought the Jell-O patent from Pearle for $450. Sales crept along, though Woodward was a marketing genius. Nicely dressed salesmen went house to house with product samples and cookbooks featuring Jell-O. He was about to sell the patent when sales shot through the roof, reaching $1 million in 1906. His company eventually would become General Foods Corporation, now known as Kraft General Foods.[x]

Pearle wanted Jell-O to be a big hit, but was unable to wait. His impatience kept him from reaping the rewards. Of course, he couldn't have known that Jell-O would be known for decades as "America's Favorite Dessert." (Unfortunately, I've never shared that sentiment, as I don't really love Jell-O. But obviously for many years, America and the world have loved it.)

We often feel like Pearle while we wait in the ministry. We share the gospel, disciple believers, preach, visit the sick, care about the hurting, wake up in the middle of the night to go help people, and we do everything we can to do the work of the ministry. But often, results don't seem to happen. The church doesn't grow. People listen to the gospel, but they don't trust Christ. An event you've been planning for months conflicts in timing with a big game or community gathering, and no new people come out to the church.

Galatians 6:9 says, "And let us not be weary in well doing: for in due season we shall reap, if we faint not." We are often weary in the work, but we have to be careful not to get weary of the work.

The most discouraging thing that can happen in ministry is when people you have known and loved try to flat-out destroy you. Surprised? If you've been in the ministry for any number of years, then you know this is true. If you are starting out in the ministry, then wait for it. Sadly, it will happen. Think of when Paul wrote in Philippians 3:18–19, "(For many walk, of whom I have told you often, and now tell you even weeping, that they are the enemies of the cross of Christ: Whose end is destruction, whose God is their belly, and whose glory is in their shame, who mind earthly things.)"

Soon after we began our Christian school, there were a few people who left our church and joined with some disgruntled people from another church. That is something that I'm always surprised about—but I shouldn't be. Sometimes people don't really know each other when they attend your church, but they become stuck together like super glue the instant they leave. They spend all of their time together, doing a lot of talking about the pastor and their perceived problem.

Matthew 18:15–17 says,

"Moreover if thy brother shall trespass against thee, go and tell him his fault between thee and him alone: if he shall hear thee, thou hast gained thy brother. But if he will not hear thee, then take with thee one or two more, that in the mouth of two or three witnesses every word may be established. And if he shall neglect to hear them, tell it unto the church: but if he neglect to hear the church, let him be unto thee as an heathen man and a publican."

Here are the principles of conflict resolution as outlined in the Bible:

1. If your brother sins against you, go to him and tell him his fault privately. If he listens, you have gained a brother.

2. If he won't hear you, take one or two people with you.
3. If he doesn't want to hear you out, then take it to the church.
4. If he neglects to hear the church, then the church should exercise church discipline.

Most of the time though, Christians in churches act like they've never heard of Matthew 18. Or perhaps they've heard of it, but they've never used the principles God has laid out so perfectly in His Word.

According to the Bible Related Ministries website, over 30,000 Protestant churches are experiencing a heart-wrenching time at any given moment. 15,000 church splits occur each year, and the pastor burnout figure is 20%. Too many churches wait too long to deal with problems. Pastors take a back seat to solving problems. Churches get destroyed when they have secret board meetings without inviting the pastor or alerting the church that there is a problem.[xi]

No wonder George Barna found that in the 20-year period from 1991–2011, a lot had changed.

- Church volunteerism has dropped by eight percentage points since 1991. Presently, slightly less than one out of every five adults (19%) donates some of their time in a typical week to serving at a church.

- Adult Sunday School attendance has also diminished by eight percentage points over the past two decades. On any given Sunday, about 15% of adults can be expected to show up in a Sunday School class.

- The most carefully watched church-related statistic is adult attendance. Since 1991, attendance has receded by nine percentage points, dropping from 49% in 1991 to 40% in 2011.

- The most prolific change in religious behavior among those measured has been the increase in the percentage of adults categorized as "unchurched." (The Barna Group definition includes all adults who have not attended any religious events at a church, other than special ceremonies such as a wedding or funeral, during the prior six-month period.) In 1991, just one-quarter of adults (24%) were unchurched. That figure has ballooned by more than 50% to 37% today.

- When asked to choose one of several descriptions of God, the proportion who believe that God is "the all-knowing, all-powerful, and perfect Creator of the universe who still rules the world today" currently stands at two-thirds of the public (67%). That represents a seven-point drop from the 1991 level.

- The biggest shift has been in people's perceptions of the Bible. In 1991, 46% of adults strongly affirmed that "the Bible is totally accurate in all of the principles it teaches." That has slumped to just 38% who offer the same affirmation today.[xii]

We should strive to teach the whole counsel of God in our churches so this type of biblical illiteracy doesn't perpetuate itself. Let's not dilute God's Word from our pulpits. Instead, let's stand on the Bible as the inerrant Word of God. In doing this, if people leave our churches seeking "lighter fare" from other pulpits, then we don't need to be disheartened. When we keep preaching, working, and praying, God will bring an increase to our churches and will bless our faithfulness.

The Reality of Life

Sometimes there are members who don't seem to understand that life isn't fair. They also haven't realized that life in a church isn't always fair. While the board and the pastor seek to make sure that people are being treated correctly, sometimes it isn't possible to make everyone happy. In fact, if pastors spend too much time trying to make everyone happy, as the old saying goes, they will make no one happy.

These were some of the principles we taught the students in the Christian school. Most of our kids haven't been trained that life isn't about them, but rather it is about Christ.

When our Christian school began in 1979, Christian education was still relatively new. You would think people would applaud that effort and get behind it. Especially Christians. But a group of people got disgruntled, left our church, and started their own Christian school. They bought an old school building. The local newspaper ran a huge article about their upcoming school year.

The article had several slams in it about our Christian school. Those who had worked so hard to get the Christian school up and running were grievously hurt. We couldn't believe the people would be so mean. (Sometimes, Christians can hurt you the worst. Never be surprised when a Christian hurts you. Trust me, when people think they have God on their side, it is like they possess no feelings for others.)

The saddest thing I've observed throughout the years is the hurt to the newer people in the church, those who just got saved. (They are easily swayed to anybody's way of thinking, and sometimes they are casualties when other people want to leave a church. That happened in this situation, and it was a big blow to us.) New Christians were affected by the disgruntled people who left the church. After all this hard work, we were at our lowest point when people who we thought loved us were instead working against what we were doing.

Our school started in the fall for its third year. The other school never started. For all their talk and bravado, they weren't able to get the school going. A year later, the building was condemned and torn down. One day when I was driving past the place where the building had been, I noticed some of the bricks were still left. I stopped the car and picked up two of them. I put them in my office as a reminder to keep on keeping on during the hard times. (In contrast, Dr. Art Rorheim has given me a piece of the floor of the gym from the first AWANA club, and that meant a whole lot more to me than those bricks.) Those who don't quit will always win in God's service. The trial of my faith has definitely been more precious than gold.

Outlive your critics. Listen for the tiny bit of good that you will learn from them, and throw away the rest. In the end, those who are persevering faithfully in the service of the Lord will finish strong.

How to Keep Going

God will let us go through trials that will help us. He will not allow us to go through trials that will hurt us. God will never let you get hurt. James 1:12 states, "Blessed is the man that endureth temptation: for when he is tried, he shall receive the crown of life, which the Lord hath promised to them that love him." The word "temptation" in this verse is *peirasmos* from the Greek and it means "trial." When you endure trials, God will reward you with a crown of life.

Have you really thought about what it will mean to receive crowns from the Lord Jesus Christ for living in service to Him? Won't it be wonderful to receive a crown from His nail-scarred hand? How do we get that crown? We get it by enduring trials, by handling hard times, and by going through hard things that are definitely going to happen in every church. Anytime you have people, you are going to have trouble. There is no way around it. And yet, there is no greater calling than to go through the difficult times with your people, to love them, and to handle the hard times.

Remember the Good

During the hard times with the Christian school, I remembered back when the Lord had called me to Bible college. Here is a real clue for you to help you get through hard times. Don't think about the present and what you are going through. Think about the past—don't remember all the bad things that have happened, but rather focus on how God has called you for this particular moment. Even in the worst of times, God always gave me a sign that all the problems would work out. There are a lot more good times than bad in the ministry.

In the same way, God has brought you to this particular moment, this particular time. The trial you are facing has been divinely allowed, and He alone knows the outcome. All you can do is lead your people through the difficult time. If you are a worker or a member of a church that is going through a hard time, this is when God wants you to support the leadership over you. He wants you to support your pastor and give him encouragement. Remember, he is being attacked by the devil and attacked by people whom he thought he could love and trust. There is almost no pain greater than that. (Believe me, I know about that pain and how it feels.)

God will get you through the hard times, and your church will come out stronger than it was before the difficulty. How do I know this? Because it's happened to me hundreds of times; and every time, God has been faithful beyond what I could ever think.

$$\sim\!\!\infty\!\!\sim$$

Remember Your Own Call

Another thing you can do to get through hard times is to remember your call. Second Timothy 1:8–9 says, "Be not thou therefore ashamed of the testimony of our Lord, nor of me his prisoner: but be thou partaker of the afflictions of the gospel according to the power of God; Who hath saved us, and called us with an holy calling, not according to our works, but according to his own purpose and grace, which was given us in Christ Jesus before the world began."

A lack of commitment can plague churches. People aren't volunteering the way they did many years ago. I've been thankful for the many wonderful workers and volunteers at Quentin Road, yet many pastors have shared with me that this is a very real problem in churches across the country.

Philippians 3:12–14 states, "Not as though I had already attained, either were already perfect: but I follow after, if that I may apprehend that for which also I am apprehended of Christ Jesus. Brethren, I count not myself to have apprehended: but this one thing I do, forgetting those things which are behind, and reaching forth unto those things which are before, I press toward the mark for the prize of the high calling of God in Christ Jesus."

The Apostle Paul went through much persecution and many difficult trials. He had to handle much opposition. In pretty much every city he went to, he encountered trials. Sometimes, though, we don't realize this. We read verses like the one in Philippians, and we don't really think about what it means.

Paul faced hard times.

Really hard times.

Paul probably faced harder times than what you are facing. This is not to minimize the very real, hard time you are facing in your church or in your life; but to make you understand that in spite of the difficulties, Paul knew his calling from God was sure. He forgot what was behind and pressed on to the high calling in Christ Jesus.

You are called with a holy calling—whether you are a pastor, a member, or whatever your role is in the Body of Christ. Remember that call when you're tempted to get discouraged.

That's what I did. When I went through the hard times, I remembered how God orchestrated our path each and every step of the way.

Going Where?

About ready to graduate from Florida Bible College, Linda and I were excited about what the Lord was going to do. But the problems and troubles we were going through seemed insurmountable in many ways. We had two young children who were still in diapers (a fact I still like to remind them about) and lots of school debt. We had no money and no support. We wanted to go and start a church, but weren't sure how in the world we were going to do this.

I had gone to the office of student relations and looked at a huge map of the United States. Pins were in all the places FBC graduates had gone. But there was no pin in Chicago. I asked why no graduates had gone to Chicago. This was kind of strange, since graduates had gone out to hundreds of cities. I mentioned it to Linda. We talked about Chicago for awhile. I was from small towns in Kentucky, and Linda was from Dayton, Ohio. We had no desire to go to a city where we would have to deal with the noise, pollution, and traffic. We had two small children. Where would we live? How would we start a church when we didn't know anybody? Our school bills were a big worry, too. We had to pay them off. We didn't see that happening if we started a church. At least if I was able to go to an already established church, I could make a salary. It might not be big and I definitely wasn't in it for the money, but it would be better than starting out with no financial support.

A St. Louis church needed pulpit supply, so we went there. I really wanted to be at the church. They liked me, and I really liked them as a congregation. Going to an established church seemed like a safer route than going and starting from scratch. We prayed about this, but God closed the door when the church called someone else.

I shoved Chicago out of my mind. I preferred cities like Paducah, Kentucky, where I'd gone to high school. Kentucky Lake was only 20 miles away. I loved fishing there. Pretty much Heaven on earth.

But something in my heart said Chicago.

I didn't want to listen.

At graduation, Dr. Mark Cambron preached. He was one of our favorite college professors. He had been dean of Tennessee Temple and worked for W.B. Riley and Lee Roberson. I still believe he was the greatest prophecy man that ever lived. He was speaking to the graduates. I'll never forget his

Dr. Mark Cambron.

message. The room was full of graduates, family, and friends. Maria Gonzalez sang one of my favorite songs, written by Mike Otto, "Let Me See This World, Dear Lord, as Though I Were Looking through Your Eyes."

That song on that particular night meant a lot. I thought about what it meant to see the world as the Lord Jesus saw it: to see the people who are lost, hurting, and alone; to feel compassion for them and to want them to know about eternal life; and how the trial of my faith was more precious than gold.

Suddenly, Dr. Cambron said something that perked up my ears. "You need to follow God wherever He is calling you. He might want you to go to some big city that you have no desire to go to."

Ouch. Did he have to be so pointed? Could he read my mind?

"You need to follow God's call, though you might have two babies in diapers."

Wow! This man was a mind reader. No question about it.

"Or school bills."

Okay. This was incredible. How did he know?

"Follow God wherever He calls you, and you will be blessed. You will win souls for Christ. You will be a laborer in His harvest."

God had called. With a grateful heart, I answered His holy calling. I knew where we were going to start a church. At the end of the service, I caught Linda's eye.

She smiled. "I know where we are going," she said.

"Where?"

"Chicago. We're going to Chicago."

Finish Line Strategies

- Know that hard times are part of life. I know this might seem basic and obvious, but it is amazing to me how many of our Dayspring graduates who go out to start churches or take churches are surprised by the fact that people leave or backstab them. If you are in the ministry, there are going to be problems.

- Remember your calling. It is a holy calling, not a man-made calling. When the hard times come, remember the goodness of the Lord.

- The Christian life isn't a game; it is a battle. There are many people who don't understand this. They want everything to be all nice, rosy, and happy. The truth is, Satan is real. God is real. Satan wants people not to hear about the truth of the gospel. He is actively trying to keep people from trusting Christ. First Peter 5:8 says, "Be sober, be vigilant; because your adversary the devil, as a roaring lion, walketh about, seeking whom he may devour."

- God is stronger than the devil, and He will help you. First John 4:4 says, "Ye are of God, little children, and have overcome them: because greater is he that is in you, than he that is in the world."

- God has a plan for your church. He has a plan for your life. The plan may not be a glorious and wonderful plan right here in the day to day, but His plan for you will work out for good. Romans 8:28 says, "And we know that all things work together for good to them that love God, to them who are the called according to his purpose."

Chapter 16
Determination in the Power of God

Therefore, my beloved brethren, be ye stedfast, unmoveable, always abounding in the work of the Lord, forasmuch as ye know that your labour is not in vain in the Lord.
1 Corinthians 15:58

Jennifer White didn't know what to think when her seemingly healthy 17-year-old son, Ryan, lost his eyesight. In an article by Robert Callovi in the *Palm Beach Post*, Ryan is described as being athletic and fit. He runs cross country and plays volleyball. He won the Palm Beach Marathon 5K men's title in 16 minutes, 33 seconds.

Ryan came out of the garage and into the house, telling his mom that he couldn't see. He said it felt like pins and needles were all over his body. She rushed him to the hospital, where they determined Ryan was having a stroke. They administered a tissue plasminogen activator, or tPA, a drug often given to stroke patients to help reduce brain damage. But tPA can also cause fatal bleeding of the brain if administered at the wrong time. Fortunately, Ryan recovered, and in a day his eyesight started to return. He didn't remember much until about his third day in the hospital. But a few months later after much determination and hard work, Ryan was back doing what he loved best: running. Nothing, not even a stroke, was going to stop him. [xiii]

Determination like Ryan had is the real key to the Christian life — determination in the power of a great God. The God who saved you is the same God who called you. The same God who called you is the same God who will help you keep going forward. Even when it is painful. Even when it seems like everyone else has gone far ahead of you. Don't worry about it. God is the One who keeps track. God knows what you are doing.

Someone asked me if I've ever felt like quitting and my reply was, "Only on Mondays."

Second Timothy 4:7–8 says, "I have fought a good fight, I have finished my course, I have kept the faith: Henceforth there is laid up for me a crown of righteousness, which the Lord, the righteous judge, shall give me at that day: and not to me only, but unto all them also that love his appearing."

❧ ❧

Onward to Chicago

After graduation, we loaded up two Cadillacs (we drove them to Chicago for people who needed them driven there from Florida; and we used them as a moving service, too). One of the cars belonged to Bill Wirtz, the owner of the Chicago Blackhawks.

We were ready to go. My dad had one last thing to say: "Son, please don't bring those grandbabies to Chicago. They'll get murdered."

He obviously didn't care too much about Linda and me, but for the grandbabies he would do anything. Of course he was kidding, but he was concerned. I felt for him at the time, but nothing like I do now that I have my own grandchildren. (Once a person becomes a grandparent, they truly begin to understand life. You've heard the saying, "If I'd known how much fun grandkids would be, we would have had them first.")

Dad loved us so much. He drove our Volkswagen Bug with the broken muffler that we couldn't afford to fix.

We started on the 1,500-mile trip with the Volkswagen Bug. Every time a police officer would get behind me as I drove to Chicago, we would pray so hard that he wouldn't stop us and give us a ticket. Every single time,

Our famous (or infamous) VW Bug.

the officer would turn off onto a ramp and we would breathe sighs of relief and praise God.

We arrived in Chicago after hours and hours of hard driving. We were young and naïve and didn't know anyone in the city. It was the greatest journey of our lives. We had no money. But we had the most wonderful thing in the universe—we had the call of God. We had a destination. And we had His grace for every moment.

We had heard of a ministry called Slavic Gospel Association, so our plan was to contact them and see if they could help us. That was pretty much our lone preparation for this journey.

As I look back over 40 years later, I think about the faith it took to do this. I can't believe we all just hopped in the car to go to Chicago.

Of course, I had planned for the future of our church: Within the first year, we probably would have a thousand people. Everyone we would meet would want to hear the gospel. Tons of people would get saved. Our church would grow, and we'd have to build within a few months of arriving there.

Now, I really didn't think it was going to be easy. I thought it would be difficult; but honestly, nothing could have prepared me for how hard it would actually be.

We met Peter Dyneka at the Slavic Gospel Association, and he allowed us to stay in a basement apartment for two weeks while we got settled. I asked Peter why there were bars on the windows of our apartment.

"After three days of living here, you will know the answer to that question," he answered,

I learned quickly. Bars weren't supposed to keep us in, but to keep people out. Chicago sure was different from Kentucky.

We started looking for an apartment and jobs. We weren't sure how both of us were going to work, but God provided a wonderful lady to watch the kids while we worked. (There are people who teach that women shouldn't work outside the home; but sometimes a family has no choice, and they have to do what they have to do. The Bible doesn't say that a woman can't work. In fact in the Bible days, everyone worked, including the children.) That was what we had to do to make it. (You have to make your family a priority, or you won't make it in the ministry. But you also have to make God a priority. If the kids don't see God is important to you, then they won't want to have anything to do with church when they grow up. If you make the church so important in your life that you neglect your family, your kids won't serve Christ, either.)

I had heard of a renowned liberal preacher whose father was also a famous preacher. (Except the father loved the Lord and had influenced many people for Christ.) I couldn't understand why anyone would want to preach about the Bible when they didn't believe it, so I went to see this young preacher and asked him why he didn't believe in the Bible. He told me, "Dad never had time for us. He was always busy studying. I never felt important to him."

From that moment on, I determined I would not be that kind of father. I have always had my office door open to my children, even when I was doing counseling. I made time for them and established early how important my family was to me. As the children got older, we'd surprise them by going to a hotel that had a swimming pool (a big deal in those lean, financial

My kids loved to swim — we always found time for them.

days). We always had fun together.

As a high schooler, Julie was asked if she would rebel. She said, "Why would I rebel? I have nothing to rebel against." Neither of my children has ever given me any trouble.

They have both, along with their spouses and children, lived their lives in service to the Lord. (I know this doesn't always happen in Christian families. It is still each child's choice to serve the Lord. If you have a prodigal child, continue to pray for them; but realize it is that child's decision to do what is right.)

Linda got a job as a telephone representative at Ma Bell in Chicago. She bypassed the entry-level job, and they put her into a better position. We were so glad the Lord was providing. I got a job as a janitor at Midwest Bible Church, and also drove the bus for their school. (By the way, that is where Billy Graham had one of his first jobs.) The first day I picked up all the kids, the route took me three hours. I got so lost I didn't know what to do. Somehow I managed to pick everyone up and get back to the school.

We moved to our first apartment on 3100 West Fullerton Avenue, a fourth-floor, walk-up style residence. We didn't know this was a gang-infested area. We heard sirens going late at night from all the violence.

Our dangerous Fullerton Ave. apartment.

Once, Jimmy threw his shoe out of the window of the apartment, and it hit a policeman on the head. I heard a knock at the door; and there was the policeman holding Jimmy's shoe in his hand.

We loved to barbecue off the porch on the apartment. It was tiny and could hardly hold even a small grill. (Several years later after we'd moved from that apartment, we drove by and saw the whole porch had fallen off. Good thing it didn't happen when we were on it.)

We didn't have money for curtains, but we did manage to buy a card table and chairs from the Salvation Army Store. We lived in constant fear that our kids would push out the screens in the apartment because the windows came all the way to the floor.

We started to search for a place to meet as a church, but it was very frustrating. Businesses weren't receptive to us using their space. We talked to store owners and other people, but couldn't find a place to meet.

I remember that summer as being so hot that our apartment was stifling. We saved our money, but couldn't afford to buy a fan. We would almost get enough money, then another bill would come up and we couldn't buy one. I sweat easily; and anyone who knows me knows that I almost always have to be in air conditioning, or I physically can't take the heat. In those days, there was no air conditioning. It was difficult for us to sleep at night. The floor of our apartment got so dirty from a suet-like substance that appeared out of nowhere on the floor. We had to mop it constantly. We shopped for a fan and finally found a good deal at Goldblatt's, a Midwest chain known for their good prices on household items. We bought it for $20. We brought that fan home, and there probably wasn't a happier family in the world. The kids were jumping up and

Leroy and his printing presses.

down and shouting. All of us were so happy. I've never appreciated a fan so much. You appreciate the little things when you have nothing.

I had witnessed to a printer named Leroy Juron. We invited Leroy to Thanksgiving dinner. When he arrived, I put the turkey on the card table and tried to carve it. The frail table from the Salvation Army Store collapsed. The turkey slid off the table and onto the floor. Grease covered the floor. We cleaned it up the best we could and tried to still enjoy our Thanksgiving. Leroy didn't have much money either, but he couldn't take it anymore. The next day he went to a used furniture store and bought a table for us.

But we still had nowhere for our church to meet. We kept searching and couldn't find anything for six, long months. We had come to Chicago full of hopes and dreams, but now it seemed like nothing was going to happen for Christ.

Waiting on God

Have you ever been to a place in your church or in your life where it seemed like you had to wait interminably for God? You needed somewhere to meet for a church, or your grandmother was sick, or maybe you were trying to finish up school and provide for your family. You took two steps forward and three steps back. Waiting on God isn't easy and not something for the faint of heart. Early on when I first got saved, it was like God answered with a huge "yes" to every prayer. But as I was saved longer and learned to trust the Lord more, I often had to wait for the answers to my prayers. Sometimes the answer to my prayers was a "no" because God knew that I didn't need whatever it was I was praying for yet.

Waiting on God is something we need to learn to do.

Did you know that if you lived on St. Paul Island in Alaska and ordered a pizza, it would take three days for you to get the pizza?[xiv] Waiting on God can feel like waiting for a pizza. It seems like the rest of the world lives in places where they can get almost instant prayer delivery. But you are in a place where it takes three days, three months, three years, or longer for your answer. Remember, God is never late. He is never early. He is always on time.

I'm not sure that any person actually enjoys waiting. Have you ever gotten in line at the express lane of the grocery store and been tempted to count the items in the cart ahead of you because you are sure it looks like there are more than ten items in there? Then you probably hate waiting as much as I do.

The apostles knew what it was like to wait. They had seen Jesus ascend into Heaven and had been told by Him to go to Jerusalem and wait in this certain place. They walked from the Mount of Olives to the Upper Room. Acts 1:12–13 shares more about this event. "Then returned they unto Jerusalem from the mount called Olivet, which is from Jerusalem a sabbath day's journey. And when they were come in, they went up into an upper room, where abode both Peter, and James, and John, and Andrew, Philip, and Thomas, Bartholomew, and Matthew, James the son of Alphaeus, and Simon Zelotes, and Judas the brother of James."

These people waited for the coming of the Holy Spirit. I can only imagine their mood while they waited. They had seen Jesus multiple times since He'd come back from the dead. They'd seen Him ascend into Heaven. Now they waited again before they could accomplish the next thing they wanted to do for the Lord. They were in the position we were in while we were trying to find a place to meet—stuck in-between. But the difference between the apostles and what we were going through was the apostles had been told by Jesus what would happen next. All they had to do was trust the Lord and wait.

Here are three things the Apostles did while they were in the upper room:

❦

Power in Prayer

First, the apostles prayed. Acts 1:14 says, "These all continued with one accord in prayer and supplication, with the women, and Mary the mother of Jesus, and with his brethren." They continued to pray and to ask the Lord for His guidance and direction.

What if one of the people in the room had said, "Oh, we don't need to pray. We already know Jesus promised us the Spirit would come." Just because we have the promises of God doesn't mean we don't need to pray. We pray because we love to commune with our Heavenly Father. And He loves to hear us pray. Contrary to what some hyper-Calvinists believe, prayer does change things. The apostles prayed as fervently as ever in unity. The word "supplication" is *deesis* from the Greek, and it means "a seeking or an entreating to God."

They knew the promise of the Holy Spirit was true, and yet they continued to pray fervently. This is a good principle for all of us to remember. Continue to pray, and don't stop. God is listening.

❦

Take Time to Study

The second thing the apostles did was study. They studied the Scriptures during their time of waiting. Peter began expounding on the Old Testament Scriptures that told of Jesus. Remember Jesus had told them during His ministry to search the Scriptures. John 5:39 states, "Search the scriptures; for in them ye think ye have eternal life: and they are they which testify of me."

They didn't sit around and complain there was nothing to do. They did something productive. They searched the Scriptures. They used the time to prepare for the ministry that was ahead of them. They had patience.

What is patience?

1.   Wait on God even when your circumstances are desperate.

2. Don't be anxious.

3. Trust God has a bigger plan and is doing a greater work in your life than the one you can see at the moment.

4. Look at today and keep doing what you know to be God's will for you, knowing beyond a shadow of a doubt God will show you the next step.

Do you have patience when you are waiting on God to work and move in your life? I know I often don't have patience when I wait for Linda while she is shopping. After Linda and I got married, we went with her family to the mall. The ladies went straight to the sales racks. Her dad looked at me with a smile and said, "Get used to it. They are like two bird dogs circling their prey."

One man visited a local department store with his wife. They had purchased a piece of luggage and a cooler. As Ed waited for his wife to finish the rest of her shopping, he dragged the luggage and cooler around with him to the shoe department. A clerk asked if he could be of assistance.

"No, thank you," Ed replied. "I'm just waiting for my wife."

A man behind him said, "I'm waiting for my wife, too, but I never thought of bringing a lunch and an overnight bag with me."

❧

Continue Helping

Like the women trying to find a bargain, the apostles continued with business as well. They decided to appoint by lot one of Jesus' followers to replace Judas Iscariot. Later on we see that Jesus appeared to Paul (then named Saul) on the road to Damascus. Paul trusted in Christ and was called to be an apostle. Nevertheless, the apostles waited for the Holy Spirit to come; but they waited with a purpose. They kept busy doing what they knew they should do for the Lord.

❧

The Reward of Waiting

So after praying, witnessing, studying, working, and asking for a meeting place, nothing happened for our start-up church. Actually, it wasn't even a start-up yet! We kept working and praying, knowing God would

answer. One afternoon I was helping Leroy with a print job. (Helping
Leroy in those early days gave me the
idea to develop the huge printshop
we have now at Quentin Road. Never
underestimate the power of waiting.
If I hadn't helped Leroy, I would never have learned about printing.)

Our printing operation prints millions of gospel tracts that are distributed around the world in many languages.

As I worked with Leroy, Otto
Knottnerus, who owned the store
next door, came into the printshop to order a job. He was a builder, and he
and his sons would do carpentry work for people. He was from Holland
and had an accent. Leroy introduced us.

Otto said to me, "I will give you the building next door for free." I was
distracted by Leroy, who, out of sight of Otto, was spinning his finger
around his ear. The secret message I thought Leroy was giving me was,

Otto Knottnerus gave us our first meeting place.

"This man is cuckoo!" I decided to heed Leroy's advice and did not accept this offer. So I said, "No, thank
you. I really appreciate your offer, but I don't want to
meet in your storefront."

Otto shrugged. He left the printshop. Immediately Leroy turned to me. "Why did you turn down
the store? We have been praying for months that God
would give us a building to meet in, and He was willing to give it to you for free!"

I was puzzled, "But you said the man was crazy."

Leroy sighed loudly. "I wasn't saying he was crazy. I
meant the man was Dutch. I was showing you a windmill so you would know he was Dutch!"

To this day, I still can't figure out why in the world
Leroy chose to use a windmill at that moment. Why
did it matter that the man was Dutch? Chicago is
a melting pot with many different ethnicities and

cultures. I loved them all.

Immediately, I called Otto. After apologizing profusely, I begged him to allow us to use his building. To my great joy, he agreed.

We finally had a place to meet. Even better, it was free. It wasn't very big, but we had our church. We named it Chicago Bible Church, and it was on West Fullerton Avenue. Our church started right down the road from where AWANA Clubs started with Dr. Art Rorheim and Dr. Lance Latham.

We were thrilled beyond words. This was one of those amazing days when you see God work. We previously had faith and determination that God would work, but the waiting was long and arduous.

God had worked in an incredible way. Now the people would start flooding in. Surely after all that waiting for a place to meet, God would bring people in by the hundreds.

But He didn't. We would have a few people one week, then the next week we would just have Linda, the kids, myself, and Leroy. One week, a gang called the Jousters came to church. The place was packed. I shared the gospel and about 40 of the gang members indicated they had trusted Christ. But then the next week came, and none of them came back. This was so discouraging. Over and over our hopes would be raised by situations like this, only for them to be dashed again.

Families would visit and ask, "What do you have for our kids?'

I would answer, "Right now we don't have anything; but if you will stay, I'm sure we'll have things for your kids." Then they would leave.

One time, we were coming home from work and we had a flat tire. I got out and changed the tire. When we got back to the apartment, the police were there. Someone had robbed the unit below us. I asked what time the robber had been in the apartment, and it was the exact time I was changing that tire. I truly believe that if we hadn't had a flat tire, we would have come home to a very bad situation with the thief being there. Who knows what the consequences would have been. It was a scary time, but God always took care of us.

Are you in a place where you need to have a little more faith in your great God? Have you felt as Linda and I did when you were waiting for God to show you what to do next? Is the waiting causing you to feel like you are at the end of your rope?

Keep trusting God. Have determination in the power of God. Faith isn't based on you and whether you can muster up enough. Rather, faith is based on God. Just as God took care of us every step of the way from the early days onward, so He will take care of you.

Trust His power.

He will show you the next step on the path.

Finish Line Strategies

- Continue studying the Word of God. Preach from what God is showing you. Always be open to looking deeper into the Word and asking God for His guidance.

- Continue praying. I know this sounds obvious, but prayer is how we communicate with God. We should always be conversing with our Heavenly Father. Some people keep a prayer journal, and this helps them to keep praying. Whatever you are doing in your life, don't stop praying.

- Learn new things while you are waiting. Figuring out how cheap and easy printing was has benefitted every aspect of ministry at Quentin Road. If I hadn't helped Leroy while I waited for a meeting place, I would never have learned this. Never underestimate the power of waiting.

Chapter 17
Despair Is Not a Factor

For we would not, brethren, have you ignorant of our trouble which came to us in Asia, that we were pressed out of measure, above strength, insomuch that we despaired even of life. 2 Corinthians 1:8

High school student Paul Chartschlaa was one of the first young men I met in Chicago. He trusted Christ as his Savior soon after I witnessed to him. His family was with the Slavic Gospel Association. He was very intelligent. He played football, and was able to set type in different languages. He became one of my best friends. He

Paul Chartschlaa.

was sort of my protector. He was a tough guy. We played tennis together. (That may sound like I'm extremely athletic, but I'm not. I'm not very good at tennis, but we had a lot of fun playing it at different places in Chicago when we could find an empty court.)

Paul Chartschlaa introduced me to the wonders of Chicago food. He would come and meet me for an Italian beef sandwich—tender, thinly cut roast beef on an Italian roll with au jus over the top. Sweet peppers were my topping of choice. Margie's Beef was our favorite. When we came back from eating one of these sandwiches, Linda would smell the garlic on my breath and say, "I can't believe you ate an Italian beef and didn't get me one." (Poor Linda. Paul didn't have money for more than one friend.)

Early one Sunday morning, Paul came with me when I preached at the

Pacific Garden Mission. Since most preachers didn't have time to speak at the mission on Sundays, I could go early before preaching at Chicago Bible Church, and at least feel like I was preaching to a crowd since I didn't have too many people coming. Paul, like a typical high schooler, refused to sit on the platform with me at the mission. He sat in the audience with the men. After the service, the workers started herding the men to the cafeteria for a meal. Paul started to come up to the platform to go with me, but the workers wouldn't let him.

"I'm not here because I'm homeless," Paul said. "I'm with him." He pointed to me. The workers asked if he was with me and I shrugged. It might do him good to experience why I wanted him to listen to me. After a little while, I went down to the cafeteria and rescued Paul before they made him spend the night there. After that, I had no trouble with him sitting on the platform.

We prayed for a song leader to come to the church. One day while I was there at the mission, I met one of the workers who had a great voice. He said he'd love to come and lead our singing. After all this waiting, we were finally getting somewhere. We would have a song leader. Our services would be better with more singing. We were so excited. The song leader came for two Sundays, and it was so nice to have music during our services. But then he didn't show up after that. We didn't know what happened to him.

Leroy Singing.

This is the reality of the Christian life. Often when you receive a big blessing like we did for a free building to meet in, you will find that opposition will come in the weeks that follow. This doesn't mean God has abandoned you. Quite the opposite. It actually means Satan has noticed what you are doing and is doing his best to discourage you.

Despair.com

I'm sure you've seen those motivational posters where an eagle is flying and it says something like, "Be like the eagle and soar through life." There is a website called Despair.com that has demotivational posters. Under "mistakes" it says, "It could be that the purpose of your life is only to serve as a warning to others." Under "humiliation" it says, "The harder you try, the dumber you look." Under "despair" it says, "It's always the darkest before it goes pitch dark."

We laugh at these sayings because often they feel very true. We are tempted to despair when this happens. One preacher wrote that we spend more time feeling discouraged than feeling encouraged. There is some truth to that.

In the early days, there were many moments when we weren't sure the church would ever get going. Our whole family lived and died every time a person came into the door of the church. If I had known what was going to be in the future, that one day I would be blessed with a church, school, and college, I probably wouldn't have ever gotten discouraged. But I didn't know the future. I had to trust that God knew the future. There were many times I felt like quitting. Those months we spent in Chicago, even after getting a place to meet, were some of those times.

✦

Elijah's Death Threat

Like our getting a free place for our church to meet, Elijah had been doing great. First, he had predicted there would be no rain; and sure enough, his prediction came true. Then God had shown up in a mighty way on Mount Carmel by sending fire from Heaven in answer to Elijah's prayer. The people saw that God was the true God. Elijah then had the 450 prophets of Baal executed. Everything Elijah had done had turned to gold.

When Queen Jezebel heard about what had happened, she became very angry. She sent a death threat to Elijah.

This stopped Elijah in his tracks. He was off his mountaintop experience and definitely down in the Valley of Discouragement.

How did Elijah respond to the death threat from Queen Jezebel? Maybe not in the way you would expect him to respond. You would think after seeing the miracles of God happen in such a wonderful way he would say, "Jezebel can only kill me if God allows her to. I stand in the strength of my God."

Actually, it is almost humorous to look at Elijah's reaction. Not because a death threat isn't serious, but because Elijah had killed 450 prophets just before that point. First Kings 19:3–4 tells us what happened, "And when he saw that, he arose, and went for his life, and came to Beersheba, which belongeth to Judah, and left his servant there. But he himself went a day's journey into the wilderness, and came and sat down under a juniper tree: and he requested for himself that he might die; and said, It is enough; now, O LORD, take away my life; for I am not better than my fathers."

Elijah wants to die. He is sitting under a tree and wishing he could die. That is how discouraged he feels. If you ever wonder if you can possibly live up to the lives of Bible heroes like Elijah, don't forget about this event in Elijah's life. Here Elijah had had the greatest miracle of his life, and now he wants to die. Some might say at this point that Elijah really wasn't saved, but he was.

Elijah reacts with the flesh instead of with the Spirit. He allows his sinful self to feel the discouragement instead of realizing he serves a mighty God.

When a discouraging blow comes to our lives, how are we tempted to react? Most of the time, it is with our feelings. We don't rely on the Lord. We don't remember all the times God has helped us in the past. We don't consider all God will continue to do in our lives. We don't remember verses like Jeremiah 29:11 which say, "For I know the thoughts that I think toward you, saith the LORD, thoughts of peace, and not of evil, to give you an expected end."

God thinks thoughts of peace toward us, not thoughts of evil. Elijah had his eyes on the problem, not the ultimate Problem Solver of the universe. Did he really not think God could deliver him after bringing fire down from Heaven two days before?

Before we get too hard on Elijah, let's consider ourselves. We are prone to do the same thing as this prophet. After the mountaintop experience, we have to go into the valley.

It is there we end up experiencing the most spiritual growth.

D.L. Moody.

The great evangelist D. L. Moody became very much disheartened because he thought the Lord was not sufficiently blessing his ministry. He would talk discouragingly of everything about his ministry. He felt this way for several months.

One Monday when at his most dejected point, he met a friend. His friend had had a wonderful Sunday service. He asked Mr. Moody what kind of a day he had on Sunday.

"Oh!" said Moody, "I had not a good one."

"Much power?"

"No."

Then Mr. Moody inquired what his friend had preached about.

"Oh, I preached about Noah."

"How did you get on?" inquired Mr. Moody.

"Oh, grandly. Did you ever study up Noah?"

Mr. Moody said he thought he knew about Noah, and that there were only a few verses about him.

"Oh, if you haven't studied up Noah, you ought to do it. He's a wonderful character."

After they parted, Mr. Moody got out his Bible and read all he could find about Noah; and while he was reading, this thought came to him: *Here is this man who was a preacher of righteousness for one hundred and twenty years, and yet never had a convert outside his own family.*

After this, Mr. Moody went to a prayer meeting and met a young man who had come from a town in Illinois. This young man was joyfully telling of ten bright converts in his recent meeting.

Why? said Mr. Moody to himself, *What would Noah have said if he had ten converts? And yet, Noah didn't get discouraged.*

From that point on, Moody decided to keep going in the strength of the Lord and not allow depression to overtake him. I'm sure like any person giving their all for the Lord, there were times he would get discouraged; but then he would remember Noah and become encouraged.[xv]

Many men and women of God go through disheartening times. You will also go through times of despair. Often these experiences come directly after God gives you a great miracle. Keep trusting.

Meeting Ralph

One week we met with a group of kids on a Saturday, and someone knocked at the door. We went to the door and met Ralph Kowalski. He had heard about our church, and wanted to come and check us out. We became friends. He had a disease that caused bumps to cover his body. He also couldn't talk very well, and would often start spitting involuntarily while he was talking. We welcomed him in and he became our third member.

Ralph.

We had three members now: Paul, Leroy, and Ralph. These people had a true pioneering spirit. Pioneers are willing to start small and keep going, even when they get discouraged. These people are few and far between, but these men were some of our first pioneers. I thanked God for them, but I wondered if it was possible for our church to ever really grow beyond three people. I think of all those who could have stayed, but left because we didn't have enough ministries. I really believe they lost a lot of blessings.

One day, Paul gave me a small, iron cannon. He meant it as a deco-

ration for my office, which I found humorous since I didn't have an office. But when I looked inside the barrel of the

A toy cannon gave me great encouragement.

cannon, I saw that he had rolled up a piece of paper and stuck it in there.

I took it out and unrolled it. The words encouraged my soul.

Dear Pastor,

I know it is really hard now, but keep going. Someday you'll have one of the largest ministries in Chicago.

In Christ,

Paul Chartschlaa

Sometimes on the darkest and hardest day, God gives the most amazing encouragement. I'll never forget Paul writing me that note. It meant more to me than I could ever express.

Whether you are waiting on God, experiencing a miracle from God, or going through a difficult time after a mountaintop, know He is with you. Despair is not a factor. He holds you in the palm of His hand.

Stay encouraged.

Finish Line Strategies

- Just like the apostles, do what God wants you to do at that moment when you wait for Him. As we waited on the Lord to help us find a place to meet, we didn't sit around. We did what we knew we should do. We talked to people. We witnessed to people. I witnessed to a teenager, Paul Chartschlaa, who trusted Christ and became a great help to me in the ministry. During the hard times in our church when we've had to wait for a permit or wait for something to happen so we can proceed, we have found that God is still working right in the moment with us. He will sometimes bring someone into our path who needs to hear the gospel; or we'll decide to go somewhere we don't normally go, and God will give us an idea about how to proceed. I often counsel Dayspring students to not sit around and wait for God's will to magically appear in their lives, but to do what they can for the Lord right now. Maybe a preschool class needs them to help. Perhaps a bathroom needs to be cleaned. It could be that the kitchen needs to be cleaned up at church and the men who work in it are weary from working for so many hours. The college student can be a blessing to so many by going and offering to help. He will benefit from being around godly people who are hard workers, and he is using his time wisely as he waits for God to show His will.

- Know that God has a purpose and a reason for waiting. You might save a lot of money because you had to wait. God might reveal to you later that if you had gone ahead without waiting on Him, you would have been in a much worse position.

- Treasure the time you wait. I really mean this. I know it goes against the grain; but sometimes while you are waiting, you can spend more time with your wife or your children. Nurture the relationships in your life. Some people say that they put God first, then family, and then the church. Others say to put God first, then the church, and then the family. The truth is, the church has to be first, but so does the family. Tend to both. They are of equal value. They go together. Wreck one and you wreck both.

Chapter 18
Facing Forward

Let no man despise thy youth; but be thou an example of the believers, in word, in conversation, in charity, in spirit, in faith, in purity. 1 Timothy 4:12

Paul's note to me was a real encouragement, but there were still many hardships that we faced. That's why we jumped at the invitation to do a revival in Ohio. Linda had a close family friend who had a church there. We thought it would be a nice break. Plus, I was ready to get out of the city for a little bit. (I wasn't used to breathing air I could see.)

About a month before we were to go to Ohio, the preacher who had invited us died. We thought they wouldn't want us to do the revival; but when we called, the board said, "No, please come. We want souls to get saved."

The revival turned out to be wonderful. Several of the young people decided they wanted to go to Florida Bible College. Many people trusted Christ.

Then the board did a surprising thing. They offered me the position of pastor. I don't exactly remember the size of the congregation; but compared to the three or four people who were coming to our church, it was huge. They had a beautiful building, a parsonage, and a two-car garage.

Remember, we were living in abject poverty for all practical purposes. We had nothing. We lived in a fourth-floor apartment. Whenever we got groceries, we had to

Steep steps at the Fullerton Ave. apartment in Chicago.

walk up four flights of stairs to put them away. We barely had any furniture. We only had a small storefront for our church to meet in. To top it all off, the house in Ohio had a trout stream behind it. (I've already mentioned several times my love for fishing.) I'm sure you can imagine how tempting this offer was.

Here we were being offered a ready-made church with everything in it that we would need. It was already established, there was a faithful group of people who regularly attended, and it was in an area that ensured there would be future growth.

I was a country boy. I loved being out in nature. I could have the best of both worlds. My wife could afford to buy things the children needed. My children would have a much more stable life growing up in that area.

These thoughts raced through my mind as I gazed at the church with the house perched invitingly off to the side of the property. Everything was as perfect as it could get.

I knew I couldn't take it. I knew absolutely, beyond a shadow of a doubt. God had called us to Chicago. That was where He wanted us.

It was hard to say goodbye to those wonderful people, but we knew God would call someone to be their pastor.

We went back to our tiny apartment. As we climbed up the stairs, each of us holding one of our children, we knew we had made the right decision.

God had called us. We needed to stay faithful to that call until He wanted us to do something else.

Eyes on the Goal

Keeping a forward focus isn't always easy. In fact, it can be downright difficult. Not only can wrong things distract you and keep you from moving forward, but also good things can be an interruption to something else God is doing in your life. Like the church in Ohio. While it wasn't a bad thing that they wanted me to be their pastor, it was a distraction from the call God had placed on our lives.

I knew as surely as I knew anything that if I had accepted that call to Ohio, I would have been hit by a Mack truck. Though Chicago Bible Church had few people, I couldn't bail out on them.

The Christian life isn't just hard, it is actually impossible to live without God's strength. Zechariah 4:6 states, "Then he answered and spake unto me, saying, This is the word of the LORD unto Zerubbabel, saying, Not by might, nor by power, but by my spirit, saith the LORD of hosts."

God isn't just saying this to Zerubbabel; He is saying it to you. You don't need to be discouraged as you face the battle. You don't need to look to the right or to the left. Instead, you need to be focused on the goal.

Second Timothy 1:12 states, "For the which cause I also suffer these things: nevertheless I am not ashamed: for I know whom I have believed, and am persuaded that he is able to keep that which I have committed unto him against that day."

Paul knew what it was to suffer. He was tempted to give up. He was tempted to do something else rather than to serve God where God wanted him to be. Paul knew what it was like to fear, to be hungry, to be stoned, to be shipwrecked, to be persecuted, to pray and not see God answer his prayer about his thorn in the flesh, and to be discouraged because other people left him high and dry and didn't help him.

Although he went through all of this, Paul never took his eyes off the goal.

Peace of Mind

What does it mean to have peace of mind? Sometimes when we work hard as pastors, leaders, members, and believers, we allow resentment and bitterness to creep into our lives. This is one way we can take our eyes off the goal. Duke University did a study on peace of mind. These points might help you to continue to go forward, even when tempted with something that you could call good.[xvi]

Factors found to contribute greatly to emotional and mental stability are:

1. The absence of suspicion and resentment. Nursing a grudge was a major factor in unhappiness.

2. Not living in the past. An unwholesome preoccupation with old mistakes and failures leads to depression.

3. Not wasting time and energy fighting conditions you cannot change. Cooperate with life, instead of trying to run away from it.

4. Force yourself to stay involved with the living world. Resist the temptation to withdraw and become reclusive during periods of emotional stress.

5. Refuse to indulge in self-pity when life hands you a raw deal. Accept the fact that nobody gets through life without some sorrow and misfortune.

6. Cultivate the old-fashioned virtues — love, humor, compassion, and loyalty.

7. Do not expect too much of yourself. When there is too wide a gap between self-expectation and your ability to meet the goals you have set, feelings of inadequacy are inevitable.

8. Find something bigger than yourself to believe in. Self-centered, egotistical people score lowest in any test for measuring happiness.

These are all great ways to avoid discouragement and keep a forward focus. Remember, God wants to work through you, but He will do it in His way and His timing.

One morning in Chicago, we brought our children to a next-door neighbor so she could babysit them. After I had taken Linda to her job at the telephone company, I went to the church to clean for the day; and felt a strong burden for our financial well-being. We were short $400 on our bills. In spite of both of us working as hard as we could, we didn't have enough money to make it. As I have said before, if anyone knows me at all, they know I have always paid my bills; so this lack was of particular frustration to my spirit.

I walked down the hallway at Midwest Bible Church to get a vacuum cleaner. God had provided miraculously for our small, storefront ministry. Souls were getting saved, and I saw real potential in some of the people. I knew God was using us to make a difference in people's lives. We had never felt more sure of our calling.

But today it was like it was all for nothing. I couldn't pay my bills. Our car insurance for six months was due. I didn't know if Linda and I could keep working full-time for the church and full-time in the workplace. We were emotionally, physically, and mentally exhausted.

As I started to vacuum the hallway, I cried out to God, "I know You haven't abandoned me, Lord, but it sure feels like it. I need Your help and strength like never before."

From the Worst to the Best

As a clergyman walked down a country lane, he saw a young farmer struggling to load hay back onto a cart after it had fallen off.

"You look hot, my son," said the preacher. "Why don't you rest a moment, and I'll give you a hand."

"No thanks. My father wouldn't like it."

"Don't be silly. Everyone is entitled to a break. Come and have a drink of water." Again the young man protested that his father would be upset.

"Your father must be a real slave driver. Tell me where I can find him, and I'll give him a piece of my mind!" the minister said.

"Well," replied the young farmer, "he's under the load of hay."

Things might not have gone much worse that day for that farmer—at least, let's hope they didn't. Often life kicks us in the face, circumstances get us down, difficulties frustrate our best intentions—and that is when God is at His best.

I'm sure as you read the above sentence, you wondered how this could be true. How is it that when things are at their worst, God is at His best?

Because our God isn't confined to circumstances like we are. He isn't burdened by time and space. The entire universe is at His disposal.

However, in our tiny universe, things can get very dark indeed.

That day when I worried so much about our bills, I tried to remember that when things are at their worst, God is at His best; but I have to be honest with you, this wasn't easy.

That night when I went to get the mail, I opened one slim letter from a friend I hadn't seen since Bible college. I hardly noticed the check as I read his letter. He'd been thinking about us and knew God had laid on his heart that we had a need. At first I couldn't really see what the check said. I thought it was for $40. *Well, that was nice for someone to send us $40. We still had $360 left to pay.*

But then Linda said, "Wait, the check says $400. The exact amount we need."

Even now as I write this, my eyes fill with tears as I remember the generosity of my friend that day. The check confirmed to me the providence and graciousness of my great God. I remember the overwhelming sense that in spite of the work of starting a ministry, it was all worth it.

◈

A Few Good Things

A man named Earl Livesay started attending the church. He owned a business and had a nice house in the suburbs. He started giving $50 a week in the offering plate. This was a huge amount of money at the time. We finally could do something more as a congregation. We found a public school, Feehanville Elementary in Mount Prospect, Illinois, near Earl's house. It was about 40 minutes from the storefront we had been meeting in. This was the second location of what would eventually become Quentin Road Bible Baptist Church. We started meeting at the school, and our family found an apartment that wasn't too far away.

Feehanville Elementary in Mount Prospect served as our meeting place in the Chicago suburbs.

I attended a mission's conference at Florida Bible College and miraculously, some of the families there started supporting us. I became the number one-supported missionary out of about 40 missionaries. How could this be? Was it because Linda and I had taken a step of faith and gone where we least wanted to go? We started receiving about $100 a week. Things were looking up. More people started attending.

Then one of my friends, Mike Floyd, came to visit our church. I really felt that God was calling him to stay with us and continue to help us out. He said, "I have no to desire to stay in Chicago. This is not where I want to be."

"I disagree with you, Mike," I said. "I'm going to pray that God will make you sick until you accept the call."

Now I was young and brash in those days; but that evening, Mike got really sick. He threw up all night. Linda said, "What did you do to this guy?"

The next morning, Mike told us he would stay and help us. He ended up marrying my cousin, Trena Ford, and the two of them have been wonderful and faithful supporters through the years. They have three children who are all in full-time ministry for the Lord.

Mike & Trena Floyd on their wedding day.

Always Faithful

Throughout the years, I can always say one thing: God was faithful. He was faithful when we were discouraged. He was faithful when things didn't seem to be going the way they needed to go. He was faithful when things were going well. He was always there. He was always supporting us and giving us strength to keep going.

Have you thought lately about the faithfulness of God? Have you considered that He holds you in the palm of His hand? Have you thought about how much He loves you? Hebrews 12:1–2 tells us about the great cloud of believers who are cheering us on to keep going and serve the Lord.

"Wherefore seeing we also are compassed about with so great a cloud of witnesses, let us lay aside every weight, and the sin which doth so easily beset us, and let us run with patience the race that is set before us, Looking unto Jesus the author and finisher of our faith; who for the joy that was set before him endured the cross, despising the shame, and is set down at the right hand of the throne of God."

⁓⁓

Sing This in Distress

Psalm 124:1–8 shares some comforting words when things are distressed.

"If it had not been the LORD who was on our side, now may Israel say; If it had not been the LORD who was on our side, when men rose up against us: Then they had swallowed us up quick, when their wrath was kindled against us: Then the waters had overwhelmed us, the stream had gone over our soul: Then the proud waters had gone over our soul. Blessed be the LORD, who hath not given us as a prey to their teeth. Our soul is escaped as a bird out of the snare of the fowlers: the snare is broken, and we are escaped. Our help is in the name of the LORD, who made heaven and earth."

If I looked at your photo albums, would I find pictures of the happy times or the sad times of your life? Do you have pictures of the day your boyfriend broke up with you or your husband left you? Do you have pictures of the moment your boss fired you or your church hurt you deeply? Most likely you don't. We take pictures of the good times, and that is something that is helpful to us. We need to remember those times.

What if you could really see a picture of yourself when your boss fired you? Would you also have a picture of the person who told you something encouraging later that day? Would you have a picture of the friend you called to confide in who helped by listening? Would you have a picture of the Bible passages you read that gave comfort like never before? Would you have a picture of your prayer and how close you felt to the Lord? In the darkest of times, we discover more about our Lord than at any other point.

Is this thought of remaining faithful convicting you? Is it making you realize you need to keep on keeping on? So many of the early pioneers of our church have realized this and lived out this truth in their lives. I'm so proud of all of them and all that they have accomplished through our great God's strength and help. They mean so much to me.

Can I ask you right here, right now, to be a pioneer for God's work, too? To realize there are going to be times of hardship, times of discouragement, times of despair. To understand God is with you in the darkest times and in the best times. His power will uphold you. Face forward. God's great strength will pour into you, and you will be used by Him in mighty ways.

Finish Line Strategies

- Go for a walk when you are discouraged. Looking at God's beautiful nature will help you to see the big picture when things feel bleak. They will give you perspective. Get out and look at a lake or ocean. Whenever I'm by the water, it reminds me of God's wonderful, creative genius, and it encourages me.

- In the early years before we had any privacy, we would turn off all the apartment lights and park our car a few streets away so no one would think we were home. We even taped our windows, lit candles, and made homemade pizza. Jim and Julie still talk about those times as being wonderful experiences for them. It's important that your kids realize being in the ministry can be fun.

- Go out and find someone to share the gospel with. You'll find no greater joy than when you are sharing your faith. You will feel the greatest encouragement you could ever feel.

- Don't be afraid to share with godly friends what you are feeling, like when you aren't focusing as well as you should. They will help you to keep your focus on Christ.

- Write down Romans 15:13, "Now the God of hope fill you with all joy and peace in believing, that ye may abound in hope, through the power of the Holy Ghost." Post it somewhere so it can be an encouragement to you. Memorize it.

- Contact someone who can give you spiritual advice about the matter. Perhaps there is a pastor who has gone through something similar or a spiritual person who you know would understand. Not too long ago, Pastor Dan Reehoff called me. He was discouraged and had gone through some hard things in his church. He and his wife, Aimee, went to a town close to Milwaukee, Wisconsin, to start a church. (Pastor Dan is my daughter-in-law Karen's brother.) They had about 20 people; then some people left, and they were down to about four people. I told him, "Pastor Dan, you are doing a lot better than I did in the beginning. You have four people. By the end of my first year, I barely had anyone. You are doing better than I did." In the past year, they've experienced a lot of growth, and now they have about 100 people coming.

- Read Psalm 1:1–2, "Blessed is the man that walketh not in the counsel of the ungodly, nor standeth in the way of sinners, nor sitteth in the seat of the scornful. But his delight is in the law of the LORD; and in his law doth he meditate day and night." Don't seek the counsel of ungodly people.

- God is with you, no matter how dark the night. If you honestly have no one you can go to with your problem, continue to pray and seek God's wisdom. He will send someone to help you.

Chapter 19
God Blesses Obedience

Having confidence in thy obedience I wrote unto thee, knowing that
thou wilt also do more than I say. Philemon 1:21

John Adams was a leading advocate for independence long before others were willing to speak up. After graduating from Harvard, he moved into the home of a lawyer as an apprentice and immersed himself in studying. He moved back to his hometown of Braintree, Massachusetts, passed the bar, and then lost his first case on a technicality. This embarrassed Adams, and he vowed never to repeat this mistake. Judging from the rest of his life, he always prepared for what he needed to do. He served as Washington's Vice President and then as President. Adams made countless sacrifices to serve his country, and is seen as one of our great founding fathers.[xvii]

Adams realized the importance of preparation and hard work. These attributes are important in every facet of life, especially in the Church. Every job you do for Christ is important. You may not understand that when you are cleaning out the Sunday School cabinet or sweeping the fellowship hall, until someone comes to church and says, "Everything here is so neat and clean."

The Obedience Test

Second Kings tells the story of a woman who obeyed God when she didn't know where that obedience would take her. Here is her story:

"Now there cried a certain woman of the wives of the sons of the prophets unto Elisha, saying, Thy servant my husband is dead; and thou knowest that thy servant did fear the Lord: and the creditor is come to take unto him my two sons to be bondmen. And Elisha said unto her, What shall I do for thee? tell me, what hast thou in the house? And she said, Thine handmaid hath not any thing in the house, save a pot of oil. Then he said, Go, borrow thee vessels abroad of all thy neighbours, even empty vessels; borrow not a few. And when thou art come in, thou shalt shut the door upon thee and upon thy sons, and shalt pour out into all those vessels, and thou shalt set aside that which is full. So she went from him, and shut the door upon her and upon her sons, who brought the vessels to her; and she poured out. And it came to pass, when the vessels were full, that she said unto her son, Bring me yet a vessel. And he said unto her, There is not a vessel more. And the oil stayed. Then she came and told the man of God. And he said, Go, sell the oil, and pay thy debt, and live thou and thy children of the rest." 2 Kings 4:1–7

Consider for a moment the circumstances of this woman. She was a wife of one of the prophets. Her husband had died, and now she and her two sons were literally starving to death. All she had was one pot of oil in her house; and she knew at any moment, someone would come and take her sons as slaves to pay off her debt.

She was at the end of her rope, or at the end of her oil. Can you imagine if you were in your home and had only one bottle of vegetable oil to your name?

She was told to go to the neighbors and ask them for pots. Notice Elisha didn't say to her, "Look, I'm going to do a miracle for you. I'm going to multiply the oil into much more oil so you can sell it to pay off your debts." He didn't give her the answer. He gave her what I call the Obedience Test. He told her, "Go to the neighbors and ask for their extra pots."

She had to take a step of faith and humble herself before God could work in her life.

Are you facing your own Obedience Test? Is God asking you to do something that doesn't make a whole lot of sense to you?

Maybe you have an upcoming test you don't know how to study for because the instructor delights in giving tests that don't make sense. You are used to getting good grades, and so you feel as though you'd rather drop the course than risk getting a bad grade. Should you go to the Lord about this? Absolutely. Should you drop the course? Don't decide this until you've spent some time in prayer about it.

Do you feel like you should cut back on your hours at work because there is some ministry work you wish to volunteer for? Are you concerned about how you are going to make it with less money? Go to the Lord and ask Him to help you. And remember, don't be afraid to put yourself out there where God can really use you. He will take care of you as He does the sparrow.

Recently, a Dayspring Bible College student shared about some of the difficulties he was experiencing. He was doing ministry at the church, carrying a full load of college courses, working a full-time job, trying to pay off his college loans, and buy a car. All of this pressure was making him want to give up. As he looked at his life, he didn't see how he had any choice but to quit doing the ministry at church and all of his college courses so he could work more hours and save money faster. Yet he didn't want to stop doing ministry, since that was what he had been called to do. He decided to keep doing ministry and his college courses, though he knew he might never have enough money to buy a car.

A vehicle became available through a person in the church whose relative had passed away. The young man was overjoyed to discover he had enough money to purchase the vehicle. He was so glad he had waited on the Lord's provision. The car he was able to purchase was much better than any other car that had been available with his limited funds.

Keep trusting God. Trust Him especially when the way is dark. He will provide.

House Visitation

Mike Floyd and I decided to visit every house in Mount Prospect to see if we could get people to come to church. It took months to accomplish this, since Mount Prospect is a big suburb of Chicago. We encountered tons of dogs. (I'm pretty sure there is a special reward in Heaven for pastors who are willing to visit people with dogs. Not that I don't like dogs.

It is just when you encounter so many dogs, or you see a sign that says "Beware of Dog," or you see a doghouse which is bigger than the house, that is when you know you need to be careful.)

One time we were about to go to a house, when a huge dog came out onto the sidewalk. I don't remember what kind of dog it was, but it didn't look happy at all. Fortunately, that dog didn't attack us. Another time when we went to the door of a home that was open with just a screen door, we heard loud, ferocious barking. Mike put his foot against the bottom of the screen to ensure the dog wouldn't be able to come out.

From that whole effort, we had only one family visit the church (Today, it is harder to go door to door in the Chicago area, though there are pastors in more rural communities who can still go door to door.); but I wouldn't say our visiting was wasted. We were doing what we knew we needed to do. We did the thing we knew to do next. God will never show you the whole picture until years go by and you look back on what He has done. But He will always show you the thing you should do today. We kept working; and little by little, we continued to see growth in the church.

I preached at Braun Manufacturing once a month. Mr. Braun would pay people whether they came and listened to the preaching, or they

Mr. August J. Braun.

didn't. So most of them came to the services. I went to him and told him we needed two buses. He found us two for $1000 each. We now had buses. We could pick people up and bring them to church.

I also drove five bus routes for the public school system. I had the routes with the most unruly kids on them, but the kids were good for me. It was a good job and paid well. Through this job, I met the superintendent of schools, and we became friends. He would let special singing groups from Florida Bible College ride the bus with me, sing to all the kids, and give their testimonies. He asked me to speak at the junior high graduation.

"You need to give the gospel when you speak," he said.

"Are you sure you want me to give the gospel? Won't you lose your job?"

The superintendent said, "I don't mind. This is my last year. You know this is a strong Jewish area."

"Exactly." I knew the area since I drove the bus. "You might have parents protest that a preacher is doing the graduation."

"I care about the souls of boys and girls. I want them to go to Heaven. Could you make sure you show that illustration with your wallet, too? They need to really understand the gospel."

I gave the gospel at the graduation, and many hands were raised to indicate salvation. At the moment I finished, the board came to the superintendent and wanted to fire him. They threatened me with a lawsuit, too. The superintendent smiled at me and said, "Don't worry, you won't get sued." The superintendent resigned since he planned to anyway.

One-Year Anniversary

We had been in Chicago almost a year, and it was getting close to our church's one-year anniversary. With all our hearts, we wanted to have 100 people for this special event. We worked hard inviting people out. We went to trailer parks, subdivisions, and apartment complexes.

On our anniversary, we had 100 people. (Of course, that was counting every child and maybe a mouse or two. Okay, I'm kidding about the mice, but we had worked so hard and were so proud.)

Right in the middle of the service, the fire alarm rang. We had to keep going through the service with that thing ringing. Fortunately, it was a false alarm. We discovered it was three-year-old Julie who pulled the fire alarm. No celebration is complete without a fire alarm going off somewhere.

Love for People

One of the most important things Linda and I had for the people of our church was love. We also had love for those who didn't know Christ as we continued to work to have them come to the knowledge of salvation through the Lord Jesus Christ.

The classic chapter on love, 1 Corinthians 13, shares the definition of what our attitude as Christians should be toward others. "And though I bestow all my goods to feed the poor, and though I give my body to be burned, and have not charity, it profiteth me nothing. Charity suffereth long, and is kind; charity envieth not; charity vaunteth not itself, is not puffed up." 1 Corinthians 13:3–4

Paul said love is more important than spiritual gifts, knowledge, faith, generosity, or a willingness to die for Christ. Yet many times we lose sight of this as believers. We begin to think our acts of service are more important than our attitude toward that service. We might do our service grudgingly, start thinking disgruntled thoughts, and say, "Isn't that person lucky that I am serving him?" or "I wish people would appreciate all that I do for them."

❧

It All Begins with an Attitude

The biggest truth of the Christian life is if we don't have an attitude of selfless love toward others, we won't have a ministry. If we don't genuinely care for others, then there is no reason for us to continue. The bottom line is the Christian life takes courage and great sacrifice. This service manifests itself in hundreds of ways in the everyday moments of our existence.

Have you ever known someone who has a spirit of meanness toward their service for Christ? This person could say things like, "I cleaned the church bathrooms last week, but no one thanked me for the sacrifice I made," or "I work in the youth group week after week, and it seems no one appreciates what I am doing," or "I worked so hard for that person, but he or she always seems to focus on everything I'm doing wrong."

It is easy—too easy—to fall into this attitude. The human heart is deceitful and desperately wicked, and we often don't realize we think these negative thoughts. We don't understand that if we don't continually do our service out of love, then our service isn't really service at all.

Paul tells us love is patient; love has a long fuse; love is slow to boil; love counts down before it blasts off. Then he tells us love is kind. We might think we are loving people, but many Christians aren't very kind.

❧

It's All About Souls

I strive to be all about souls — from running camps, to starting schools, preaching overseas, printing tracts, and global broadcasting — I always want to see people get saved.

Above: Preaching and teaching at the Solid Rock Theological Seminary in India.

Left: Wallet hand gesture illustrating the clear gospel of grace given every time I preach.

Right and bottom: I spent a lot of time reaching families and children.

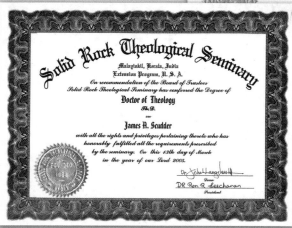

Florida Bible College

Hollywood, Florida

on recommendation of the Board of Trustees

Florida Bible College has conferred the Degree of

Bachelor of Arts in Biblical Education

on

James A. Scudder

with all the rights and privileges pertaining thereto

who has honorably fulfilled all the requirements prescribed by the college

Done at Hollywood, Florida this 5th day of June

in the year of our Lord, 19 71

Dean _____ President _____

I never liked school, but college was different. I was doing well as a senior at the University of Kentucky when God got a hold of me. I transferred to Florida Bible College. I cherish my time studying the Word of God the most.

The Board of Trustees of

Calvary Theological Seminary

on the recommendation of the faculty

hereby confers upon

James Allan Scudder

the degree of

Doctor of Divinity

with all the rights, privileges, and honors appertaining thereto

in consideration of the satisfactory completion of the studies

and requirements prescribed by the Seminary.

In Witness Whereof, the seal of Calvary Bible College

and the signatures authorized by the Board of Trustees

are hereby affixed.

this tenth day of May, 2005, at Kansas City, Missouri.

_____ Chairman of Board _____ President

_____ Secretary of Board _____ Academic Dean

Solid Rock Theological Seminary

Malayinkil, Kerala, India
Extension Program, U.S.A.

On recommendation of the Board of Trustees

Solid Rock Theological Seminary has conferred the Degree of

Doctor of Theology

Th.D.

on

James R. Scudder

with all the rights and privileges pertaining thereto who has

honorably fulfilled all the requirements prescribed

by the seminary. On this 13th day of March

in the year of our Lord 2005.

_____ Dean

DR. Ron R. Leecharan
President

Our life in ministry is about people, but we track our progress by buildings.

Building #1 under construction in Palatine, Illinois — 1973.

Finally, a real church with pews and a pulpit.

Soon out of room, we began our second building project.

Dedication of our second building in 1978.

We started celebrating the completion of our building projects with
a service of dedication and cake in
the shape of the new building.

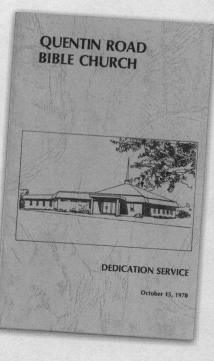

QUENTIN ROAD
BIBLE CHURCH

DEDICATION SERVICE

October 15, 1978

Our first member, Ralph.

With a growing church, school, and now college, we needed more land. God gave us 40 beautiful acres in Hawthorn Woods (now Lake Zurich) with lots of room to grow.

Bottom: Trusses going up after thinking we might not get them at all (We had to finish building them ourselves because the truss company went bankrupt).

Dedication service of our third building
(and, of course, cake).

With the steady growth of our youth ministry and schools, we needed a gymnasium. Yes, we also built this one ourselves.

You guessed it! Time to build again. But this time we would attempt to build a massive, 76,000-square-foot, steel, multipurpose building with a 3,000-seat auditorium.

Ralph breaking ground. He went to be with the Lord halfway through this project.

Our faith may have wavered a bit as we looked at the actual size of the project.

Left: God gave me the idea of a pool which saved thousands of dollars, as it is used as a reservoir for our fire sprinkler system.

Bottom: The day of the beam lift was one of the longest of my life.

We used a new exterior system that looks like stone, but is much lighter and cheaper.

Congressman Phil Crane, who attended church almost every Sunday, helped build the heating and cooling ducts.

Many of the young people of the church volunteered to do the many jobs of the project.

We had an impromptu service in the uncompleted auditorium. These moments really helped morale.

Quentin Road Bible Baptist Church
Building Dedication • May 3, 1998

Praise the Lord, we finished! God even prevented serious injury of our staff and volunteers. Contractors tell us they have never seen a building this large and complex built mostly by volunteers. This certainly was no piece of cake!

Dayspring Campus

Student Union

Women's Residence

Cafeteria
Gym

Administration Building

Men's Residence

Executive Offices

Maintenance Building

Married Housing

Caretaker

Academic Building

In 2012, God provided an amazing miracle for Dayspring Bible College & Seminary — a new, 13-acre campus less than 5 miles away.

We believe in using every means possible to influence the world. From this old-fashioned tent meeting in the '70s to a modern leadership conference, we have always emphasized God's grace.

We use large events like the Christmas pageant, where thousands hear and see the true message of Christmas.

Our Mother-Daughter Banquets now have over 1,000 ladies attending, again hearing the clear gospel of grace.

We recently celebrated our 40th year of ministry. We invited the community, and 3,000 people attended. We were able to serve all of our guests an old-fashioned chicken dinner in less than 10 minutes, thanks to the amazing dedication of our faithful members.

President George W. Bush
—we share a common
birthday—July 6, 1946 (what an
amazing day for the world!)

Congressman Dennis Hastert
—former speaker of the House.

Congressman J.C. Watts.

Senator Bob Dole.

Congressman Phil Crane.

Although I gave up politics to
become a pastor, God has
allowed me to be an influence
for righteousness to many
people in state and federal
offices.

I was privileged to open
both the U.S. House and
Senate in prayer.

Congressional Record

United States of America

PROCEEDINGS AND DEBATES OF THE 107th CONGRESS, FIRST SESSION

Vol. 147   WASHINGTON, WEDNESDAY, OCTOBER 3, 2001   No. 131

House of Representatives

The House met at 10 a.m. and was called to order by the Speaker pro tempore (Mr. LaHood).

DESIGNATION OF THE SPEAKER PRO TEMPORE

The SPEAKER pro tempore laid before the House the following communication from the Speaker:

WASHINGTON, DC,
October 3, 2001.
I hereby appoint the Honorable RAY LaHOOD to act as Speaker pro tempore on this day.
J. DENNIS HASTERT,
Speaker of the House of Representatives.

PRAYER

Dr. James A. Scudder, Quentin Road Bible Baptist Church, Lake Zurich, Illinois, offered the following prayer:
Dear heavenly Father, because You love the Almighty Creator, the everlasting, omnipotent one, the one who loves more than we could ever imagine, we come before You right now to humbly seek Your face. I beseech You to watch over this great Congress of the United States of America as they make important decisions and endeavor to accomplish that which is best for our great Nation. We pray for the ongoing investigation for the attack on America. Oh, Lord, how we grieve at the atrocities that were performed within our borders.

Each of these men and women are facing decisions more significant, more extensive, and more intense than any decision they could have imagined just 3 weeks ago.

We are a Nation indivisible, undivided. We thank You for our amazing heritage of freedom, and we acknowledge right now that all of our blessings come from You. We thank You for the great patriotism that is sweeping our land, and pray that we will continue to fight, acknowledging You as the source of all our strength.

I pray You will put Your umbrella of protection over each Member of Congress. Please give Your great assistance for the essential responsibilities that You have assigned to them. I pray for each person here, that they might know the peace that passeth all understanding. I ask You this in Your Son's name, Jesus Christ. Amen.

THE JOURNAL

The SPEAKER pro tempore. The Chair has examined the Journal of the last day's proceedings and announces to the House his approval thereof.

Pursuant to clause 1, rule I, the Journal stands approved.

PLEDGE OF ALLEGIANCE

The SPEAKER pro tempore. Will the gentleman from Illinois (Mr. CRANE) come forward and lead the House in the Pledge of Allegiance.

Mr. CRANE led the Pledge of Allegiance as follows:

I pledge allegiance to the Flag of the United States of America, and to the Republic for which it stands, one nation under God, indivisible, with liberty and justice for all.

ANNOUNCEMENT BY THE SPEAKER PRO TEMPORE

The SPEAKER pro tempore. The Chair announces that we will have 10 1-minutes on each side.

WELCOMING DR. JAMES SCUDDER, SENIOR PASTOR OF QUENTIN ROAD BIBLE BAPTIST CHURCH IN LAKE ZURICH, ILLINOIS

Mr. CRANE asked and was given permission to address the House for 1 minute and to revise and extend his remarks.)

Mr. CRANE. Mr. Speaker, today it is my honor to welcome Dr. James Scudder as our guest chaplain. Dr.

Scudder is a senior pastor of my church, the Quentin Road Bible Baptist Church, in Lake Zurich, Illinois.

In 1973, Dr. Scudder founded the Chicago Bible Church in a storefront. He migrated up to Chicago area from Kentucky. Well, actually, I do not know whether he went by way of Indiana en route, as Lincoln did, but he finally got to Illinois and he founded the church there. Then he expanded that church by moving out to Lake Zurich, Illinois. He has gone from a storefront church to a church that is 70,000 square feet. It is one of the biggest, or the biggest, in our area there. In addition to that, it has one of the largest congregations, in the thousands.

Dr. Scudder is the president also of Dayspring Bible College. He founded a school, grammar school, high school, and a college there. He is the host of the weekly TV broadcast, the Quentin Road Bible Hour, which is seen here on WGN-TV. He is the host of a radio program called Victory and Grace. In addition, Dr. Scudder is the author of several books.

He simultaneously is married to one of the most remarkable talents, Linda Scudder. She is an expert pianist, but she also leads the choir, and they have one of the largest choirs in the entire State of Illinois, and do remarkable performances every Sunday.

To show his additional talents, he has a son, one son named Jim, Jr., who is now also a pastor in his father's footsteps. He does as stirring a job in the pulpit, almost, as his father does. He is challenging him already. So whenever Pastor Scudder is traveling on missionary work, and he does that around the world, his son, Pastor Jim, Jr., fills in for him.

There is someone else, Pastor Bob Vanden Bosch, that I would like to recognize, who also works in the Quentin Road Bible Baptist Church, but spends a lot of time down in our State Capitol of Springfield, Illinois, trying to convert the heathen in Springfield.

Dr. Art Rorheim, co-founder of Awana, serves on our college board and is the closest of friends.

My good friend, Dr. Curtis Hutson, preached for us many times until God took him home with cancer.

More important to me than the president of the United States were the spiritual men and women God put in my life.

"Doc" Lance Latham, co-founder of Awana and accomplished pianist, played for our second building dedication.

Jo Norris (the amazing woman who prayed me into the ministry) with my granddaughter, Amy.

God has really blessed Linda and me, with all of our children and grandchildren serving the Lord and active in ministry.

This is my sister, Pauline, and her husband, Mike Holovak. He was the first coach for the Patriots and the general manager for the Houston Oilers.

Clockwise from left: Our grandchildren, Erica, Jamie, Amanda, and Amy.

My amazing wife, Linda, has been very effective in our music ministry. She has stood by my side through thick and thin, and I will forever be grateful for her love for the Lord and for me.

The True Spirit of Christ

Let me share something that will change your life: working hard is part of life. The person you are working for has the right to criticize your work. It won't feel pleasant, but beware of getting offended over it. When you get offended, it is hard to keep on going for Christ; but you must realize that in reality as you serve others, you answer ultimately to our Lord. As you work for Him, keep in mind that the slights and insults you are bound to feel from others are par for the course in the Christian life. Jesus is keeping track, and you will be rewarded for your faithfulness at the Judgment Seat of Christ. As the old song says, "It will be worth it all when we see Jesus."

Known by Kindness

Are you known as a kind person? Are you someone who will drop everything to help someone, or are you always nursing a grudge against others?

How do you feel when you are in line at a crowded supermarket and everyone is making negative comments under their breath? How about when you are trying to travel the speed limit and you have someone behind you honking?

It is easy to adopt the "me-first" attitude of the world inadvertently. We have deadlines to meet and places to be. We fall into this rush-rush attitude where we don't ever have time for other people.

What if our Lord had this attitude, and didn't heal the blind and the deaf or preach whenever He had opportunity? We shudder to think what would have happened had our Lord been selfish. Many times we are too busy to stop and remember people matter; and if we don't have an attitude of selflessness toward them, we won't have a ministry. Take a moment right now and ask God to give you the strength to look at the people around you with new eyes. Ask Him for help in realizing that if we don't show genuine, Christ-like love to others, people won't be drawn to the Savior.

Our attitude of love for others will supercharge our ministry to them.

❦

Your Obedience Test

Working to get 100 people was kind of like what the widow did with Elisha's order of getting pots. She didn't just get one pot, go in and close the door, and see if God would do a miracle. If she had done that, she would have had one extra pot of oil. Instead she got as many pots as she could, went into her house, and saw God work big time for her. I wonder if she said to herself afterwards, *I'm glad I got so many pots, but it's too bad I didn't go around and get a few more. Then I would have had more blessings.* (By the way, we did get to 100 that Sunday, but the very next week we had a much smaller crowd. Still, we believed that if you threw enough mud at the wall, some would stick.)

When it comes to the Lord, sometimes we don't know why we are doing certain jobs. You are faithfully completing the work and don't always see the end result. But you will. Just as the woman with Elisha saw the blessing of God, so you will see it as well. God always blesses obedience and faithfulness to His Word, and He will bless you. He will bless your church, too.

Finish Line Strategies

- Don't get sidetracked by things that don't matter. Stay focused on the goal.

- God will keep revealing His will to you as you continue to obey Him.

- Use Ivory soap. It does the best job at getting rid of fish odor. (Okay, I threw that in to see if you were really reading this book instead of skimming, but I do love Ivory soap the best.)

- Sometimes a person in authority will correct you for something you are doing wrong. Confess your sin and go on the best you can. God has forgiven you. Don't let your past keep you from serving in the present. Remember, Proverbs says the difference between a wise man and a fool is that a wise man wants correction, while a foolish man doesn't.

Section 3

Thru many dangers, toils and snares,
I have already come;
'Tis grace hath brought me safe thus far,
And grace will lead me home.

Chapter 20
A Life Full of Purpose

Be strong and courageous, be not afraid nor dismayed for the king of Assyria,
nor for all the multitude that is with him: for there be more with us than with him:
With him is an arm of flesh; but with us is the LORD our God to help us,
and to fight our battles. And the people rested themselves upon the words of
Hezekiah king of Judah. 2 Chronicles 32:7–8

The elementary school was an okay meeting place for the church, but not ideal. More people attended, but we wouldn't be able to grow unless we had somewhere to call our own.

We needed property, but we had very little money.

We looked at every available piece of property in Mount Prospect and the surrounding suburbs. All of them were way out of our price range.

A lady named Barbara came to help us with the music when we were still meeting in the school. She lived with us for awhile. The kids slept on the floor in our bedroom. Although this wasn't ideal, it was infinitely better than the fourth-floor, walk-up apartment.

Mike Floyd and I would go to a restaurant named Golden Bear. We would order coffee (they had free refills) and plan our future church building by drawing on a napkin. I wish I had kept some of those napkins instead of throwing them away. They would be interesting to look at now.

Property was valued at $40,000 an acre. We didn't see how we could afford it.

Linda and I also wanted to buy a home. We had lived in the small apartment for quite awhile, and the kids were almost old enough for school. We found a townhome in Vernon Hills, Illinois, and thought it was perfect. It was big enough that we could meet in it for church. We scraped enough money together for the down payment of $1,000. (That was a lot of money to us.)

I was at the Randhurst Shopping Mall right by our current apartment, when I went to a pay phone to call the bank and see if we got approval for our loan. The bank said no. They couldn't approve the loan. Not only could we not move into the townhome, but we had lost $1,000. I remember telling Linda and seeing the tears in her eyes. The blow couldn't have been greater. It pretty much ripped our hearts out. We could not think coherent thoughts for a few days, we were so devastated. Losing $1,000 also almost sunk us financially. It took us a long time to recover from that blow.

We had so wanted stability as a family. My wife and kids had sacrificed a lot to come to Chicago to start a church. We had worked hard and had focused on getting the church going. Now, we weren't getting the townhome. There was little hope for a future loan since this first bank had turned us down.

Looking back with all the hindsight that time provides, I see it would have been the worst thing in the world if we had gotten that townhome. The location would have been too far away from the people who were attending. We couldn't keep meeting in an apartment or townhome if we hoped for church growth, and there would have been no money to purchase property for a church building. Our church wouldn't have survived. God had other plans for us, but we didn't know it at the time.

To this day when I go by that mall in Mount Prospect, I remember my phone call to the bank, the bad news, and the sick feeling in the pit of my stomach at not being able to get that townhome.

The third verse of "Amazing Grace" came true in my life. *Thru many dangers, toils and snares, / I have already come. / 'Tis grace hath brought me safe thus far, / And grace will lead me home.* God would help us keep going. We had to believe this.

We determined our joy couldn't come from possessions, houses, or anything else. Our joy had to come from Christ. First Peter 4:13 says, "But rejoice, inasmuch as ye are partakers of Christ's sufferings; that, when his glory shall be revealed, ye may be glad also with exceeding joy."

Defining Your Purpose

How do you react when something happens that deters you from your purpose? When we lost that money and that home, it was like all hope was gone. Yet we spent much time in prayer, Bible study, and sharing with our church members. We remembered, once again, that God had called us and He would continue to be faithful to us. Looking back, I see this as an important part of making it in the ministry and in life. Every time we had a setback, we went back to our calling. We remembered all God had done already in our lives; and we chose to continue to trust, knowing God would eventually bless.

What is your purpose in life? God's purpose for you will always begin as a God-given concern. I don't mean just a passing concern. As the old saying goes, "Everybody ends up somewhere in life. Some end up there on purpose."

Billy Sunday said, "More men fail through lack of purpose than lack of talent."

None of us want to feel this way about our lives. As believers, we have a higher calling that is far beyond our human imagination.

Adoniram Judson sweated out Burma's heat for 18 years without a furlough, and went six years without a convert. Enduring torture and imprisonment, he admitted he never saw a ship sail without wanting to jump on board and go home. When his wife's health was failing, he put her on a homebound vessel with the knowledge he would not see her for two full years. He confided to his diary: "If we could find some quiet resting place on earth where we could spend the rest of our days in peace...." But he steadied himself with this remarkable postscript: "Life is short. Millions of Burmese are perishing. I am almost the only person on earth who has attained their language to communicate salvation...."[xviii]

Nehemiah's Higher Call

Nehemiah discovered God had a calling for him. Nehemiah's greatest joy was to fulfill that calling.

Nehemiah 2:12 tells us that Nehemiah "arose in the night, I and some few men with me; neither told I any man what my God had put in my heart to do at Jerusalem: neither was there any beast with me, save the beast that I rode upon."

In 587 B.C., the Babylonians invaded and destroyed the city of Jerusalem. The temple was destroyed. Some years later, the Jews returned to Jerusalem, but things did not look good. The temple was not being maintained. Sacrifices had ceased. The Jews had adopted the lifestyle and culture of the surrounding nations. Deplorable spiritual and social conditions existed in Jerusalem.

But one man back in Persia was about to be used by God. Nehemiah was about to discover God's purpose for his life.

Do You Have a Divine Purpose?

What is your divine purpose? What has God called you to do? As you start out upon life's crossroads, be sure your heart's purpose is prompted by the Lord. How can we tell whether the secret purpose of our heart is implanted by God?

Winston Churchill wrote these words when he was asked by King George VI to form a government after Neville Chamberlain stepped down. "As I went to bed at about 3am, I was conscious of a profound sense of relief. At last I had the authority to give directions over the whole scene. I felt as if I were walking with Destiny, and that all my past life had been but a preparation for this hour and for this trial....Therefore, although impatient for the morning, I slept soundly and had no need for cheering dreams. Facts are better than dreams."[xix]

Maybe some of you are reading this and are thinking, *But I'm no Churchill.* No matter who you are, God has placed you here for a purpose. You were put on this earth with gifts and talents that are waiting to be used to fulfill God's purpose for you.

The Purpose Test

Here are four guidelines to determine whether the desire in your heart is God's purpose for your life:

Test 1

If your purpose was accomplished, would it be for the good of others as well as yourself? Any success that doesn't help other people is not in accord with the mind of Christ.

Test 2

Would the accomplishment of your purpose be for God's glory? Nehemiah knew God wanted the walls of Jerusalem rebuilt. He had a divine purpose, and he knew God had put this in his heart. He knew God would be glorified when the walls were rebuilt.

Test 3

Is your purpose in accord with the Word of God? Remember, God never goes against His Word. He considers His Word higher than His name. I've had people tell me through the years, "Pastor, I prayed about it and I have peace." Time and time again, these people were willing to go against the Bible because they had a peaceful feeling. (Remember, feeling peace about a situation doesn't necessarily mean you are doing the right thing.)

Test 4

Have you sought godly counsel about your purpose? Have you gone to someone, a pastor or spiritual friend, and asked for advice? Don't just go to the person that you know will agree with you. Go to someone who will give you advice from the Word of God.

Fulfilling God's Promise

Why was Nehemiah concerned about the broken-down walls? God had made a promise to His people. God said that if His people returned to Him, then He would restore them. He would bring them back from exile and make them prosperous again. Nehemiah's concern wasn't really about a wall. His concern was about God's people.

When we fulfill God's purpose for our lives, we help God's people. We are giving to others and sharing the gospel with them. We live a life of graciousness and love that draws people to the Savior. We consciously look out for our fellow believers. We follow a divine call.

First Thessalonians 5:14 states, "Now we exhort you, brethren, warn them that are unruly, comfort the feebleminded, support the weak, be patient toward all men." When we comfort those who need extra support, when we give a helping hand to someone in need, when we help pay for someone's car repair, when we go above and beyond in our service to others, we, along with them, will see them drawn closer to the Lord.

Endurance for Your Purpose

The difficulties of Nehemiah's task might well have given a strong man excuses to turn back, but Nehemiah's faith in God gave him the grace to endure.

Whatever purpose God has brought to your heart, know one thing: God will give you the endurance you need to fulfill it. Whether God has called you to be a pastor, deacon, or Sunday School teacher, remember just as He gave Nehemiah grace to finish his task, so He will give you the strength to endure over the long haul.

Understand the barriers to achieving the purpose God has given you will be high. They will sometimes be treacherous. Second Timothy 2:3 exhorts, "Thou therefore endure hardness, as a good soldier of Jesus Christ." James 5:11 tells us, "Behold, we count them happy which endure. Ye have heard of the patience of Job, and have seen the end of the Lord; that the Lord is very pitiful, and of tender mercy."

Psalm 138:3 gives us comfort when it states, "In the day when I cried thou answeredst me, and strengthenedst me with strength in my soul."

Fred Craddock, in an address to ministers, caught the practical implications of giving everything to the Lord. "To give my life for Christ appears glorious," he said. "To pour myself out for others... to pay the ultimate price of martyrdom—I'll do it. I'm ready, Lord, to go out in a blaze of glory."[xx] God will strengthen you to do His purpose. I encourage you to grab hold of His plan for you and give that plan all your heart, soul, and strength.

We Need Property

As a last-chance effort to find our first property, we put an ad in the paper: "Small, independent church looking for one acre."

The ad ran once.

My faith was strong that the ad would work, but nothing happened. We kept looking for property, but everything we found was way out of our price range.

A few weeks later, I got a call from a realtor who was obviously drunk. He was perusing the paper (he was a bit behind on his reading) and came across our ad. He had a piece of property he wanted to show us in the morning. I didn't put too much stake in what he said because of him being drunk.

Palatine property—future location of the first building of our own.

In the morning, he actually met with me and took me to a piece of property on Quentin Road in Palatine, Illinois. It was two and a half acres with a very small, rundown house. I asked how much it was going for and he said, "$40,000."

I couldn't believe it. $40,000 for two and a half acres? And a house? We'd searched out property enough to know that this was an excellent price and within our range. Granted, the house was completely falling apart and would later be condemned as not fit for human habitation; but it was good enough for us to live in and a place for the church to meet. I could afford the payment on the property because we could use the money we were paying for rent.

I went to the bank in Palatine and asked the bank president for a loan. He was a nice gentleman who believed in us. The bank gave us the loan.

We almost jumped out of our skin with excitement. I drove to the property just to walk around again and see all that God had done. On the way, I was stopped and got a speeding ticket. I had been too excited to look at the speed I was traveling. I hadn't ever gotten one before or since, but that day I didn't care. God was so good.

I appreciate Linda for going through all of this with me. In appreciation for her being married to me and putting up with me, I bought her some Kindness curlers. They were items she had been wanting for awhile, but I couldn't afford to get them for her. I smile when I think of her getting curlers, but I did want to show her how much I appreciated all she had done.

In spite of the extreme disappointment with the townhome, God gave us something far better: a place to live and a location to build a building. We knew our lives were full of purpose.

The miracle of it all gives me chills to this day.

Finish Line Strategies

The following are from the book called, *You Might Be a Preacher If...* by Stan Toler.

- You might be a preacher if you've ever received an anonymous U-Haul gift certificate.

- You might be a preacher if you find yourself counting people at a sporting event.

- You might be a preacher if you have ever wanted to wish people Merry Christmas at Easter, because that's the next time you're going to see them.

- You might be a preacher if you've ever wanted to give the sound man a bit of feedback of your own.

- You might be a preacher if you've ever walked up to the counter at the Dairy Queen and ordered a church split.

- You might be a preacher if you've written a letter of resignation on Monday morning.[xxi]

While these are humorous, remember no matter how difficult things are, no matter how tough and terrible your boss is, or how bad your child acts, no matter how difficult that subject in college that you can't understand, these are simply opportunities for God's grace to shine through in your life.

Chapter 21
Managing, Planning, and Volunteers

Wherefore also we pray always for you, that our God would count you worthy of this calling, and fulfil all the good pleasure of his goodness, and the work of faith with power. 2 Thessalonians 1:11

The following message was on a pastor's answering machine: "I'm not in right now, but I'll get back to you as soon as possible. For a quicker response, please volunteer to teach Sunday School."

A lack of volunteers is sometimes the single, most difficult thing churches face today. This doesn't mean there aren't many people who serve in their churches, but often these are the minority rather than the majority. It is the "faithful few" who do most of the work. Often these are behind-the-scenes jobs like washing the dishes after an event or cleaning the bathrooms. (Thankfully, at Quentin Road we have many people who give of their time day after day. We couldn't make it as a ministry without them.)

Take Helen, for example. This wonderful lady sent our books and tapes to prison chaplains around the country. For many years, she used most of her own money to do this. We received hundreds of letters from these prisoners, telling us their lives have been changed forever because of the gospel message.

Don was another faithful volunteer. He answered phones for *Victory In Grace* at almost every broadcast. His upbeat attitude and loving spirit brought joy to all who knew him. He has gone home to be with the Lord now. (I wonder if he still asks the Lord if he could answer the phones of Heaven.)

We've had so many volunteers throughout the years who have made such a difference at Quentin Road. We have also been blessed to be able to hire many people to help out in the various ministries like the preschool, radio and television department, schools, college, kitchen, horse barn, dyslexia tutoring, and more. What an incredible sacrifice these people have made throughout the years. I appreciate each one of them more than they could ever know.

Some people think a church should be run like a business. Years ago, I had a man say to me, "As a businessman, I say that you should run your church like a business." My reply was, "A church is not just an organization; it is a living organism."

While smart business practices are a very important part of the church's day-to-day operation, the management and running of a church is very different than a business. That's because the church is not a building. It's a body. The local church is the Body of Christ in this spot on the planet. As such, a pastor needs great wisdom from on high to successfully lead this living entity.

Practical Management

Here are some practical tips for administrating our ministry and handling volunteers and staff. Most of these principles I picked up along the way as I was actually running the church. Some of these I learned the hard way by first making mistakes and then discovering how to do it in a better way.

Inspire people to do the job God has called them to do. Find out a person's special gift and a way to give that person a job in the church that fits their gift. You can't do everything yourself. Maybe you love to cook, but you find someone in your church who is a great cook. Give that person the job of cooking so you can be freed up to do other things.

People can always contribute more than they realize they can. That's because we serve a great God. Give people opportunities to grow and develop as they work. Bring them with you when you are going to go witnessing or running errands for church. Spend time listening to them and finding out what their passion in life is.

Care about your staff and volunteers. This seems obvious, but there are a lot of preachers who seem oblivious to the hard work of other people. I take my staff out to a special restaurant at least once a year to show them how much I appreciate them. I want them to know that I care about them and appreciate all they do.

Don't micromanage every aspect of every job. You need reports, and you need to oversee; but if you get bogged down in micromanaging, you will never move forward as a ministry.

Find people who are good at managing. Give them opportunities to learn more and discover more about their particular position.

Allow people to grow into their positions. I remember when we first hired Cindy Holler as our preschool director. She was a dental hygienist by trade and didn't know if she could run such a big preschool and staff of over 100 women; but she had a great personality, and I knew she could do it.

Train your young people to serve in the church. Many of our main staff now were students in our Christian school and were in our church at a young age. We gave them opportunities to serve. Through time, they have developed into amazing leaders. When Pastor Dan Reehoff was 14 years old, we taught him how to run a small print-ing press at the church. By the time he was in his twenties, he was running a huge printing operation with four-color printing and a huge Heidelberg press. When my son, Jim, was in his early teens, he mowed the grass at the church and took care of the landscaping before moving up to other duties in the church. He installed all the lights on the outside of our big building. Of course, now he is the president of Dayspring Bible College and Seminary.

Dan Reehoff started our printing ministry with very little to work with.

When Pastor Paul Julian was out of Dayspring, he became the main administrator of our latest building project, proving his ability in so many ways. When he was in high school, he never stood out; but when he helped build our latest addition along with Dave Lively, his true genius came out.

Paul Julian studies our latest building plans.

Our high school girls worked on the outside of the building doing the exterior. Now every one of them is in full-time Christian service.

So many others have come alongside and con-

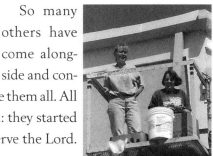

High school girls applying
the exterior material.

tributed so much. I could never name them all. All of them share one thing in common: they started out young and they continued to serve the Lord. God has done great things in their lives.

Praising the Lord

After we were approved for the loan and we bought the property, we were able to make the payment on the property because we were no longer paying rent. We were also able to have our church meet in the house—an additional savings.

God was doing so much. We could hardly believe it. The time we had been in Chicago had been tougher than anything we ever could have imagined; and yet, here we were. We had property and we had a place to live.

It was like I had been born again. Now I know you can only become born again once when you trust Christ as your Savior; but in many ways, this property was a rebirth for me. A renewing of my spirit to continue serving the Lord. A reminder to always have joy in the Lord no matter what the circumstances.

What Is True Joy?

We had true joy the day we bought the property; but we also had true joy when we had lost the townhome. (Of course, we weren't happy when we lost it, but we had joy from our Lord.)

"For I think that God hath set forth us the apostles last, as it were appointed to death: for we are made a spectacle unto the world, and to angels, and to men. We are fools for Christ's sake, but ye are wise in Christ; we are weak, but ye are strong; ye are honourable, but we are despised. Even unto this present hour we both hunger, and thirst, and are naked, and are buffeted, and have no certain dwellingplace; And labour, working with our own hands: being reviled, we bless; being persecuted, we suffer it: Being defamed, we intreat: we are made as the filth of the world, and are the offscouring of all things unto this day." 1 Corinthians 4:9–13

Most television preachers talk about the rewards of this life if you give and if you serve the Lord. They say if you have enough faith, then you are guaranteed prosperity and a wonderful life now. And yet, if that was true, then these verses from the Apostle Paul wouldn't be true. It doesn't sound very wonderful to be despised, hungry, thirsty, naked, buffeted, not to have a home, to work hard all the time, to be persecuted, defamed, and made as the offscouring of the earth.

Of course, if we believe this idea that our rewards as believers all come in this life, then any suffering we experience would make us assume we have failed, we don't have enough faith, and we aren't giving enough or doing enough. This attitude leads to frustration and a lack of hope.

This is one of the main reasons I am on television and have the program, *Victory In Grace*. I want to preach the truth of the Word of God that there is no promise that this life is going to be easy for the believer. This doesn't mean that God won't bless us and won't give us material possessions. There were some very rich men in the Bible like Abraham, Job, and others, but riches didn't possess them; they possessed riches. There is a big difference.

Human nature wants to avoid suffering at any cost. We treat it like the plague and reject it. We need to equip believers in our churches to handle suffering. We need to be examples in the way we handle suffering as well.

The prophets in the Old Testament lost everything as they communicated God's message to the people. They lost their property; their freedom; and ultimately, many of them lost their lives. So did the apostles, if you remember. They didn't exactly have an easy life once Jesus rose from the dead. Instead, they endured much suffering and hardship. Most of them were imprisoned for many years and then executed.

This may not be how you envisioned your life to be once you became a Christian. Perhaps you thought life either wouldn't be that difficult, or if it was difficult, you would soon get out of the hardship and things would be easier.

Have you gone through something really difficult lately in your church? Or maybe in your family? Or perhaps in your job? Have you been tempted to think as you've been going through the entire hardship, "If I could get out of this hard time, then things would be easier and I would be able to serve the Lord better."

Guess what? Things are always going to be difficult in our lives. I don't write this to frustrate you and make you want to give up. I write this because I care about you. It is better to think realistically about a situation.

I have to admit—I have the same feeling. I have gone through over 40 years of ministry and often I want to say, "I shouldn't keep having these hard things in our church. I shouldn't keep having people disappoint me, not after all I've been through."

And yet, God still puts me through these hard things. Difficulties will never end until we get to Heaven and receive our new bodies.

But this doesn't mean that through all of the hard times we can't have joy.

Joy comes from the inside.

Joy doesn't come from our circumstances.

Joy comes despite our circumstances.

Joy is there no matter what we are facing.

Joy can be there no matter how difficult things are.

You can have joy right now.

Dear friend, do you realize that having joy isn't about what is actually happening in your life right now, but rather it is because of Jesus giving you joy? Has this been a difficult concept to grasp as you've gone through your Christian life? Why don't you take a minute and write down a gratitude list. Think about some things you are thankful for.

Thank God for all He has done for you.

❦

Getting to Work

The new property was full of old, rusted-out cars. The weeds had grown up everywhere, but we knew we could work. That was something we already knew how to do. We had workdays at the property and got rid of the cars, removed the weeds, mowed the waist-high grass, cleared out the rocks, and cleaned out the house.

Small trees grew all over the property. Mike Floyd worked using a mower that chopped down small trees. One day he mowed grass behind our house, not realizing that the previous owners didn't have sewer or septic; but instead all the waste went into the ground. He hit a huge pile with his mower by accident, and a huge amount of mud and other unmentionables covered him from head to toe. His eyes were covered. His face was covered. The stuff was pretty much everywhere. Since Mike was a well-dressed and meticulous person, it was especially funny to see him covered with excrement.

I laughed so hard I almost started crying. I'm sure by this point Mike was considering murdering me as an alternative to me laughing at him. He kept saying, "This isn't funny. This isn't human stuff like you think it is; they had a dog that used that part of the yard."

Then I'd catch a whiff and laugh harder. Mike couldn't clean up at the property because we didn't have water there yet. He went to a gas station nearby, but they wouldn't let him use their bathroom. Finally, he found a hose and was able to clean up.

After we moved into the house, we began to have other problems. The well turned out not to work at all; and for awhile, we had to go to the pond across the street and use buckets to bring water back to our house to flush the toilets.

We never regretted any of those times. In retrospect, they were some of the greatest circumstances of our lives.

We began meeting in the house for church. Mike and Trena got married that December in the house. Jimmy's head was just above the table

This wedding cake was almost too tempting for my children.

that had the wedding cake on it. He enjoyed swiping the frosting from the cake.

I thanked God over and over for doing such a marvelous thing. He had worked miracles that I couldn't have ever planned or figured out on my own. I praised Him for His goodness. He had taken our sadness at not getting the townhome and turned it into joy by giving us 2 ½ acres and a home—except at each point, it took extra faith to jump in and do what God wanted. (The fact we had weak faith doesn't mean that we didn't trust God, but the truth of the Christian life is it's always a battle to trust God. It is the great battle of the universe.) No matter how much God has done for you in the past, you still have to trust Him for the future.

To go forward, you must remember God will always provide. As you manage, plan, and encourage your volunteers, watch in wonder as He does great things in your life.

Our young family in our first home in Palatine.

Finish Line Strategies

- Volunteers will give of their best when they feel appreciated. Make sure they know that you care about them. Send them a thank you card. Thank them specifically for what they do.

- Volunteers will do whatever it takes to minister if there is flexibility. Don't make the schedule so rigid that they feel like there is no way for them to live their life. People have hectic lifestyles, and you will get more help if you understand this and make volunteering easy for them to do.

- Make sure your volunteers and workers know what their job description is. Take the time to share with them exactly what you need done. Write it down if you can. That makes it much easier. One idea to help organize a work day or project is to have a large white board filled with all the jobs that need to be done, with the name of the person who is heading up that job. When the workers come, they know to come to the board, see the job they need to do, and then go and see the person who is heading up that job. Another church I know of writes down each job on a separate piece of paper that people can grab when they come to the work day. When the job is finished, the paper is turned in to the office. That way the pastor doesn't have to spend all day telling each and every person their job. The workers will be happy because they have a lot going on in their lives, and it is a sacrifice for them to come and help. When they come and the jobs are spelled out, they get more accomplished.

- Give the volunteers authority over their job. Even if you can do a better job, resist the urge to jump in and do it. Instead, train them and disciple them as they do the job, but allow them to do it on their own. The results will be better when they have freedom.

Chapter 22
Confidence in God's Plan

*But my God shall supply all your need according to his riches
in glory by Christ Jesus. Philippians 4:19*

Ready

God miraculously provided for us to purchase property for our third
location on Quentin Road in Palatine, Illinois. Three years after arriving in
Chicago, we started meeting in the home.

Set

We met three times a week in our living room, moving furniture and

bringing in folding chairs,
a laminate wood pulpit,
hymnbooks, and Bibles.
(Throughout the years we've
bought more chairs and
tables than I could ever
count. If your church is
always buying tables and

Meetings started in the house in Palatine.

chairs, count it as a good sign.) The living room/dining room combination
could only seat about 25 people. The home had limited parking space,
plus the strain on our family was immense. After every service, we cleaned
the house to prepare it for the next day. People visited day and night for
counseling, help, and prayer. We had no privacy. God had provided the
property, but what was the next step?

Go

Time to build. We needed a bigger place to meet. We could only
grow to a point while meeting in the house. But how would we do

it? Where would we get the money? We continued to seek the Lord's direction. Through a lot of counsel, I decided I would go and ask my friend August Braun, who I've mentioned before was the owner of Braun Manufacturing, to co-sign for the loan. I dressed in my only suit and made an appointment to meet with him.

Sitting across from him in his office, I explained I needed him to co-sign for the loan.

He raised his eyebrows, "And what is your plan to build this building once you get the money?"

I sat back in my chair. I had thought that if I could get him to co-sign for the loan and we got the loan, that I would then develop a plan. I swallowed. "I don't have a plan," I admitted.

He leaned forward. "Son, you'd come and waste a busy factory owner's time by asking for me to co-sign for you to get a loan, and you don't have a plan?"

I left his office feeling like I had let him and the whole church down. I was determined to come up with a plan and come back to meet with Mr. Braun again. I didn't know if he would make an appointment with me the second time, but I had to try.

❧❦❧

The Balance between Planning and Trusting God to Work

As you read about how I had to come up with a plan, you might be thinking, *But how is planning a part of trusting God?*

There is a balance between these two things. Living the Christian life is a partnership between us and God. He works through us, and that means we also have to work for Him. As we do what we need to do each day, we will be led by the Holy Spirit into the fullness of God's plan.

For example, if we hadn't searched for property and put an ad in the paper, I don't think God would have blessed us with property. God delights in us working hard. Work was something that God gave to Adam and Eve before the Fall, so work itself is not part of the curse. Now the work is much harder because of Adam and Eve's sin, but we were created to work.

In the end, God gave us the property through a realtor reading newspapers in the middle of the night. By the time he finally read the paper, we had almost forgotten that we had placed the ad. God expects us to work and have a plan; but He also wants us to be open to what He will do in a situation, which is always above and beyond what we could imagine.

Jeremiah 33:3 states, "Call unto me, and I will answer thee, and shew thee great and mighty things, which thou knowest not."

When we pray to our great God, He will hear our prayers. He will give us the strength to accomplish His will, but we also need to guard against planning that would be dishonoring to our Lord Jesus. Some Christians think that if they make a plan, then God will fall in line with that plan.

That's not the proper perspective. Going forward in ministry or in your life takes planning. The key is not to get so attached to your planning that you aren't aware of what God is doing in your life.

In Luke 12:16–21, Jesus says,

> "And he spake a parable unto them, saying, The ground of a certain rich man brought forth plentifully: And he thought within himself, saying, What shall I do, because I have no room where to bestow my fruits? And he said, This will I do: I will pull down my barns, and build greater; and there will I bestow all my fruits and my goods. And I will say to my soul, Soul, thou hast much goods laid up for many years; take thine ease, eat, drink, and be merry. But God said unto him, Thou fool, this night thy soul shall be required of thee: then whose shall those things be, which thou hast provided? So is he that layeth up treasure for himself, and is not rich toward God."

Jesus gives us the perfect balance here between hard work and God's plan for our lives. When we count only on our plans, we are doomed for failure. If we have no plan, then we aren't working and thinking of how we could do the will of God.

❧◈❧

Other People's Plans

Also, be careful about criticizing other people's plans. James tells us in chapter two, verse eight, "If ye fulfil the royal law according to the scripture, Thou shalt love thy neighbour as thyself, ye do well."

A Charlie Brown cartoon depicts Linus sitting with his security blanket and his thumb in his mouth. He turns to his sister, Lucy, and says, "Why are you always so anxious to criticize me?"

She always had a quick and mean response. "I have a knack for seeing other people's faults," she said.

"But what about your own faults?"

Lucy smiles. "I have a knack for overlooking them."

Sometimes it is easy to criticize other preachers or ministry leaders. Maybe we don't realize how much this will hurt them or how much they will be discouraged by our words. It is easy to explain away our own faults and lack of a plan while criticizing the plans of others. (Sometimes you have to take a stand on the Word of God, and then it is okay to criticize. It isn't okay to get personal when taking a stand. Do it for the right reasons.)

The great M.R. DeHaan said, "Speak words of comfort, words of praise, and words of cheer. Do your part to silence gossip and not repeat it."

You'll find in the ministry that some people think it is their God-given right to dish out criticism. They see it as their knack. Some might consider it a spiritual gift. These people are often blind to their own weaknesses or failures. (In our first building, we had an older couple who mentioned that our church wasn't organized. We took this seriously and got everything structured so it would run smoother. We went to visit them and their home was a total mess, but we still needed to learn from them.)

Dealing with People

Here are some principles that I've learned in dealing with disapproval from other people.

Criticism always hurts. Don't be surprised when it does hurt. That is the nature of it. Most of the time criticism doesn't come in a loving way, and there is nothing good said in the conversation.

Give yourself time to respond to the criticism. You may need to respond right away if the situation warrants that, but don't react without thinking about what you are going to say and do.

Think about the fact that there could be a grain of truth in the criticism. We can learn from everyone—even our enemies. Throughout the years at Quentin Road, I've learned every criticism can help me. The assessment might be just or fair. Many times the criticism comes from people who are doing nothing in their life spiritually, and that is always going to hurt; but more times than not, I've learned from criticism. That experience with Mr. Braun taught me a lot. He didn't mean the criticism in a mean way, but he did need to speak the truth to me; and I had to learn to take it, or I wouldn't be able to grow in my own life. There is always some truth in what they are saying, even if it is just a tiny kernel. When I have a humble spirit and take criticism in the right way, I find that God teaches me through those painful times.

One family that left our church said I was quenching the Spirit with my sermons. They started attending a liberal church where the Bible wasn't believed. I could never understand that; but the criticism made me look at my sermons, and I started working harder on my titles and my messages.

Always consider the source. Sometimes the disapproval isn't warranted at all, and the person is simply trying to make himself or herself feel better for committing sin. A college student once criticized me for going on mission trips. He said they were extravagant. He said other hurtful things, too. Not much later he was caught on camera stealing a computer from a large store. He was wearing the t-shirt of the company he was working for, so he was easy to identify. In this case, the student didn't have truth to offer in his criticism, and he was soon caught in his own sin.

❦

Coming Up with a Plan

After talking to Mr. Braun, I went home and started a plan. I drew the size of the building I thought we should build, and I figured what it would cost. I also found out what it would cost to make the payments at a certain percentage. We had a few people coming to the church and enough money coming into the offering for us to make the payments.

Making a new appointment with Mr. Braun, I met with him and showed him my plan (As I look back, I see it was not a very good plan—but at least it was a plan). Mr. Braun called his bank, one of the large Chicago banks, and said, "I want you to go out and loan this money to this church and I'll co-sign." If you have the right co-signer, you can have the worst situation in the world, but you'll get your loan.

I went to the bank to sign some papers. The banker came out and said to me, "This is not bankable."

For a moment, I was taken aback. But I swallowed and said, "It doesn't have to be bankable. If you don't want to lose Mr. Braun's account, you have to loan it."

He had a twinkle in his eye. "I'm seeing how strong you are. You are right, I do have to loan it."

We got our loan. What a glorious day! I will never forget it. We were going to be able to build a building. I can't tell you how great it was.

This was a valuable lesson for me to learn. Any of you who plan to do something for God, whether it is work in a ministry, start a church, or help someone in need, remember this lesson. Have a plan before you go forward; but then be willing to be flexible with the plan, knowing God is the ultimate Authority in your life.

What is your plan? I know we've gone over some different aspects of planning in this book already, but I mean this question in a particular way. I want you to take your plan to the Lord. Do all the research you can and study all you can. Find out as much information as possible about it. Talk to others about it, especially those who have traveled down a similar path. But ultimately, you must leave your plan with the Lord to see if He is going to bless it. He may say no to your plan, and you must be prepared for this. He might say, "I love you too much to have your plan get accomplished," or He may decide to bless the plan.

God also might look at your plan and in time, reveal He has a much more amazing plan for you. I now bring my plan to God, expecting Him to show up with a much greater and more wonderful plan. If I didn't work to come up with a plan in the first place, then I would never see God is trying to do something bigger and better in my life.

Take a moment to think about some of your plans.

Study those plans out and research them, then leave them in God's hands so you can see Him work in a mighty way. Be prepared for your plan to be rejected. If that happens, God has something better around the corner.

Finish Line Strategies

Here are some of the principles that have helped me through the years to figure out what we need to do for a new project:

- Do a ton of research on the type of project you are planning. Whether it's for a new building, computer program, or phone system, find out as much information as you can. Make those phone calls. Talk to people who know about those types of things. Find experts in that field. Find ordinary people who are doing the type of project you are thinking about doing. (With the Internet, there is no excuse for a person who doesn't do a lot of research.) Talking to people and finding out their ideas will help the most. Be aware of what your church can afford. I believe churches can borrow money, but it needs to be reasonable. If we had built a huge building for our first one, our church would have never made it. We decided on a 50 by 100-foot building with a basement. That was exactly what we needed. As the years went by, we realized we could build our own buildings a lot cheaper; but with that first building, it was important we get it built so our church could grow. Meeting in the house was working, but it wasn't a long-term solution.

- Our latest building cost us $3 million and it appraised for $15 million. We saved money on everything from labor to materials. A good builder will get three bids on something. We would get up to 20 bids, trying to get a good price.

- Give people opportunities to serve on projects in the church or to help build the building. They will take ownership of the project. Your church will become stronger as a result.

- Know there will be setbacks and problems when you build or when you do anything. The devil is alive and well, and doesn't want the gospel preached; but also understand God will continue to help as you continue to trust Him.

- Never react right away to someone who is really angry. Even if a person gets in your face or someone is a hothead, give that person a little time. Pray about what to do before going back and doing something impulsively because you are angry. The Bible says to be angry and sin not. There is no way that you can do the work of the Lord without getting angry at the people around you sometimes, but then seek the Lord's guidance and that of other godly leaders on what to do next. By that time, you will have cooled down and you will have regained perspective. Definitely never send an email, text, or a voicemail when you are angry. Take the extra time and try to talk to that person face to face, even if you have to wait a few days. As Dr. Mark Cambron used to say, "Never put something in writing if you don't have to."

- Deal with problems. Don't react in anger to a problem right away, but as a leader you are going to have troubles. It is important that you deal with them in a godly manner. Go to the person and talk to him in a kind way, but be firm if needed. Conflict comes with the territory when you do ministry.

Chapter 23
The Key to Success

A man's pride shall bring him low: but honour shall uphold the humble in spirit.
Proverbs 29:23

We had come to Florida Bible College and loved all the teaching. But before long, Bill, Rance, Ed, and I started to disapprove of what we thought was a lack of real prayer going on at our campus. We already met together regularly to pray. Honestly, sometimes our prayers were arrogant. We were fresh out of the university, and foolishly thought of ourselves as "lowering our standards" to come to a smaller school. We loved

The Florida Bible College purchased the Hollywood Beach Hotel in Florida.

learning the Bible, but because of our pride it was common for us to focus on ourselves rather than on the Lord.

We invited other students to our prayer meetings, and soon outgrew the space we were in. We found an island we could get to by a small bridge, and decided to have the prayer meeting there. Pretty soon, many more FBC students joined us. We would pray prayers like this, "Oh Lord, there aren't enough souls getting saved at Florida Bible College. There isn't enough prayer going on there for souls to be won to You."

Even as I write this, I cringe thinking how arrogant and full of pride we were. We continued to pray and were excited to see so many people coming out to pray with us.

A few weeks later, Dr. Stanford spoke for our chapel service. He was not a happy man.

"I have heard that there is a group of you that are from Kentucky," Dr. Stanford said. He glared at us sitting in the middle of the chapel service. Bill Adams elbowed me in the ribs.

"These students are getting together on an island to pray," he said. "Do you have the arrogance to think that you are so superior that you can meet together and think that not enough souls are being won at this college?"

Rance, Ed, Bill, and I were all looking down at this point. Several of the students who had been coming to the meeting stared at us.

Dr. Stanford continued, "There are many souls being won through this college. I can't believe you all would have the audacity to think you are super-spiritual and can pray more than we do for souls."

His words were making me feel downright uncomfortable. I wished there was a hole that I could climb into; but I had to keep sitting there throughout the chapel service, getting angrier by the minute. What right did Dr. Stanford have to tell me what to do?

Then I remembered, our college president was in authority over me. I had willingly put myself under his leadership. I remembered the verse I should have thought of before we started the prayer meeting. Hebrews 13:17 says, "Obey them that have the rule over you, and submit yourselves: for they watch for your souls, as they that must give account, that they may do it with joy, and not with grief: for that is unprofitable for you."

Dr. Stanford would give an account for me, and for all of us Kentucky boys (as he had called us). I decided to humble myself, even if it was difficult to do so.

After chapel, Ed, Rance, and Bill were hopping mad. "How dare he call us out like that in front of everyone?" they said. "We're going to leave this Bible college. We don't need to go through stuff like this."

I cleared my throat. "Hey, guys, I'm going to go and talk to him."

"No, way! That wouldn't be a good idea after how mad he is."

"I'm going to talk to him," I repeated. I walked over to his office and knocked on the door. As soon as he came to the door, I felt so guilty and ashamed of what we had done. "Dr. Stanford, I apologize. We shouldn't be so full of pride that we think this school isn't winning enough souls to Christ. I promise to stop the prayer meeting. I humbly ask you to forgive me."

Dr. Stanford smiled. "Of course I will, son. Thanks for coming and apologizing."

My friends calmed down, too, and we stopped the prayer meeting, learning an important lesson in humility along the way.

∽∾◠∿

Always Be Humble

I spoke about receiving criticism in the last chapter. Now I want to further elaborate about how to receive instruction from those in authority over us. No pastor is above getting rebuked. No layperson in the church is above having someone in authority speak to them. That's because all of us sin. But how do we respond to those who rebuke us?

The National Institute of Standards and Technology in the Washington, D.C. area helps the US keep our measurements straight. Before we had more accurate ways to define the length of a meter, they stored a platinum-iridium bar that was made in France. At 0 degrees Celsius and at the right atmospheric pressure, this bar was exactly one meter long. This bar was known as Prototype No. 27 (France originally made 30 of them for use in various countries around the world). This bar was our standard for the length of the meter for many years. Today, we use characteristics of light to more accurately define a meter.

The standard that all of us have is the Bible. This is a measuring stick for us as believers. Second Timothy 3:16 states, "All scripture is given by inspiration of God, and is profitable for doctrine, for reproof, for correction, for instruction in righteousness."

Those in authority over us know what the Word of God says, and they sometimes have to rebuke members of their flock because what someone is doing or saying isn't lining up with Scripture.

Hebrews 4:12 says, "For the word of God is quick, and powerful, and sharper than any twoedged sword, piercing even to the dividing asunder of soul and spirit, and of the joints and marrow, and is a discerner of the thoughts and intents of the heart."

Scripture is a revealer of what is in the heart. I know the day I went to see Dr. Stanford was an important day in my Christian development. I learned I could trust the leadership to know what was best for me and to help me to become more like Christ. His rebuke was good for me, and I needed it.

❧

How to Give Rebuke

Benny came home from his first day of school and said, "Mommy, the teacher was asking me today if I have any brothers and sisters who will be coming to my school."

"That's nice of her to take such an interest in your family, dear. What did she say when you told her that you are the only child?"

"She said, 'Thank goodness.'"

Now that I've covered how to receive a rebuke, I want to share some principles for giving rebuke. This is a necessary part of any leader's job, whether you are a pastor, boss, or parent. There are ways to do it that will either help your church, or destroy it and hurt your family.

One way to describe the Corinthian church is trouble, trouble, trouble. In 1 Corinthians, Paul had rebuked the church for their sin. In 2 Corinthians, the people had read Paul's painful letter. They had asked forgiveness of their sins and disciplined the church members who had created the problems. Paul had suffered a lot from the situation with the Corinthian church, but he benefitted greatly because he was willing to stand up and do the right thing.

❧

Going Forward

We need to give and receive rebuke in a biblical and godly way so our churches can survive and thrive. Too many pastors don't want to deal with problems in their churches. They would rather take a "wait-and-see" or "let-the-dust-settle" approach. Sometimes a situation warrants that approach, but most likely the situation needs to be confronted.

Life is a continuous process of getting used to things we hadn't expected. Rebuke is one of those things. The more we learn to give rebuke in a gracious way and receive rebuke when it hurts, the more we will grow in our Christian lives.

Second Corinthians 4:1–5 says,

"Therefore seeing we have this ministry, as we have received mercy, we faint not; But have renounced the hidden things of dishonesty, not walking in craftiness, nor handling the word of God deceitfully; but by manifestation of the truth commending ourselves to every man's conscience in the sight of God. But if our gospel be hid, it is hid to them that are lost: In whom the god of this world hath blinded the minds of them which believe not, lest the light of the glorious gospel of Christ, who is the image of God, should shine unto them. For we preach not ourselves, but Christ Jesus the Lord; and ourselves your servants for Jesus' sake."

Paul wrote these verses to the Corinthian church because of false accusations they had written about the Apostle Paul. (I can tell you from firsthand experience that if I had a penny for every false accusation that has come upon me, I would practically be a mega-millionaire.) Paul had purity of motive when he wrote the letters to the Corinthian church. His desire was that the gospel would continue to be preached. He was honest. He served this church because he loved the people. In our own lives, we need to remember that if our motives are pure, then we will have the opportunity to keep sharing the gospel.

We might think of Paul as a physically strong man who could take any accusation hurled against him; but the truth is, when you look at 2 Corinthians 4:7, you can see he really considered himself frail pottery. It was the treasure inside the pot that was his strength. His pot was weak like every other pot.

We continue forward in our churches and in our lives, not because we will receive any glory, but to get our W.D. (Well Done) Degree. We can't wait to hear the Lord say, "Well done, thou good and faithful servant."

Matthew 25:21 says, "His lord said unto him, Well done, thou good and faithful servant: thou hast been faithful over a few things, I will make thee ruler over many things: enter thou into the joy of thy lord."

Dear friend, part of receiving your W.D. Degree is learning how to receive and give out rebuke. As much as we would like to shove this part of the ministry away from us, it is a very real and important part that we don't dare ignore.

More Help Arrives

Shortly after finishing the first building, more help arrived—John and Kristine Julian. They had two children who were close to the ages of our kids, so that was really nice for them. Later, they would have another

son named Mark. The Julian family has been a wonderful support through the years. Linda and Kristine had met in Florida while we were still going to Bible college. They would often go to the laundromat together. (This was in the days of cloth diapers. After we'd go in the laundromat and fill up the washers with those dirty diapers, it didn't take long for the place to clear out of people.)

While in Florida, we had asked John and Kristine to come and help us out. We didn't expect they would; but they did come, and they

The Julian family was a great addition to our ministry.

were a huge blessing.

John and Kristine's three children have been a wonderful help in our ministry over the years as well. Their daughter, Joy Laegeler, works in our church and college music ministry. Her husband, Jon, runs our kitchen, turning out

about 700 meals a day. Their son Pastor Paul Julian is our administrator at Quentin Road. He handles so many things all the time. (I don't know how he does it.) I appreciate him and his family's dedication. His wife,

Molly, runs our preschool and does an excellent job. John and Kristine's third son, Pastor Mark Julian, is the Dean of Students of Dayspring Bible College and Seminary. His wife, Courtney, teaches in our Christian school.

Who Did We Serve?

As a church, we wouldn't go with trends. We would go with what the Bible said. I loved Florida Bible College and its emphasis on the gospel, but I didn't learn about local church until I started one. This wasn't because FBC didn't believe in the local church—they did—but because they didn't emphasize it. As we continued to move forward with the church, we saw its importance in people's lives. After people got saved, they would get discipled in the local church. They could then go out and share the gospel with more people who would get saved. The church would grow, not by addition but multiplication.

A devastating blow came my way when I learned Dr. Stanford had fallen into sin by having an adulterous affair. The news made me physically sick, and I doubted at that time I would ever recover from the blow. He had come to visit us three times as we were starting the church, so I had to tell our people the news as soon as possible. It was one of the hardest things I have ever had to deal with. Fortunately, I shared the news with my church before it made the headlines of all the city papers around the country, including the *Chicago Tribune*. (It also made the front page of the *London Times*.)

I would say this to any pastor: Always share the truth with your church. Do it carefully, trying not to hurt anyone, but you need to be as honest and upfront with your church as you possibly can. Do it with counsel, as I've mentioned before, but do it. When you are honest and upfront with your congregation, the people will learn to love and trust you. No pastor has a following unless he has earned it. You earn it when you are humble, truthful, and open with your people. You don't get respect because you have the title of pastor. You only get respect when you are as open as you can be with your people. The people have to know that you think more of them than you think of yourself.

I had to decide once again who I followed. Was I going to follow Christ only? I could no longer lean on Dr. Stanford. I used to call him with every problem and he would give me advice. He would say, "Don't worry about that problem, Jim. That isn't very big at all," and I'd hang up the phone feeling at peace. After he sinned, the pain was beyond words because I would no longer have that advice-giver in my life.

Have you had something this devastating happen to you in your life? Maybe your parents divorced, a sibling committed suicide, or your wife or husband betrayed you. Whatever happened, I'm sure you can still remember the day you found out about the news and how you handled the news. These things are always really difficult, but they are important times in our lives. They are times when we have to determine who we are going to serve. These devastating circumstances bring us to our knees for months, even years. They bring us right to the breaking point. There are many people who break as a result of news like this. Honestly, I don't blame them. These types of situations are difficult beyond belief.

We need to discover how to go on when devastation comes our way. Even when a major Christian falls. Moses' successor, Joshua, said to the people in Joshua 24:15, "And if it seem evil unto you to serve the LORD, choose you this day whom ye will serve; whether the gods which your fathers served that were on the other side of the flood, or the gods of the Amorites, in whose land ye dwell: but as for me and my house, we will serve the LORD."

While I had already chosen to serve the Lord when I was called to preach, I discovered that day I also had to choose to go forward no matter who fell around me.

One of the early church fathers, Polycarp, lived his life for the glory of God. At 86 years old, the officials called upon him. Before this, he had a vision that he was to be martyred. He could have fled; but he said, "No, the will of the Lord be done."

The officials that came to arrest Polycarp asked what harm would it be if he would say, "Lord Caesar," and make a sacrifice to save his own life. Polycarp's great response was, "Eighty-six years I have served the Lord, and

He never once wronged me. How then shall I blaspheme my King who has saved me?"

The men said to Polycarp, "If you do not worship Caesar, we will bring out the wild beasts to kill you."

He replied, "Bring them on."

They replied, "If the beasts do not scare you, then we will burn you at the stake."

"You threaten me with fire, which burns only for an hour, but soon is extinguished. The fire of future judgment and eternal punishment reserved for the ungodly you are ignorant of. Why do you delay? Do what you do," was Polycarp's bold reply.

As they burned Polycarp, there was a great testimony that went out, inspiring the early Christians. When people stand for what they believe about Jesus Christ, it produces a testimony that enables all to see what Jesus claimed is true. How we live and how we react to our difficulties makes a big difference in the testimony we are giving before a lost world.[xxii]

You need to know people are watching you to know how you respond to your difficulties. They want to see how you will react when you have these problems. How you react will make a difference in your testimony and whether other people will serve Christ as a result of you standing for Him.

While it took me awhile to recover from the news of my mentor's infidelity, I remembered my own calling was sure. I discovered I wasn't serving a man; rather, I was serving the Lord Jesus Christ. He is the One who had never let me down, the One who had laid down His life for me. I was indebted to Dr. Stanford for helping me to understand the gospel and providing the Bible college as a place to go, but I needed to keep going in my Christian life no matter what happened. I knew that people around me were watching to see how I would react to this crisis.

First Peter 2:9 states, "But ye are a chosen generation, a royal priesthood, an holy nation, a peculiar people; that ye should shew forth the praises of him who hath called you out of darkness into his marvellous light."

When a crisis comes, how will you react? How will you stand up for what you believe in? Will you continue to serve the Lord, even if a person whom you greatly admire falls? Will you continue to do the right thing no matter what? Will you realize the key to success is staying humble?

Serve God fully and with single-hearted devotion.

Finish Line Strategies

Here are some helpful principles on how to receive rebuke from someone in authority over you:

- Learn to accept rebuke. Don't bristle at it. Take it humbly.

- Apologize and mean it. If you have really been rebuked strongly, it might be good to apologize when you receive it and then to find a way to apologize again the next day. You want to make sure to clear up any resentment that might be between you and that person.

- Don't stomp off when you are getting rebuked. Don't close your ears to the truth of what is being said.

- Don't get so defensive that you really aren't listening to what is being said to you. If you need to defend yourself, do it as humbly as possible.

- Thank the person for the rebuke and mean it. I know this is hard to do, but I can promise you will look back later on your life and be so thankful you accepted the rebuke in a good way. You will find you learned more from that rebuke than probably anything you went through in your life.

Here are some principles about giving rebuke:

- Rebuke privately. Don't do it publicly if you can help it. Sometimes the person is willing to say something hurtful or damaging in public, and it is like they are taunting you to rebuke them publicly. Sometimes you will need to go ahead and say something publicly, only because other people aren't going to follow your authority if someone can say whatever they want about you and get away with it.

- Assume the best about the person. Give them an opportunity to explain what happened.

- Be encouraging if at all possible. Mention the good work the person does or the kind of people they are so they know you don't just see the bad but also the good.

- Go to the person in the next day or week and talk to them to make sure the air is clear between you.

Chapter 24
Church Growth

Then had the churches rest throughout all Judaea and Galilee and Samaria, and
were edified; and walking in the fear of the Lord, and in the comfort of the Holy
Ghost, were multiplied. Acts 9:31

Our church turns out hundreds of homemade pizzas a week. It is one of the ways we can minister to the community. Many folks have first entered our doors because we were offering great food. Our kitchen ministry has been a blessing since the beginning. From the early days of making Easter breakfast for 100 to today where hundreds of people are fed daily, the kitchen, headed up by Chef Jon Laegeler, has been as much of a ministry as any other ministry. (On our 40th anniversary, we fed 3,000 people in ten minutes with only church help.)

Even a smaller church can find ways to use food to minister to people. It is a great way to encourage discussions and fellowship as we sit down and eat together.

Jon Laegeler making pizza from scratch.

As pizza dough takes time to create, so it takes time to grow a church. It doesn't happen overnight. When I look back, I see all the miracles that God has done throughout the years. I see how He faithfully led us every step of the way.

During those years, though, there were some bleak times. I often remember thinking it seemed like we weren't growing at all. Unlike pizza dough that rises in only a few hours, Quentin Road has always grown slowly. We've always grown more like an oak tree, slowly but surely. This is the best way to grow.

Basics for Church Growth

Maybe you are reading this and thinking, "I'd sure like to get my church to grow." Congratulations. That is a worthy goal. We wouldn't be human if we didn't want things to grow. What I want you to look at is ways we should use to grow a church and ways that we shouldn't use to grow a church.

Don't Water Down Messages

The preaching of the Word of God will grow a church, but be aware that strong preaching will offend people. There is no way around this. Paul says in Galatians 6:6, "Let him that is taught in the word communicate unto him that teacheth in all good things."

We are to teach the whole counsel of God as preachers. I believe in verse-by-verse teaching and also topical preaching. I do both on a regular basis. When we teach verse by verse, we cover the whole Bible and can't pick and choose what we teach. Verse-by-verse saves time as well because a pastor doesn't have to figure out a topic, but can simply preach the next passage. We do an occasional topical message or series to cover an important area of life such as child training; but when we do, our expository experience helps us stay true to Scripture.

Many preachers today think they need to water down their messages to make them more palatable for the listeners. We never need to do this. The Word of God can speak for itself. We should not use just one verse for a whole sermon while only threatening to open the Bible again the entire rest of the sermon. If doctrine is not taught in a church, the church might grow for awhile; but it will be a weak growth that will wither away when opposition arises.

Use the time that you have to learn from the best preachers that are out there. Listen to good preachers when you exercise. Read other sermons. Read commentaries. Keep your eyes open for illustrations that you can use in your messages. (Some of the best illustrations happen right in your own life and family.)

The bottom line is this: Stay in the Word of God. Teach from the Bible. Your church will grow solidly like a strong oak. There is a lot of pressure on preachers to grow large churches. They think they need to grow by any means possible. This might tempt them not to teach the Word of God as strongly as it should be taught. Never allow this thinking to compromise your preaching. Instead, realize your church might grow a little more slowly when you teach the full counsel of God, but that growth will be solid and sure.

***

Becoming Like the World

The world has its own music, its own entertainment, and its own amusements. These are things we don't need to bring into our churches. In fact, they are directly the opposite of God's ways. Rock music comes from rebellion in the first place. How can changing the words make it less rebellious? Our young people don't need more music that has a terrible beat and isn't uplifting to the Lord Jesus. They need to be given good, godly music that will bring them closer to the Lord. Our churches don't benefit when we try to have our services like the world. Churches that do this are destroying their young people. They think they are helping them, but instead they are tearing them down.

Psalm 149:1 says, "Praise ye the LORD. Sing unto the LORD a new song, and his praise in the congregation of saints." Sing a new song. Don't take the world's garbage music and try to make it work for your church.

***

Commonsense Strategies for Growth

Be aware of how easy you make it for people to attend your church. Have you ever driven into your parking lot and thought about what a new visitor to your church might think? Maybe your parking lot is hard to navigate, or it isn't easy to find a place to park. Do you have signs throughout your church that make it easy for visitors to find the restrooms, Sunday School classrooms, and the nursery? Colossians 4:5 says, "Walk in wisdom toward them that are without, redeeming the time." We need to walk in wisdom in front of those we are trying to reach and redeem the time. We don't have much time left before the Rapture. Let's do our best to reach those who don't know Christ as Savior; and then bring them into the church, mentor them, and disciple them in the knowledge of Christ.

One church I know of had such an old building that the nursery had a mildew odor. They had to spend a good amount of money to make the nursery a safe place for the children. This church could not grow with the nursery in such a state. Make sure that your buildings and parking lots are safe and inviting.

One pastor I know went as a "secret visitor" to another church. He had a difficult time locating the church because the sign in front was broken and hard to read. The parking spots were all filled except for some in the very back. When he got inside, he went to the restroom to wash his hands, and there were no towels. When he came back out, four men were talking in the lobby. One of them gave him a bulletin as he approached, but then they kept talking to each other. When he got inside the auditorium, he sat down in the back. The pew he sat on was so old it almost collapsed. These kinds of things can easily be fixed in a church. Sometimes we go to our own churches week after week without thinking how a visitor might feel.

Strong Leadership

If there is not strong, godly leadership in the church, then the church will not grow. Second Timothy 2:1–2 states, "Thou therefore, my son, be strong in the grace that is in Christ Jesus. And the things that thou hast heard of me among many witnesses, the same commit thou to faithful men, who shall be able to teach others also." Building your leadership may take some time, but churches will attract people who want to grow to be like their leaders. As they learn more about God's Word, they will want to grow stronger in their faith.

Don't put people on your board who aren't qualified to be leaders of the church. I've seen many churches fall because they did not have a godly board. First Timothy 3:6 says, "Not a novice, lest being lifted up with pride he fall into the condemnation of the devil." A novice is some-one who hasn't been tested. He is new to the faith or may be a carnal

Christian. He has never been in leadership, so the first time he is in leadership, he is lifted up in pride.

Personally, I've seen this principle at work in condominium associations. A president is elected for the association, and this person has never been in leadership before. This person takes the opportunity to come up with all of these rules and regulations which make it extremely hard for all the people living in the condominiums. (I call them condo commandos.) This isn't the job of a president. Instead, the job is to make the association grow and go forward. It is the same in a church. A leader's job is to help the church grow and move forward. When people are on the board who aren't devout followers of Christ, they can easily be lifted up in pride and drag the church down. Be smart and don't put someone on your board who isn't godly. That is a sure way to avoid a lot of problems in a church.

A Pastor Needs Checks and Balances

I appreciate my board so much. They are such a help in the leadership of our church. They do a great job and are such a blessing. I never dread board meetings because I appreciate the checks and balances we have. As a pastor or leader, you need to feel the same way about your board. All of you need to be on the same page when it comes to the growth of the church, ministries of the church, and the general direction of the church. I talk to my board about what is going on in the church, and they review the finances each month. One person sees every check, along with the treasurer. If you do this on a regular basis, no one can say that you weren't honest. (I have known of several churches which really had no books and no accountability, and this wasn't a good situation. For almost 30 years, I have had an outside CPA review all of our books.)

I talk to people and confide in them. I'm not afraid to trust people, though sometimes that has hurt me. That doesn't mean I can't trust people in the future.

So many people at Quentin Road have been a wonderful support through the years. They have been with me through thick and thin. I don't think I could ever adequately thank them for all that they have done for the Lord.

❧

Sometimes People Will Leave

Willie McCarrell, the founder of IFCA International, said, "A pastor is like a train conductor. Sometimes people get on the train and sometimes they get off." Unfortunately, this is true. We'd like to think that no one will ever leave a church, but sometimes it happens. Philippians 3:17–19 says,

Willie McCarrell.

"Brethren, be followers together of me, and mark them which walk so as ye have us for an ensample. (For many walk, of whom I have told you often, and now tell you even weeping, that they are the enemies of the cross of Christ: Whose end is destruction, whose God is their belly, and whose glory is in their shame, who mind earthly things.)"

People will leave, and sometimes they will even become enemies of the cross of Christ. This is one of the saddest things that can happen. But don't let it discourage you to the point where you don't want to keep trying. God will continue to grow His Church. Sometimes people will leave, but a lot more people will stay.

❧

Our First Parking Lot

I remember being so happy when we got our first parking lot for the new building. Previously we had to park in the street in Chicago or in our apartment parking lot, so having our own parking lot was a big deal.

Dozers cleared the area that was to be our parking lot, and then the big trucks came in with gravel. (For some reason, a person had recommended we get large gravel rather than small gravel. During our first

Our first parking lot caused some problems for high-heeled shoes.

Sunday using the new parking lot, many of the ladies weren't too happy because their high heels sunk down into the gravel. One man who came out to visit our church got his car stuck in the gravel, and didn't come back to visit for seven years.) Finally, someone paid to get the parking lot paved, and it looked like we had a real church.

To this day I still really like our first sign.

We renamed the church Quentin Road Bible Church because we were no longer in downtown Chicago. Because our property was located on Quentin Road, we decided to name it after the road. Many years later when we bought 40 acres, the property just happened to be on the same road, but eight miles farther north.

We could not believe this 40-acre property was available and affordable.

We kept the name the same as we moved to the new town, which helped people know we were the same church.

Maybe you are at the point where you feel like your church isn't going to grow. You have worked and worked, but you don't see it happening. May I encourage you not to feel discouraged? Consider how happy I would have been when I first came to Chicago to know that someday our church would have its own parking lot. I didn't know it at the time, but I did trust God would do mighty things.

Pastors and lay people, continue doing what God would have you to do.

True church growth happens slowly. It takes time for a church to develop strong leaders and mature members. Leaders, be aware of new ways to reach out to your community that will bring people into your congregation. Members, keep being faithful to attend all the church services and see God bless in your family. Believers, if you haven't yet found a good church, commit the next few months to finding one. Pastors, as your congregation grows, God will give you His strength as you lead.

Finish Line Strategies

Here are some danger signals that will alert your church to serious problems:

- A church that preaches about the Bible but does not preach the Bible (Romans 10:17; 2 Timothy 4:2).

- A church with an annual vote for the pastor, thus creating a "we-call-the-shots" atmosphere (1 Peter 5:3).

- A church so dignified it is petrified. But neither should a departure from doing all things decently and in order be advocated (1 Corinthians 14:40).

- A church with a constitution that contradicts God's Word (2 Corinthians 2:11; 2 Timothy 3:16, 17).

- A church with no stand on separation (2 Corinthians 6:14–18).

- A church so carried away by its own definition of "love" that it fails to exercise discipline among its membership when needed (Matthew 18:15–20; Romans 16:17, 18; 1 Corinthians 5:12–13; 2 Thessalonians 3:10–15).

– by Dr. Charles Svoboda

Two other thoughts are...

- All worry is a control issue. When we worry constantly about what could happen with certain situations in the church, who is really in control, you or the Lord? Philippians 4:6–7 states, "Be careful for nothing; but in everything by prayer and supplication with thanksgiving let your requests be made known unto God. And the peace of God, which passeth all understanding, shall keep your hearts and minds through Christ Jesus."

- Take a moment to think about some practical ways you can learn to lean on the Lord Jesus Christ so you don't have to worry. How can this help you in your church, in your leadership, in your home, and in your life?

Section 4

When we've been there ten thousand years,
Bright shining as the sun,
We've no less days to sing God's praise
Than when we'd first begun.

Chapter 25
Burn Out or Rust Out

Being confident of this very thing, that he which hath begun a good work in you will perform it until the day of Jesus Christ. Philippians 1:6

Finally, we had a real blacktop parking lot, a real building, a real sign, and other things that most churches take for granted. But one day the county was repaving the roads and came into our parking lot with their heavy trucks, breaking our blacktop.

After enduring all we went through to get our first property perfect, now we were looking at broken blacktop. When

I was so happy to have a "real" church building. We would rent no more.

you are a pastor, sometimes you can't win for losing. You can count on this kind of thing happening when you work in a church. For every two steps forward, you take fourteen steps back. That's what it feels like, anyway. We went to the construction guys whose truck had done this and asked them to come and fix it, but they said they wouldn't. They explained that breaking the blacktop was our problem. Fortunately, we were able to go to the county and the county listened. They made the men come back and fix our parking lot.

We started AWANA, and before we knew it, we had over 200 kids coming out. It was so exciting. We were having AWANA clubs up to four nights a week; but after awhile we realized that people were getting burned out, so we combined all of our AWANA clubs into one night. We didn't want to burn out the people in their work for the Lord.

Burn Out or Rust Out?

Some churches have the philosophy, "I'd rather burn out than rust out."

Other churches have the opposite philosophy, "I'd rather rust out than burn out."

These are both extremes. We shouldn't burn out for Christ (do so much that we neglect everything else in our lives) or rust out (do nothing and get to the point where we are useless for Christ).

AWANA Clubs were really growing and helped our church grow.

Galatians 6:9 states, "And let us not be weary in well doing: for in due season we shall reap, if we faint not." God tells us that sometimes we are going to get weary. We shouldn't be surprised by being weary. Fatigue is part of being in the ministry. The key is that you figure out how to keep going and not be weary.

Throughout the years, I've been careful to watch for people's level of weariness. When they are at their limit, I do all that is in my power to ease their burden. But sometimes the ox is in the ditch, and we have to keep going. (One time when we built our third main building, we had to work on a Sunday because of the weather, or the building would have taken weeks longer to complete. The rest of the congregation met outdoors, and the workers could hear the service as they worked. All of us bonded that day because we had to keep going. We had no choice. Even the kids in the church who are now grown say they remember that special time.)

After the hard work, I make sure to give the people a break so they can recuperate. They need time to relax and be with their families so they don't burn out. This is the balance of the Christian life.

The churches in Galatia were weary in the work. The Judaizers had come in and told everyone in the church they had to have works to go to

Heaven. The leaders were fatigued from proclaiming the truth and fighting heresy.

The fourth verse of "Amazing Grace" encourages me like no other verse in a song. "When we've been there ten thousand years, / Bright shining as the sun, / We've no less days to sing God's praise / Than when we'd first begun."

One preacher liked to sing these words instead, "When we've been there forever more" because he said there was no time in Heaven. But I like singing "ten thousand years." It gives me comfort to consider that in Heaven I will be singing (even me with my terrible singing voice) for ten thousand years, and it will be like I just began. When things are at their roughest, I remember Heaven and the last verse of "Amazing Grace." These thoughts give me the strength to keep going.

I hate the casualties that come from false teachers the most. There are people in the church who are strong in doctrine and aren't going to be swayed no matter what someone tells them. They go to the Word of God. But there are others in the church who are new believers. They don't know the difference yet between sound and shaky doctrine. When false teachers get a hold of these new believers, they often get discouraged and quit the church altogether.

One time, I gave a preacher free tuition for his three children. When I attended a pastor's conference, he tried to take over the church. Our board and people stood by me and kept that from happening.

The word for "weary" in the previous verse is *ekkakeo* from the Greek, and it has the idea of fainting or failing. So Paul, warning the Galatian Christians not to get weary, was the same as if he was warning them not to give up and not to fail.

Consider Moses. There were many times when he got weary in the work of leading a million or more people around the desert. When the people fought a battle, Moses stood and watched the people fight. When he held up his arms, the people prevailed. When his arms grew tired, the enemy would start to win. After awhile, Moses got pretty tired of holding up his arms, so two of his men came and helped him.

When it comes to burnout, we begin to feel our arms grow weary like Moses' arms did. We push hard; we give it our all—and then we hit a wall. We are tired, weary, exhausted. We don't think we can go on. This is when other people come in and help us. They have to come alongside in the work of the ministry. They start to feel the burden and also the necessity of praying for you, upholding you, and helping you make it for the Lord. That is the secret to not allowing hard work to burn us out. When we feel like we are going to burn out, we need to figure out how to share the burden so the work still moves forward. Ultimately, the work will proceed more than when we were trying to do it all by ourselves.

Frame Building and Beyond

Many of our key families who have stuck with us throughout the years joined the church while we were in the first building. Many of them got married in our church. One of the things that sets our church apart is dedicated people. I thank God for every one of the people that attend Quentin Road. Each one of them has a special place in my heart.

Gary and Terrie Birginal on their wedding day.

Al Smith, the great hymn writer, visited us in the first frame building. He could lead a group of people in singing hymns like no one I have

The great singer and songwriter Al Smith with me in our first building.

ever known. As we went out the doors of the church and down the steps, he looked over at the property next door. He said, "God told me that you will own that property."

Normally, when people tell me that God has told them something, I don't give it much credence. We get our advice and help directly from the Word of God, but there was something about the way Al said it that made me take notice.

Several days later, out of the blue the owner called and said she was selling the property next door. I told the lady that we had no money to think of buying the property. She said, "Are you sure about that? Where is your faith, pastor? Why don't you go to your congregation and at least let them know about it."

Not knowing what else to do and highly doubting we could consider such a thing having just built our first building, I went to our church and let them know about the property being sold for $40,000.

The next Sunday, someone gave us $40,000 in stocks, telling us to sell them and buy the property. What an answer to prayer. Up to this point, it had taken us months to find our first meeting place, then a year to find our first property, then another six months before we built our first building. Now, with just a word from Al Smith and a call from the property owner, we had our second property.

Never underestimate the power of God.

A year after we bought the land, we started to plan what kind of a bigger building we needed. We knew we wanted it to be brick and to be

Ground breaking for our second building.

beautiful. We needed a gymnasium, fellowship hall, and more classrooms.

A group of contractors were hired. We had an agreement that they would oversee the building project. At that point, we never dreamed of building a building by ourselves. We wanted to build a hexagon-shaped auditorium out of brick. It would truly be a beautiful building for the area.

We sold bonds in order to finance the project. By doing this, we were able to raise $250,000. The only problem with the bonds was when we later sold the property, we had to find every single person who had bought them to clear the title. Some people had died and we had to find out who owned their bonds, but we did finally find every person and paid them all off.

The agency we hired to contract the project was full of good and

Dave Lively saved the day as he was able to lay out a complex building.

reputable people, but the bids came in about $200,000 more than we had raised. For a little church, this amount over budget would have devastated us. There was no way we could afford to build. Fortunately, the contract said we could get out of it at any time, so we made the radical decision to completely do the contracting ourselves. A man in our church named Dave Lively, who got saved through an "Am I Going to Heaven?" tract I gave him, became one of the main contractors. The man is absolutely brilliant. He figured out how to lay out the building in the hexagon shape, and that wasn't easy.

Have there been people in your life who have helped you to figure out difficult problems? Maybe you haven't taken the time to thank them for what they have done for you. I know I've tried to thank all the people who have helped through the years, but there is no possible way I could. So many people have come alongside and given their lives for the ministry. Appreciate what these people have done in your ministry. I appreciate

Our 2nd building was a complicated hexagon shape, and we always seemed to have to work in the snow.

my people standing behind me through thick and thin.

I've written a lot in *Finish Strong* about how we need to trust God during the difficult times and to trust His timing when it seems like it is taking a long time for something good to happen. I also want to mention there are times when He brings things to pass we aren't expecting at all. This shows how great our God truly is. When you lean on the Lord, you won't burn out or rust out. He will give you insight into what ministries are helping your church and which ones may not be as beneficial. He will give you the wisdom to know when to take a break to refresh yourself in the Lord so you can continue in His mighty work.

Thank God—whether you are feeling blessed, or whether you are going through a trial. God is always working on your behalf.

Finish Line Strategies

- Listen to the Bible on CD or on your smartphone when you are feeling weary. The words of God coming directly into your ears will refresh you.

- Meditate or memorize all or parts of the following verses. Isaiah 40:28–31 states, "Hast thou not known? hast thou not heard, that the everlasting God, the LORD, the Creator of the ends of the earth, fainteth not, neither is weary? there is no searching of his understanding. He giveth power to the faint; and to them that have no might he increaseth strength. Even the youths shall faint and be weary, and the young men shall utterly fall: But they that wait upon the LORD shall renew their strength; they shall mount up with wings as eagles; they shall run, and not be weary; and they shall walk, and not faint."

- Find ways for ministries in your church to pay for themselves. Our preschool helps the financial needs of the whole ministry at Quentin Road; and yet, we are charging about the same as other preschools in the area. We offer a quality experience for the children. This is a huge value for the parents in our community, and they don't mind paying for something they know is excellent quality.

- Sometimes there are unavoidable financial situations where your home has been foreclosed because of a bad economy, medical reasons, or something like that. Don't beat yourself up for that. There are inevitable situations like this, and they happen at some point to many people in a bad economy.

- Be generous. Money is a gift from God. The ability to live is a gift from God. I have always believed that a giver is so much more blessed than a non-giver.

Chapter 26
God Recycles People

We are troubled on every side, yet not distressed; we are perplexed, but not in despair;
Persecuted, but not forsaken; cast down, but not destroyed; Always bearing about
in the body the dying of the Lord Jesus, that the life also of Jesus might be made
manifest in our body. 2 Corinthians 4:8–10

God is the ultimate Recycler. In every situation you face as a pastor, leader, member, or believer, you will learn something that will help you in the future. You may not think what you are learning will help you. You may not see how in the world the knowledge would assist you; but I promise you, God doesn't waste anything.

We always ended up building through the winter in Chicago. This hexagon-shaped building was no different. (I'm not sure how it always happened, but we froze every time we built. Maybe it made every person who helped out, including me, appreciate the building more when it was finished.) We used a straw idea we had used for the foundation of the first building. The straw kept the ground from freezing, and we were able to keep going through the freezing cold.

Our 2ⁿᵈ building finally finished.

We did a lot of the work ourselves, but not all of it. We did the contracting. Still, the work we did opened our eyes to what we could do in the future.

All Things Work Together

I remember when I met Jon Laegeler, our chef. He worked in a bakery and made beautiful wedding cakes. A few years later, he came on staff full-time to work in our kitchen. God used his talent for His glory.

My son-in-law, Neal Dearyan, was a land surveyor

before he came to Dayspring Bible College. He was able to use his talent to help lay out our buildings.

Mike Darling is a plumber, and has used his talent too many times to count on many of our building projects.

My son-in-law, Neal, lays out our 5th building.

Our Chef Jon has prepared many meals.

One preacher said he was traveling to Chicago when he saw an elderly man and his wife waving for help. They had pulled over to the side of the road. The man said they were on the way to town, but were almost out of gas. They wondered if the pastor would mind getting them a

Mike Darling was always faithful.

gallon. The preacher suggested that he would drive behind them to town and if they did run out, he would go ahead to town and get them some. They accepted gratefully. They drove for 20 miles. The man would look in his rear view mirror and wave at the preacher. They made it all the way to the gas station.

At the station, the man thanked the preacher. He said, "Just knowing you were behind us just in case we did run out of gas allowed my wife and me to drive without worry."

The preacher said God works the same way; He is behind us all the way. When we think we are at the end of our rope, out of strength, out of energy, He is there to keep us going. He recycles every event in our lives to help us grow and learn more about the future.

❧

Ready to Expand

As the church kept growing, we began the Christian School and then Dayspring Bible College. This recycled our buildings. Now we could use them not only for church, but for AWANA, school, and college. It became clear that we would have to find more property to build. At our current location, we didn't have enough land

The 1st day of the Quentin Road Christian School.

Dayspring Bible College's early years.

to build again. We started looking for property. About eight miles away, we found twenty acres, exactly what we needed. The price was right. The property was located in a less-congested area so the prices were cheaper.

When we went to inquire further about the property, the price had changed. They wanted more for the land than they had originally said. We decided not to buy the property. It didn't seem like we could ever expand.

❧

Joseph

Consider Joseph's life. At 17, his father gave him a coat, showing him favoritism. (I counsel parents all the time to be careful of favoritism in their families. It definitely doesn't lead to anything good.) Still, it wasn't Joseph's fault that his brothers became so jealous of him that they wanted to kill him. At the last minute, they decided to sell him into slavery.

Think of Joseph in chains on his way to Egypt with the Ishmaelites. It's ironic that a descendent of Ishmael, who was Joseph's grandfather's half-brother, would be the one to bring him to Egypt.

Joseph is away from everyone in Egypt. There are a lot of people who have gone to other countries to live, and they have felt lonely being away from their families and loved ones. Picture a 17-year-old going through this. He isn't just in another country studying at a different college or living with a family; he has actually been sold into slavery.

Joseph is a slave in the house of a rich man named Potiphar. He learns a lot there and things are looking a little better, at least for a little while. Genesis 39:1–6 states,

"And Joseph was brought down to Egypt; and Potiphar, an officer of Pharaoh, captain of the guard, an Egyptian, bought him of the hands of the Ishmeelites, which had brought him down thither. And the LORD was with Joseph, and he was a prosperous man; and he was in the house of his master the Egyptian. And his master saw that the LORD was with him, and that the LORD made all that he did to prosper in his hand. And Joseph found grace in his sight, and he served him: and he made him overseer over his house, and all that he had he put into his hand. And it came to pass from the time that he had made him overseer in his house, and over all that he had, that the LORD blessed the Egyptian's house for Joseph's sake; and the blessing of the LORD was upon all that he had in the house, and in the field. And he left all that he had in Joseph's hand; and he knew not ought he had, save the bread which he did eat. And Joseph was a goodly person, and well favoured."

Things are getting a little better for the kid. Don't forget all Joseph learns while he oversees Potiphar's house. He is discovering how to manage many different aspects of life. He is in charge of everything: the food, the servants, needs for the family, and more. Potiphar completely trusts him. But then Potiphar's wife wants him to sleep with her and Joseph flees, leaving his coat behind.

This wicked woman promptly uses the coat to accuse Joseph of rape. Joseph's situation goes from bad to worse. Now he's in jail, but it isn't that long before the keeper starts putting more and more into Joseph's hand. Soon Joseph is running the whole prison. (Can you imagine what an amazing administrator Joseph is? He is young, without any real training. God uses everything to train us, even life's difficulties.)

When Joseph finally gets out of prison, he is promoted to the second-highest position in the land. God uses Joseph's wisdom and training to help him handle the pressures of his new situation.

Ultimately, he is able to save all of Egypt and the surrounding areas from starvation. And most of all, he is able to save his brothers and his father.

His brothers.

Did you catch that? He saved his brothers.

The brothers who despised him.

The brothers who wanted to kill him.

The brothers who threw him into a pit.

The brothers who sold him into slavery.

Yes, those brothers.

Joseph has amazing words to say to them when he finally reveals who he is in Genesis 45:4–8.

"And Joseph said unto his brethren, Come near to me, I pray you. And they came near. And he said, I am Joseph your brother, whom ye sold into Egypt. Now therefore be not grieved, nor angry with yourselves, that ye sold me hither: for God did send me before you to preserve life. For these two years hath the famine been in the land: and yet there are five years, in the which there shall neither be earing nor harvest. And God sent me before you to preserve you a posterity in the earth, and to save your lives by a great deliverance. So now it was not you that sent me hither, but God: and he hath made me a father to Pharaoh, and lord of all his house, and a ruler throughout all the land of Egypt."

Joseph says, "But as for you, ye thought evil against me; but God meant it unto good ..." (Genesis 50:20a). Isn't it incredible all that Joseph went through that prepared him for this amazing place in history? Joseph didn't burn out or rust out in his service to the Lord. He kept going forward. He didn't allow his difficult situation to make him bitter. Instead, he allowed his difficult situations to mold him and make him into a man of God.

What about you? Where are you at in your situation? Do you understand that God has a bigger plan for your life than you could ever dream? He might not tell you at every point what the plan is, but I can promise you every situation you go through will prepare you for the next situation. God is a God of mercy. He also orchestrates the universe in amazing ways. He has the ability to recycle the bad stuff in your life and turn it into good. I've seen this over and over again: from the time we lost the loan for the townhome, to the time we contracted out the building only to have to do the contracting ourselves because all the bids came back too high. Each of these events had a bigger purpose than we could have imagined for the future of the ministry.

Now you need to do the same thing in your own life. You need to take a moment and consider all that you have gone through. Think about what God has brought your way. Ask Him to give you discerning wisdom about how to keep the people He has entrusted to you from either burning out or rusting out. Then thank Him for all that you have gone through.

That's right. Thank Him.

I know this isn't always easy to do; but when you thank God, you are showing that you understand the bigger picture of what is happening. Everything that you experience in your life will be for your ultimate good.

❧

God Recycles People

Not too long ago, the news in my area reported people were becoming angry because all the stuff they recycle is being dumped into a huge pile. All the agonizing work the residents were doing to separate out the garbage was being wasted because in that city there weren't enough people to put separate containers into separate places.

Only God can recycle without there being waste. God is continually working on us and making us more fit for His use. The Apostle Paul's greatest fear was becoming a castaway—this means he didn't want to be put on a shelf and not used for the Lord. First Corinthians 9:27 states, "But I keep under my body, and bring it into subjection: lest that by any means, when I have preached to others, I myself should be a castaway."

In order for us not to be put on a shelf, God has to continually take circumstances in our lives and use them to shape us for His glory.

Does that include circumstances like breathing death on Christians, thinking you're doing God a favor? Acts 9:1–2 states, "And Saul, yet breathing out threatenings and slaughter against the disciples of the Lord, went unto the high priest, And desired of him letters to Damascus to the synagogues, that if he found any of this way, whether they were men or women, he might bring them bound unto Jerusalem."

How about going on a rampage against Christians? How about being mean-spirited enough to join with other religious leaders to destroy more Christians?

Acts 8:1 says, "And Saul was consenting unto his death. And at that time there was a great persecution against the church which was at Jerusalem; and they were all scattered abroad throughout the regions of Judaea and Samaria, except the apostles."

Paul (then Saul) consented to the death of Stephen, the first martyr. Can you imagine having this on your conscience?

God appeared to Saul on the road to Damascus, which I find interesting. Here he was traveling to Damascus, and he ended up getting saved on the way to destroy the very thing that he would become—a believer. Then he was directed to a believer's house. The man was Ananias.

Can you imagine if a murderer of your fellow believers, maybe even friends and family, came and knocked on your door claiming to be saved? Would you invite him into your home? Fortunately, the Lord had already appeared to Ananias and told him Saul was for real. Ananias did have some questions about what the Lord had asked him to do.

Acts 9:10–22 says,

"And there was a certain disciple at Damascus, named Ananias;

and to him said the Lord in a vision, Ananias. And he said, Behold, I am here, Lord. And the Lord said unto him, Arise, and go into the street which is called Straight, and enquire in the house of Judas for one called Saul, of Tarsus: for, behold, he prayeth, And hath seen in a vision a man named Ananias coming in, and putting his hand on him, that he might receive his sight. Then Ananias answered, Lord, I have heard by many of this man, how much evil he hath done to thy saints at Jerusalem: And here he hath authority from the chief priests to bind all that call on thy name. But the Lord said unto him, Go thy way: for he is a chosen vessel unto me, to bear my name before the Gentiles, and kings, and the children of Israel: For I will shew him how great things he must suffer for my name's sake. And Ananias went his way, and entered into the house; and putting his hands on him said, Brother Saul, the Lord, even Jesus, that appeared unto thee in the way as thou camest, hath sent me, that thou mightest receive thy sight, and be filled with the Holy Ghost. And immediately there fell from his eyes as it had been scales: and he received sight forthwith, and arose, and was baptized. And when he had received meat, he was strengthened. Then was Saul certain days with the disciples which were at Damascus. And straightway he preached Christ in the synagogues, that he is the Son of God. But all that heard him were amazed, and said; Is not this he that destroyed them which called on this name in Jerusalem, and came hither for that intent, that he might bring them bound unto the chief priests? But Saul increased the more in strength, and confounded the Jews which dwelt at Damascus, proving that this is very Christ."

Saul wasn't just recycled; he was transformed.

Be patient with the people in your congregation. It takes time for them to grow and change. God will transform them, but sometimes Christian growth is a slow process. Teach your people how to be patient with new believers. They don't know everything about the Christian life yet. They need to be treated gently. The Word of God will teach them and they will change, but give them time. Be patient with yourself as well. Take the experiences you have in dealing with people and allow them to help you to be a more patient and kind person.

God can change anyone. Don't look at people for their outward appearance; look at them through the eyes of our loving God. Our God loves people and wants them to go to Heaven. You'll never know who is going to be recycled and transformed.

Finish Line Strategies

- When you are weary, you are the most vulnerable to taking everything that is said to you personally. Guard against that.

- Go for a walk or a bike ride. Better yet, go for a walk with someone who understands and will listen to you.

- Brainstorm about some ways you can lighten the work load for everyone. Work smarter, not harder.

Chapter 27
Thankful or Thankless?

Enter into his gates with thanksgiving, and into his courts with praise: be thankful unto him, and bless his name. Psalm 100:4

After the owners of the 20 acres changed the price, Jim Rende, a faithful man in our church, learned of a 40-acre property across the street. It

The 40-acre property was an amazing deal.

was close to the price of the other property, and this new property was better. They would sell it for $240,000 and would finance it at 10%. Back in the days of Jimmy Carter, 14% was a deal. Ten percent was an unbelievable deal.

Palatine Township was interested in our current property. This was really exciting; because if we could sell our current buildings, then we would have enough money to build a new building. Our church voted unanimously to go ahead and sell, and then buy this property in Hawthorn Woods, Illinois. My daughter, Julie, was 14 at the time, and she remembers that meeting. She has mentioned that this was a key point in her life to decide to serve the Lord.

The *Daily Herald* newspaper covered our sale and move.

On the night that the township bought our hexagon building and our first building, we had a zoning meeting for our new property. We needed to get zoning from the city of Hawthorn Woods.

A bunch of our people who lived in the Palatine Township went to that meeting. Others who lived closer to Lake Zurich also went to the meeting. Our kids babysat for other families that night. My daughter and Joy Julian (Laegeler) babysat for the Floyd family. My son and Paul Julian babysat for another family.

Paul and Jim went outside to play basketball with the son of this family. When they tried to go back inside, they found they had accidentally locked themselves out of the house. There was a two-year-old girl sleeping inside the house. They didn't know what to do. (This was in the time before cell phones.) The boys went to a neighbor's house and phoned the meeting. The township people paged the family over the loudspeakers. The family and all the other church members present got worried when they heard the loudspeaker announcement. They wondered what was wrong. Everyone was very tense during the meeting, but they were later

relieved to find out the simple problem of a locked door. The family was able to go and take care of the situation.

In one night, both items were approved. The township agreed to buy our old buildings, and Hawthorn Woods agreed to zone us so we could build a church. This new property was 8 miles north on the same road. We didn't even have to change the name of the church. How's that for God's provision?

Now we had to build. We would meet in a public school gymnasium for the summer. (It reminded me of when we had to meet in the Feehanville School when we were looking for our first property.) Don't despair if your church has to meet somewhere else besides a church building for awhile. I've seen God work in mighty ways when we've had to meet in other places besides our building. God isn't confined by money, building materials, or property. He owns the cattle on a thousand hills and can do mighty things even with weak things.

We decided we wouldn't contract out the new church. We would completely build it all by ourselves. Sometimes when churches say they built their own building, they mean they tiled and painted and maybe dry-walled, but we wanted to do it all. We knew we could do it cheaper than a builder could do it. We already had experience with building in the past. Now it was time to do the whole thing.

The school was hot with no air conditioning, so it kept us working hard toward having our own building. We had to get the building done by September (this was late May) because we needed to start our Christian school in the fall. We had a goal. So the people went to work.

The Miracle of the Rain

Earlier in this book, I described to you when it didn't rain on our property the Saturday we poured the concrete foundation. It was at this time we had this miracle.

Building 3 took a lot of planning and prayer.

Soon after that, we encountered a new problem. The trusses — or rather, the lack of trusses. They were delayed time and time again.

Understand this, dear friend, whenever you are serving the Lord and trying to do something for Him, you will have problems. Don't be surprised by this. Don't be shocked. Expect problems. When there are trials and troubles in our lives, we know God is working. He is doing something bigger. He is always doing something better than we can see at the time.

✦

God's Character

We should learn to expect problems in our Christian lives and not be completely surprised by them. When we go through difficult times, we can look to God's character to discover how to best make it through the problems.

God lives outside of time. He can see the end from the beginning, and He always knows what is best for us. I find when I'm concerned or worried over a problem I'm facing, it helps to think about God's character.

Let's look at three men in Scripture who understood they needed to stand up for what was right. They also had a God who would answer them and help them. Daniel 3:13–18 says,

"Then Nebuchadnezzar in his rage and fury commanded to bring Shadrach, Meshach, and Abednego. Then they brought these men before the king. Nebuchadnezzar spake and said unto them, Is it true, O Shadrach, Meshach, and Abednego, do not ye serve my gods, nor worship the golden image which I have set up? Now if ye be ready that at what time ye hear the sound of the cornet, flute, harp, sackbut, psaltery, and dulcimer, and all kinds of musick, ye fall down and worship the image which I have made; well: but if ye worship not, ye shall be cast the same hour into the midst of a burning fiery furnace; and who is that God that shall deliver you out of my hands? Shadrach, Meshach, and Abednego, answered and said to the king, O Nebuchadnezzar, we are not careful to answer thee in this matter. If it be so, our God whom we serve is able to deliver us from the burning fiery furnace, and he will deliver us out of thine hand, O king. But if not, be it known unto thee, O king, that we will not serve thy gods, nor worship the golden image which thou hast set up."

These three men had amazing courage. (An easier way to remember their names is Shadrach, Meshach, and Under-the-Bed-I-Go. That last name reminds me of the dog we had when the children were young. Her name was Shadow; but we often called her Shadrach, as she loved going under the bed, especially after she had gotten in the garbage.)

These three men knew about God's character. They knew He was omnipotent—all powerful.

The word *omnipotent* is derived from the Latin, and indicates that God's power is infinite and unlimited. God is called Almighty in the Bible, and this word *omnipotent* means "Almighty."

Psalm 89:8 states, "O LORD God of hosts, who is a strong LORD like unto thee? Or to thy faithfulness round about thee?"

God is omniscient—He knows everything.

God knows the past, present, and the future. Everything. He knows what would have happened and the hundreds of millions of scenarios that could have happened. The three men could rest in the fact that God knew what a precarious situation they were in. He knew and understood what they faced.

God is omnipresent—He is everywhere.

Paul Little states, "God is not a substance spread out in a thin layer all over the earth; all of Him is in Chicago, in Calcutta, in Cairo, and in Caracas, at once and the same time."

Psalm 139:11–15 says,

"If I say, Surely the darkness shall cover me; even the night shall be light about me. Yea, the darkness hideth not from thee; but the night shineth as the day: the darkness and the light are both alike to thee. For thou hast possessed my reins: thou hast covered me in my mother's womb. I will praise thee; for I am fearfully and wonderfully made: marvellous are thy works; and that my soul knoweth right well. My substance was not hid from thee, when I was made in secret, and curiously wrought in the lowest parts of the earth."

God is everywhere. Knowing this, the three men who were about to be thrown into the fiery furnace could rest in Him.

You can do the same no matter what happens. God's omniscience, omnipotence, and omnipresence are His character. He knows what you are going through. He knows how difficult things can be in your life. He knows what you are facing. He knows the hardships, the turmoil, the strife, the frustration.

Keep going in the Christian life, my friend. Even if things are difficult, know that God's character remains the same. He will carry you through.

The Trusses

We had bought the trusses from a company that was in bankruptcy; but of course, we didn't know that fact at the time. The trusses weren't getting delivered, and we desperately needed them. We sent over some of our

Our men went to the defunct truss factory and built the remaining trusses, pulling the last one out as the door was padlocked.

own workers to build the trusses. The men did a great job. We finished the last truss and carried them out to the truck. Precisely at that moment, the bank came and padlocked the factory doors.

Getting those trusses enabled us to stay on schedule.

These kinds of things have happened over and over again throughout our ministry. (It is like Murphy is a member of our church.) Praise God that He intervened and we got those trusses. We would have been in big trouble if we hadn't gotten them. The building would have experienced a huge delay.

There were times during that building project when the 40 acres

Building 3 on our new 40 acres is finally complete – just in time for school to open!

mocked me. I would say, "Why in the world did I think we could use up all this land? There is no way on earth that could ever happen."

Some of my pastor friends thought I was crazy for getting such a huge amount of land and building a huge building. (Looking back, I see we could have used even more, as we were soon out of room.) But I hung on during those times of doubt, because I knew God was in it.

When people saw how sincere we were, businesses would give us a better price for materials. Our church people came out every single night and worked on the building, and the ladies provided food every day of the week. We had a wonderful time together. Many people in our church would tell you that was one of the best times in their lives because of the fellowship and fun that went along with all the hard work.

When I was on the board of an organization, an expert came in and said if he wrote the missionary letters, the organization would raise their support by at least 30%. However, when the guy wrote the letters, the support went down because it didn't seem like the letters were real.

That's an important part of doing Christian

John Julian working, even with a broken foot.

work. We always have to be humble and real with others. We have to give of ourselves, and then people will want to get on board with that thought. As we worked on the building, we shared our burdens and grew closer the more we worked together.

❧

My Encounter with a Semi Truck

God taught me to lean on Him early because I got into so many scrapes and dangerous situations as a child. Dad got me a go-cart when I was about

nine years old. I loved that thing and would drive it all over the roads in Morehead, Kentucky. There were no brakes on the go-cart, so I had to reach back and pull off the spark plug wire to get it to stop.

Morehead, KY, was the place where I almost met my Maker.

There was a hilly road on the back of the campus of Morehead State University. As I careened down the hill, a semi appeared out of nowhere. It was barreling right at me, and I couldn't stop my go-cart. I prayed in the name of the Father, Son, and Holy Ghost (rather than just in the name of the Father) for good measure. I got down as low as I could, and I went all the way under the moving semi truck.

Somehow, the truck didn't hit me. I could have gotten killed that day. The angry driver stopped as soon as he could, and came back and gave me a well-deserved tongue lashing.

Dad was a worrier, so I thought it better that he not know about this incident. (It's a good thing he didn't know about everything I did. It might have killed him earlier than his time.)

If Mom was late, Dad was sure she probably had an accident. He would name the bridge where he was sure it happened. (If cell phones and Internet were around then, I have no doubt that my dad would have been on the phone every second she was on the road and checking the Internet for possible road construction or traffic to try and keep her safe.) If she was

15 or 30 minutes late, he was sure she had been killed or was in a hospital somewhere.

Dad always worried something had been stolen. He would come home from the church, look for something, not find it, and say it had been stolen. I lived in constant fear of robbers coming in the house. But we would always find the things that were "stolen." They were simply misplaced.

Mother was the opposite of a worrier. Two more contrary people than her and my dad could not have gotten married. Nothing bothered her. She never met a stranger. She could go in a restaurant and, within a few minutes, know everyone by name.

When I was a young teenager, we built a cabin below Kentucky Dam. We loved going there to camp out. It was

Kentucky was a great place to grow up.

a rustic cabin with a wood stove. I spent some of the greatest times in my life there. We bought the lot for $200. (I can't imagine doing that now; but of course, $200 was a lot more money then.)

My friends from high school would come and camp out in the cabin with me. We'd make a meal out of potatoes and onions fried in a cast iron skillet. (It was some of the best food in the entire world.)

One time Mom opened up a rollaway bed, and there was a snake inside. I'll never forget her scream. It alerted the neighbors in the town five miles away. I took a small .22 and shot the snake in the head.

Mom gave me a lot of confidence about life. She could do anything. My sister, Pauline, told me that when we were living in a more well-to-do town where most of the people had maids and butlers, she asked Mom why she didn't have a maid. Mom replied, "You never talk about what you don't have. You appreciate what you have."

Thankfulness

The lessons my mother taught me about being thankful have helped me all my life. G.K. Chesterton said, "True contentment is the power of getting out of any situation all that is in it."

William Chisholm wrote the wonderful hymn, "Great Is Thy Faithfulness." The words "morning by morning new mercies I see" came from his day-to-day walk with the Lord. He didn't write the song because of a single tragedy, as some of the hymns were written, but rather from His daily walk. He knew how to be thankful. (My father was the best man I ever knew for many reasons, but one of the most important reasons I admired him is that he taught me to be thankful.)

Choosing thankfulness is a way to make it across the finish line.

❦

Preacher in the House

Upon his conversion, the Apostle Paul was given an incredible vision. This man wanted to spread Christianity throughout the world. The journey wasn't as easy as Paul probably thought it would be. He got the opportunity to preach to thousands of people and plant churches throughout Asia Minor; but he was also stoned, beaten, ridiculed, and betrayed along the way.

When Paul wrote Philippians, it seemed as if his vision had been derailed. The churches desperately needed his attention, and there were more areas that needed to hear the message. Unfortunately, Paul was stuck inside a sort of half-way house, chained at all times to a Roman guard.

For Paul, these misfortunes were opportunities. He shared Christ with every guard forced to be with him. Even high-ranking members of the government came to hear his incredible message. During this time, Paul wrote Ephesians, Philippians, Colossians, and Philemon—without which the Church today would suffer greatly.

Like Joseph in Egypt, what men had meant for evil in Paul's life, God had meant for good. The gospel would spread throughout the Roman Empire faster with its main proponent, Paul, in prison. Only God could devise such a plan. Only a committed and contented servant could carry it out.

How did Paul cultivate the gift of gratitude? Can 21st-century

Christians adopt that same philosophy in a culture that constantly pushes us to ask for more? The secret lies in three powerful truths that can remake a believer's life.

1) It's on the Inside

Madison Avenue and Hollywood tell us happiness only comes when we reach the pinnacle. The problem with this idea is once we reach that elusive level, we find there is always more to be had: bigger cars, bigger houses, bigger boats, more money, more power.

For Christians, it is so easy to try and look or feel put together. *Then I'll be happy*, we tell ourselves. We live in a fallen world, and there will never be a right set of circumstances that can bring us true joy.

I'm not talking about houses, boats, and jobs. Even those who don't covet the big things can have poor perspective. We may hope for a little more pay at work, one more child in our family, or a slightly bigger garage. Then we tell ourselves once we get that one thing, we will be happy.

If we desire a grateful heart, we have to refuse to allow ourselves to rely on external circumstances for happiness. We have to determine whatever happens to us, we'll take it in stride, knowing full well God has ordained it all along.

2) Needs Versus Wants

I've traveled to India on many occasions; and each time I visit, I am amazed at the happiness of the children compared with most American children. These kids have so little—more well-to-do kids have one or two toys made from discarded items.

The children in India were so happy with even little things.

When you give them a piece of candy, they light up like you just gave them an expensive gift. Their joy in the middle of despair drives home a powerful principle: joy isn't based on getting everything we want out of

Preaching to thousands is an amazing and humbling experience. Many were saved that night.

life. By all accounts, these kids should be unhappy, but they are not. (I've been blessed to address large crowds in India for many years and share the gospel with these precious people. Although very hard physically, I loved traveling on mission trips to other countries, too, like Thailand, Trinidad, the Philippines, and more.)

Those who get everything they want discover things bring only temporary euphoria. That's why many of the rich and famous commit suicide, overdose on drugs, and engage in other high-risk behavior. They are looking for that elusive level of happiness, but cannot find it.

Content Christians understand God knows their needs better than they do. The devil's lie, echoed throughout the ages, is that fulfilling our lusts and desires will make us happy. Popular culture shouts this to today's teens: "Follow your heart, and you'll be happy," they say. Yet we see from the life of Job that joy remains in the heart when everything else is taken away. Joseph was happy both in prison and in the palace. We need to teach our teens to lead their hearts rather than to follow them.

As long as our peace and joy hinge on getting what we want, then we are on an emotional roller-coaster ride. Up one day, down the next, never fully settled in our minds.

It takes looking at the needs of those less fortunate to cultivate a sense of thanksgiving. You will not only realize there are others who are worse off than you are, but you will also realize how much God provides your needs and gives blessings. Here are some ways you can reach out no matter what you are going through:

1) Visit a nursing home.
2) Visit a veteran's hospital.
3) Read a missionary biography.
4) Volunteer for a short-term mission trip.

❧

3) It's All About Trust

C.S. Lewis said, "We ought to give thanks for all fortune; if it is 'good,' because it is good, if 'bad,' because it works in us patience, humility, and the contempt for this world, and the hope of our eternal country."

Trust is the essence of gratitude. If we really believe that God is all-powerful, all-wise, and all-knowing, then it will help us when life doesn't seem to go our way. We don't have to fall apart inside when everything falls around us. Faith gives us stability, maturity, and peace. Thankfulness helps us to see our life for what it truly is, and enables us to live out our faith.

It was Paul's resolute faith and thankfulness to God that helped him see through his circumstances to the larger picture. Instead of despair, he saw hope—hope that the entire world would be reached from his jail cell; hope that souls seeking the Savior would find Him because of Paul's imprisonment.

Can you truly look at your life and say, "God is working"? Even when you lose your job, your finances run short, you experience illness, or have to face death?

Thankfulness helps us praise God in the bad times. It gives us joy in the middle of heartache and smiles through our tears. In the situations you are going through right now, have you taken time to thank God? Why don't you do that right now?

Finish Line Strategies

What are some ways you can make sure you remain open, real, and humble to the people around you? Here are some principles I have learned:

- Be open with the people as much as you can. You can't tell your congregation everything, but you can be honest with them. They need to know when things are difficult and when things are frustrating. They will pray for you when you are going through rough times. They will also be more understanding of you and what you are doing. If they don't know about what you are going through, then don't expect them to care.

- Do the work of the church with the people. At every building project, I was always with everyone. My family was, too. This way the people knew I really cared about them. They saw I was willing to roll up my sleeves and sweep the floor, too.

Chapter 28
Continue in the Work

I press toward the mark for the prize of the high calling of God in Christ Jesus.
Philippians 3:14

It was time to build again—this time, a gymnasium for the growing number of children we were ministering to. Now we had more than enough room—for awhile.

Fifteen years later, it was time to build the biggest project we'd ever attempted, and we needed a permit. Desperately. It was just the beginning of the process to build our 76,000-square-foot addition. We were bursting at the seams in our old building, removing the chairs from

Our 4th building was a beautiful gymnasium for our school kids. It was also built by our members.

Building 5 would be by far the most challenging and difficult for our members and staff to build.

our auditorium several times a week to set up a place for preschool classes to meet. Pretty much every storage area had become someone's office, simply because there wasn't enough room.

Get a permit. It

seemed like a simple thing. We knew the building process would be difficult, since we had done it several times before; but we thought getting a permit should not be that hard. For once, we were right. We received the permit right away. We had a great reputation in the community. We had a huge preschool with tons of kids from the area enrolled. Our church had been a great testimony for many years, and we had done nothing but help the community.

We didn't know it at the time, but someone had called our village and said unfavorable things about us. (One of the things you can count on when you are a pastor is there will be people who don't like you. I have stayed in one place for over 40 years of ministry, so all my enemies have congregated.)

This man called the village, and told them people in our church rented out their basements to college students. This was perfectly legal. All of the people claimed the apartments on their taxes. The village thought he meant the church had a basement under our concrete slab. (I guess they thought we had dug it by hand.)

The village board showed up to inspect our church. A board member asked a preschool teacher where people went when there was a tornado. She joked, "Oh, we go to the basement."

The inspectors never did find a basement or a trap door that went down to it since there wasn't one.

Although we had a permit to build, the village acted like we couldn't build after all. The board said our building was going to be ten feet too tall, and we would have to make the building shorter if we were going to build. We already had the plans drawn up and had started bidding. We couldn't afford to change the height of the building. Besides, they had already approved the permit.

We had plans and renderings, but could not move forward. We needed another miracle.

Quentin Road is so used to having setbacks that this new one should not have surprised us at all. Nothing we have done has ever come easy; and obviously, this was no exception.

More Trouble, Lord?

As much as I've written about all the difficult things that have happened, you would think we would know we couldn't go forward without the devil attacking. Satan doesn't want souls to get saved. That is his fundamental goal. Whenever there is going to be growth for the Lord, Satan is right there to squash it.

Growing older and wiser in the Lord doesn't diminish the troubles that will come our way. In fact, the stronger we get in the Lord and the more we trust Him, the more Satan will want to fight and keep the work from going forward.

This doesn't mean there isn't hope. God is greater. He is the greatest Power in the universe. At Quentin Road, we have seen every time the greater the hardship, the greater the blessing; but that doesn't mean the adversity wasn't difficult.

Matt Floyd and his family are great encouragers.

Recently one of our pastors in Iowa, Pastor Matt Floyd, mentioned he has been going through so much hardship lately that he plans to wear a floatation device at all times. When he remembers me saying the greater the testing, the greater the blessing, he thinks of the song, "There Shall Be Showers of Blessing." Wearing the lifejacket will insure that when the blessings start pouring out of Heaven, he won't drown. I love Pastor Matt's humorous take on life. It is how we should all be living. We should realize God is with us and wants to bless us, especially when we are going through difficult times.

I'm sure if you have children, you are familiar with water parks and the lazy river. (This is the place all the adults want to go because water parks are really quite tiring.) I was thinking about the lazy river and the current that goes through it. The current is strong enough to propel your tube down the river, but not so strong that you can't easily get in and out of the river. You know the current is there, especially if you get out of your tube and try to stand still. While it isn't impossible, it is a bit uncomfortable to do this. You can walk against the current, but it is still not the easiest thing to do. Other tubers get a little angry when you try to go against the current and you bump into them.

Compare this to the Christian life. Most Christians want to take the lazy way out. They want to go with the current, go downstream, not make a big fuss, and not really take a stand.

It is when you get out of your tube and try standing that you will first notice the current is uncomfortable. When you attempt to go against the current, it gets downright frustrating to others who are not spiritual. People won't like it that you are moving in a direction contrary to everyone else; and the current from the river will pull at you to get back in your tube, kick your feet back, and do nothing.

Don't allow yourself to stop serving the Lord because there are hard times ahead. God is faithful. He will help you through those hard times just as He has done in the past. I love the old saying, "God has brought you too far in His name to bring you to shame."

∽◦C✑

The Art of Waiting

Think about Zacharias in the temple. He and his wife, Elizabeth, had waited a long time to have a baby, but now it didn't seem like it was going to happen. They were also waiting for the Messiah. Now every Jewish woman wanted to be the mother of the Messiah, and I'm sure this couple was no exception. One day an angel appeared to Zacharias and gave him a surprise announcement.

Luke 1:5–20 says,

"There was in the days of Herod, the king of Judaea, a certain priest named Zacharias, of the course of Abia: and his wife was of the daughters of Aaron, and her name was Elisabeth. And they were both righteous before God, walking in all the commandments and ordinances of the Lord blameless. And they had no child, because that Elisabeth was barren, and they both were now well stricken in years. And it came to pass, that while he executed the priest's office before God in the order of his course, According to the custom of the priest's office, his lot was to burn incense when he went into the temple of the Lord. And the whole multitude of the people were praying without at the time of incense. And there appeared unto him an angel of the Lord standing on the right side of the altar of incense. And when Zacharias saw him, he was troubled, and fear fell upon him. But the angel said unto him, Fear not, Zacharias: for thy prayer is heard; and thy wife Elisabeth shall bear thee a son, and thou shalt call his name John. And thou shalt have joy and gladness; and many shall rejoice at his birth. For he shall be great in the sight of the Lord, and shall drink neither wine nor strong drink; and he shall be filled with the Holy Ghost, even from his mother's womb. And many of the children of Israel shall he turn to the Lord their God. And he shall go before him in the spirit and power of Elias, to turn the hearts of the fathers to the children, and the disobedient to the wisdom of the just; to make ready a people prepared for the Lord. And Zacharias said unto the angel, Whereby shall I know this? for I am an old man, and my wife well stricken in years. And the angel answering said unto him, I am Gabriel, that stand in the presence of God; and am sent to speak unto thee, and to shew thee these glad tidings. And, behold, thou shalt be dumb, and not able to speak, until the day that these things shall be performed, because thou believest not my words, which shall be fulfilled in their season."

Zacharias couldn't believe the Lord was going to work in this amazing way. He could have received the commission from the angel, but instead he asked for a sign so he would know it would happen. The angel said he wouldn't be able to talk until the baby was born. (Good thing this didn't happen to a woman. I can only imagine how difficult that would be. [Just kidding.]) I know it was hard for Zacharias; but he believed God, even at an older age, because he knew God was in charge and he trusted Him.

We all need to trust God during continued hard times. If you want to have a church where the people are truly spiritual, then you are bound to have hard times. If you ignore all the problems and hope they go away, you'll end up with no church. It is better to expect problems and trust God when they come. He is the greatest Problem-Solver in the universe.

∾↻↺∾

Town Meeting Time

Another town meeting was scheduled to review our permit for the church. Several people from our church who lived in the village attended. The rest of the people gathered at Quentin Road and prayed throughout the meeting. There was a hint of victory in the air at that prayer meeting. People believed the meeting was going well, and it would only be a little while before we would have approval to move forward with the permit we already had.

Enthusiasm ran high, and people praised God because He was going to answer their prayers. The meeting ended, and our people waited anxiously to find out the news.

The news wasn't good. The village was not going to let us build at all unless we incorporated all their new regulations. The new regulations would cost us money we didn't have.

I should have been used to the difficult times by this point, but does anyone really get accustomed to hard times? Can anyone be prepared for everything to come to a screeching halt after months of hard work, planning, and praying?

I sure wasn't.

∾↻↺∾

Time to Do Something Drastic

The more we looked into building with the new regulations, the more difficult we realized it was going to be. Trouble piled up, and things were getting desperate. We really needed to get going on the construction, but it seemed like there wasn't any hope.

Then someone suggested de-annexing from the village. At first, this seemed like a radical idea. We didn't think it sounded like a good suggestion at all; but the more we thought about it, the more we thought it might work. We researched what it would take, and found out there were seven criteria we had to meet in order to de-annex.

We met all seven.

I was honestly amazed at God's provision. We started calling attorneys to find out how much it would cost to de-annex, and every attorney wanted more money than we could pay. Some said it would cost $200,000–$300,000. We definitely didn't have that kind of money to throw around.

We made one more phone call. I always believe in making that last call—the phone call you may not want to make because you've made so many in the past. (This is a principle I've used throughout my whole ministry. Even when you think there is no hope and you absolutely can't get a lower price, pick up the phone one more time and dial one more number. You might be surprised at what will happen. That last phone call could save you a ton of money.)

The last attorney we called said it would cost $2,000 to de-annex. I almost fell off my chair when I heard the news. We hired the attorney and in 31 days—a record in our state—we were out of the village and into unincorporated Lake County. The village let us out without opposition.

Because we were in unincorporated Lake County, it was much cheaper to build. We saved more than two million dollars by de-annexing because the county has fewer building restrictions than the village.

All these blessings came because someone wanted to stir up trouble.

Led by Your Enemies

We ended up getting direction from an unlikely source, our enemies. Events were set in motion by someone who didn't like us. These are my top five verses when I think about being led by my enemies.

Psalm 5:8 states, "Lead me, O Lord, in thy righteousness because of mine enemies; make thy way straight before my face."

Psalm 8:2 says, "Out of the mouth of babes and sucklings hast thou ordained strength because of thine enemies, that thou mightest still the enemy and the avenger."

Psalm 27:11 gives insight, "Teach me thy way, O Lord, and lead me in a plain path, because of mine enemies."

Psalm 54:7 says, "For he hath delivered me out of all trouble: and mine eye hath seen his desire upon mine enemies."

And then in Proverbs 16:7 it says, "When a man's ways please the Lord, he maketh even his enemies to be at peace with him."

Throughout the years, I have seen God do something unique. He has led us in a new direction through our enemies. (No, you don't have to go back and re-read the previous sentence to make sure I wrote it correctly. It's true.) I have seen this as a principle in Scripture, in my life, and in my ministry. In reality, I have been led by my enemies more than anything else. If you are going through a lot of opposition, look at it as an opportunity to be led by your enemies. Dear friend, this is true.

Earlier I mentioned that Joseph said to his brothers who had sold him into slavery, "You meant it for evil, but God meant it for good." I have seen over and over again God leading and guiding us by the opposition. We would never have considered de-annexing if the village hadn't given us trouble about the permit. We wouldn't have had any trouble with the permit if one person wasn't trying to stir up trouble with the village by saying we had built this secret basement. Did I mention that Congressman Phil Crane attended almost every Sunday during this whole time? That didn't hurt, either.

We wouldn't have dreamed we could save so much money. God led us in the most peculiar of ways. Psalm 23:5 states, "Thou preparest a table before me in the presence of mine enemies: thou anointest my head with oil; my cup runneth over."

A top leader in the village called me after all this happened and said, "You're not going to bring up the thing about the basement, are you?"

"I won't if you won't," I said.

We remain on good terms to this day.

One lay leader mentioned that while attending church, a member, a woman who had been making vicious attacks on the pastor, stood up and started to say more mean things about how badly she thought the pastor led the church. The leader couldn't take it anymore. He said, "You are not acting like Jesus would act."

The woman replied, "I don't care what Jesus would do. I'm not Jesus."

The leader was tempted to say, "Well, that's obvious."

The truth is, we often have to humble ourselves. When we get attacked or when our church gets attacked, we sometimes don't have a chance to defend ourselves. This is particularly frustrating because all of us want to at least be able to stand up for ourselves.

Consider our Lord Jesus Christ. Think of what He did for us on the cross. He actually asked His Father to forgive those who nailed Him to the cross. Philippians 2:5–11 states,

> "Let this mind be in you, which was also in Christ Jesus: Who, being in the form of God, thought it not robbery to be equal with God: But made himself of no reputation, and took upon him the form of a servant, and was made in the likeness of men: And being found in fashion as a man, he humbled himself, and became obedient unto death, even the death of the cross. Wherefore God also hath highly exalted him, and given him a name which is above every name: That at the name of Jesus every knee should bow, of things in heaven, and things in earth, and things under the earth; And that every tongue should confess that Jesus Christ is Lord, to the glory of God the Father."

Jesus humbled Himself. He was obedient even to the point of death. When things happen to us that we don't deserve, we need to remember the mind of Christ. Stay close to God and to the Word. If something happens that seems to put a huge stop to a project your church is doing, don't despair. Know God is in charge and might be using this new difficulty to save you time, money, and energy.

❧

The Gift

Isaac saw the gift next to his plate. Wrapped in brown paper and tied with twine, the package wasn't as brightly wrapped as the presents in the department store window, but the boy didn't care. Times had been hard.

Isaac hadn't thought he'd get anything for Christmas.

His mother put a platter of potatoes on the table. "Open your present, son."

His father folded up the newspaper. "Go ahead."

Isaac untied the twine and pulled off the paper. A pocketknife. *I've wanted one of these for forever*, he thought.

His father spoke, "I'm sorry that the pocketknife is used. My father gave it to me when I was young."

But Isaac was already opening up the tool, examining each part of it. "I don't care that it's used," he said, "This is the best Christmas gift I've ever received."

My father, Isaac Scudder, is the boy in this story. During the Depression, Christmas wasn't anything like what we celebrate now. Decorations were handmade and presents were rare. That used pocketknife was a gift that warmed Dad's heart throughout his whole life.

When it comes to the church, sometimes we have to realize the gift God gives us as we try to do something for His glory might seem like it is used at the time. You may look at the sudden opposition and wonder what kind of a gift God is really giving you.

And yet, like us, you might be surprised that opposition could be one of the greatest gifts you have ever received. The opposition will change you, grow you, and make you more like Christ. It will ultimately grow your church and bring many people into the doors who don't know the Savior. Without that one enemy, we would not have all that we have today.

Time for breaking yet another piece of God's earth.

Don't be discouraged when you get a "used" gift from the Lord. Thank Him for it.

The gift just might be the greatest gift you've ever received.

The foundation takes shape.

Our members and staff working in the winter (again!).

A Testimony of God's Grace

Soon we poured our foundation and put up the steel for the structure. Then it was time to set the huge beams going across the entire auditorium and building. That was an amazing day that I wrote about in the first chapters. Throughout the entire winter and summer we built the building. Even during this incredibly busy time, we went from broadcasting only on local television to broadcasting worldwide. We also started *Victory In Grace* radio.

Even during this huge project, the Word still went out.

Members and new attendees came out and worked every day and every night. The ladies brought food. The men worked on the roofing and did

an amazing job. (They did the roofing a new way which at first took a very long time; but then they got the hang of it, and it was much easier.)

During the building project, I had to go to India. It was January of 1997. We were putting exterior drywall on the building, when one night there was a terrible storm and an entire wall blew out.

That same night, our charter member, Ralph Kowalski, died of a heart attack. The next

Ralph loved life, but he especially loved the Holy Land.

morning I called from India and asked how things were going.

My secretary and daughter-in-law, Karen Scudder, answered but didn't seem to want to tell me how it was going. She kind of hesitated when I

asked her, and said I should speak to my other secretary, Jane Vasquez.

I asked Jane how it was going, and she gave the phone to my daughter, Julie.

I was getting worried. What was going on at the church? Had everyone died? Finally, through tears, Julie told me about Ralph passing away and about the wall blowing out of the building.

Ralph with my young son. He had been with us through it all.

I grieved for Ralph, but I knew Ralph was busy showing Jesus all the wonders of Heaven. Ralph might have just gotten there, but I'm sure he was already an expert on how Heaven was run and everything about it. Ralph was just that way. When a new person came to Quentin Road, Ralph was sure to go up to them, introduce himself,

and say he was a charter member. Everyone loved him for it. He would be sorely missed; but I didn't regret at all that he would be free of his body that shook when he talked and his mouth that inadvertently spit. He would be free of the bumps that covered him and free of all of his physical limitations. I would definitely miss Ralph for his love for souls. There was probably no one who was a greater soulwinner or who had more of a love for souls than Ralph Kowalski.

Ralph loved to be teased, and I loved to tease him.

The news about Ralph was difficult, but I got through it. The news about the wall wasn't really going to be a problem. While it would take a lot of work to repair it, fortunately no permanent damage had been done. This wasn't really a serious problem, in my opinion.

When you've been in the ministry for as long as I have, you quickly realize what real problems are.

How Do You Face Problems?

What kind of a person are you when you face problems? Are you power-conscious or problem-conscious? Many people only look at the problems. In fact, they aren't happy unless they are facing a problem. They might moan and complain to everyone within yelling distance about the problem they have to face; but in reality, they do better when there are problems.

These are the kind of people who go to their bosses or their pastors and say, "This is the problem." When they are asked what the solution is, the person has no idea. He or she is excellent at finding problems, but not so good at thinking of solutions.

This doesn't mean you should go to your boss thinking he should use each and every solution you come up with. You should remain open to ideas and whatever insight he or she might have about the problem. It does mean you should remain power-conscious about problems. After all, we have the greatest Power in the universe at our disposal. We are blessed beyond measure with God's great power, wisdom, and strength.

James 1:5 states, "If any of you lack wisdom, let him ask of God, that giveth to all men liberally, and upbraideth not; and it shall be given him." When we lack wisdom, we need to ask of God, and He will give us that wisdom. This is a promise you can hold onto no matter what is going on in your life.

Maybe you are going through a difficult problem at work, or your church is going through many issues, and you have no idea what to do. Can I implore you to go straight to the Lord about your problem? Talk to Him about what you need. Give Him the specifics about what you are facing.

Wait for Him to work. He will give you wisdom, strength, and help. Continue in the work.

He might lead you in a new direction because of something you learn from your enemies.

Finish Line Strategies

- Here's another church that believes in searching for a deal. Dr. Rod and Cindy Holler, founders of the Cape Baptist Church in Cape Coral, Florida, desperately needed a building for their newly started church. They searched for land, but the prices were way too high for them to consider buying, much less building on top of that. Through a "chance" encounter at the grocery store, they learned of a church that desperately needed to sell their building at a greatly reduced cost. They ended up getting the land, the building, and everything else they needed at a fraction of what they should have paid.

The Cape Baptist Church is one of many church plants we have done over the years.

- Look at opposition to your church as a chance to see God work. Don't get frustrated. Instead, concentrate on the power of God. He will use the opposition to bring great growth to your congregation.

- Ask for advice from many different people when you are facing opposition. One person might have the answer you are looking for, like the person who suggested that our church de-annex from the village.

Chapter 29
Pour Courage into Others

Let Israel hope in the LORD: for with the LORD there is mercy, and with him is plenteous redemption. Psalm 130:7

Once we hired an expert in church busing to come and teach us how to get more kids into Sunday School. He came and taught seminars; and then went with a large number of people from our church, visiting hundreds of homes in the community. He said he had never signed up less than 100 kids to ride the bus. Well, that day only one kid signed up to ride the bus.

Quentin Road is in the affluent Northwest Suburbs of Chicago, which is a strong Catholic area. Techniques and ideas that work well in other church locations do not work well in our church. Streamlining ideas is an important part of adapting to your area and to your culture. You find the things that work and the things that do not work. There is a lot of trial and error in ministry. Don't get discouraged if you plan a huge event, do a ton of work promoting it, and then it flops. Chalk the incident up to experience, and try something else. Whatever area you are in will determine the kinds of events and ministries that work.

If you had told me the day we had flopped trying to get 100 kids to ride our bus to church that one day we would have 1,400 children coming to our preschool, I would have told you you were crazy! Every day of the week we teach the Bible, share the gospel, and give the kids a safe place to be. We do this for people who need to work and need somewhere for their kids. Our preschool kids learn more and better than the kids in the public school system and almost any other preschool. The best part? We don't need to pick anyone up on the bus or drop anyone off. The parents bring their kids and pick them up afterwards. Plus, the parents are happy to pay us for taking such good care of their children. It is a win-win for all involved, but I didn't know that at the time.

Since I'm from Kentucky, I've been privileged to eat at the very first Kentucky Fried Chicken Restaurant. At age 65, Colonel Sanders received his first Social Security check, and it was only for $105. Instead of getting angry, he decided to do something about it. He thought restaurant owners would love his fried chicken recipe. He thought if they would use it, sales would increase, and he'd get a percentage of those sales. He drove around the country knocking on doors, sleeping in his car, and wearing his white suit. People said no 1,009 times before he got his first yes, but Colonel Sanders didn't let the no's stop him. He knew that if he kept going, he would finally get a yes. (I got to work for Colonel Sanders for one day in Paducah when a friend's mother asked me to work with her opening a new Kentucky Fried Chicken. And yes, his original recipe is still my favorite. I never met the Colonel again, but it was sure nice to work with him that one day.)

The billionaire owner of the NBA's Dallas Mavericks got rich when he sold his company to Yahoo for $5.9 billion in stock. Mark Cuban admitted he was terrible at his early jobs. His parents wanted him to have a normal job; so he tried carpentry, but hated it. He was a short-order cook, but a terrible one. He says of his failures, "I've learned that it doesn't matter how many times you failed," Cuban says, "you only have to be right once. I tried to sell powdered milk. I was an idiot lots of times, and I learned from them all."

Chicago athlete Michael Jordan is famous for being cut from his high school basketball team. He turned out to be the greatest basketball player ever, but never let failure deter him. He said, "I have missed more than 9,000 shots in my career. I have lost almost 300 games. On 26 occasions I have been entrusted to take the game-winning shot, and I missed. I have failed over and over and over again in my life. And that is why I succeed."[xxiii]

Failure is part of life. It is part of ministry. There is no success without failure. People in the Bible weren't perfect, either. God used them in their imperfections to do great things for Him.

Consider Abraham, one of the patriarchs. God had spoken to him multiple times to tell him that He would bless him and make him a great nation. But there was a problem, and it was a serious one. He didn't have any children.

For a long time, Abraham trusted. For a long time, Abraham kept going forward. But then Sarai suggested he have a child with her handmaid, and the resulting son gave their family a lot of problems. Abraham should have kept trusting God, but he probably thought he was helping God out. Then God sent three angels to see him. Abraham was sitting by his tent looking over the horizon when he saw three men approaching. He told his wife to quickly prepare a meal. The men sat and told him startling news. Genesis 18:9–15 says,

"And they said unto him, Where is Sarah thy wife? And he said, Behold, in the tent. And he said, I will certainly return unto thee according to the time of life; and, lo, Sarah thy wife shall have a son. And Sarah heard it in the tent door, which was behind him. Now Abraham and Sarah were old and well stricken in age; and it ceased to be with Sarah after the manner of women. Therefore Sarah laughed within herself, saying, After I am waxed old shall I have pleasure, my lord being old also? And the LORD said unto Abraham, Wherefore did Sarah laugh, saying, Shall I of a surety bear a child, which am old? Is any thing too hard for the LORD? At the time appointed I will return unto thee, according to the time of life, and Sarah shall have a son. Then Sarah denied, saying, I laughed not; for she was afraid. And he said, Nay; but thou didst laugh."

God still gave Abraham and Sarah a son as He promised He would do. Although Abraham and Sarah had failed by not fully trusting, God chose to continue to use them.

God will continue to use us after we fail. Sometimes pastors react to situations instead of thinking through their actions. I've done my fair share of this. Our reactions rather than our actions show us for who we are. God will still use the situation for His good, even if we inadvertently or purposely mess something up. He is not only the Ruler, but He is the Overruler. He can make everything come out for good, and it takes a powerful God to do this.

Don't become impatient along the way. Don't let yourself act impulsively about a situation. Get counsel. Follow it. Think and pray and talk about what you are planning to do. That way, while we will all still fail, we will at least minimize the effects.

Still, when we go through difficult times with people, we do get discouraged. In fact, it is one of the most frustrating parts of ministry. It is one of the most difficult things about being a pastor. And yet, I encourage you to take heart. Don't get discouraged when you don't see the results you planned on seeing. Keep plugging away, knowing God will bless your diligent effort. He isn't in the numbers game; rather, He is doing a great work whether you see the actual results or not. You don't know it, but maybe the ministry that isn't working today will be a stepping stone for a future ministry that will blow your mind with its effectiveness and outreach.

Be a Barnabas

Barnabas was known as an encourager. We first hear of him in Acts 4:36–37, which states, "And Joses, who by the apostles was surnamed Barnabas, (which is, being interpreted, The son of consolation,) a Levite, and of the country of Cyprus, Having land, sold it, and brought the money, and laid it at the apostles' feet."

The word *consolation* here means "encouragement." Barnabas' very name meant that he was an encourager. This was the name given to him by the apostles. Can you imagine if your friends thought of you as such an encouraging person that they named you Encouragement?

What are some of the things we know about Barnabas that can translate into our lives? First, Barnabas had a generous spirit. He gave things away. He sold land, took the money, and laid it at the apostles' feet.

When some people are asked to give during a Sunday morning service, they might reach into their pockets and take out the change they have rattling around. Or maybe they will open their wallets and take out some cash (though it probably wouldn't be much because people don't carry much cash these days). If they are more generous, they will write a check. (On the funny side, one time Dad and I were at a Methodist regional meeting. When they were about to take the offering, Dad leaned over and whispered in my ear, "Do you have change for a nickel?" I laughed so hard, I thought I would have to leave the meeting.)

The most generous ones go home and think about what they are going to do for the need. They might sell something they own and bring the money; they might go to the bank to withdraw money; or they might be like Barnabas and sell some land, and then give the money to the need. This shows me what a generous person Barnabas really was.

There are people at Quentin Road who are like this. They are extremely generous. Money does not have a hold on them. They have given and given to the Lord's work, and never begrudged a dime they have given. Generosity has nothing to do with financial status. I've known people who had a lot of money and were generous and people who had very little money who were generous. A giving spirit has to do with the heart.

In his heart, Barnabas was a generous person. He immediately responded to a need and immediately did something monumental about it. This is one of the first things that is written about him after it says that the apostles called him Encouragement as his name. So one of the marks of encouragement is generosity.

The Second Characteristic
Barnabas was also known as a man who could be trusted. Three times in the Bible, Barnabas was called on to do a job that required another person's trust. In Acts chapter 11, a church was being built, and they called on trustworthy Barnabas to encourage the new believers in the church. In the same chapter, the church at Antioch collected some money to give to the church in Jerusalem as it was going through tough times. Who did they call to transport the offering? They called someone they could trust,

Barnabas.

⟨~⟩◦⟨~⟩

The Third Characteristic

Barnabas was a person who saw the good in others and encouraged them. He stood by other people who needed a friend. The first time was when the Apostle Paul got saved. You remember from earlier, right—he dragged Christians off that were killed for their faith; he held the coat of Stephen, the first martyr, when he was killed. After Paul got saved, there were many Christians who were skeptical. They didn't believe he could possibly be saved after all he had done. They didn't want to accept Paul into their number because they didn't think they could trust him.

But Barnabas stood up for him (Acts 9:27). Barnabas stood with Paul and lent his support during a time of crisis. I've had people do this for me throughout the years. When the going gets tough and things are at their worst is often when God is at His best. It is also a time when you see who your true friends are.

Are you an encourager? Do you take the time to "pour courage" into others as Barnabas did? Maybe you are thinking of someone who could use a helping hand and a word of encouragement. Why don't you email or call them right now?

Finish Line Strategies

- Write down the worst thing that can happen in a bad situation. This may not sound very encouraging, but it is. When I look at the worst thing that can happen, I realize that God is bigger than the worst thing that could happen. The truth is the worst thing that can happen to a Christian is to die and go to Heaven. That doesn't sound like a "worst thing" to me.

- Write down the names of all the people who have encouraged you in the past. Thank God for them. Be power-conscious. If God is for you (Romans 8:31), who can be against you?

- Read Psalm 46, 22, 31, 42, 146, and 77.

Chapter 30
The Sign of the Moose

Therefore, brethren, we were comforted over you in all our affliction and distress by your faith. 1 Thessalonians 3:7

The sports teams at QR were always in the game.

After building on the 40 acres, we decided to begin a sports program for our Christian school. We began boys' basketball and girls' volleyball. It was a lot of fun and the kids had a blast playing sports. (If you know anything about Quentin Road, then you know that the whole church supports the school, not just the parents who have kids in the school.)

At that time, we had some people who had become disgruntled in our church, and they had started attending another church. One of the girls attending our

Our fans were always there and loud.

Christian school had parents who didn't attend our church. These disgruntled families tried to get this girl out of our school by taking her to another church and Christian school and saying untruths about us. The whole situation was very difficult for everyone, especially for this girl who wanted her parents to understand how important Quentin Road was to her. We brought up the situation to the Christian school association we were in, and asked them to deal with the problem since both of our schools were part of the association.

A few weeks later, men in our church attended the annual meeting of the association and were shocked when it was publicly announced that our school had been kicked out of the association. They said many untrue and unkind things about our school publicly. All of this was done without notification or warning. They hadn't sent us written notice or given us the courtesy of a phone call. We were shocked and devastated. Being kicked out of the association of Christian schools was terrible. We didn't know what to do.

I remember the exact spot I was standing when these two men told me what had happened. My heart sank. I didn't want our school to have any kind of bad name. This association had believed lies about us and never bothered to contact us to see if they were true.

There were two schools that did stand with us, though. They stood up in the meeting and said, "What are you talking about? Quentin Road has poor sportsmanship? They feed us free pizza after their games, even when we beat them." To this day, these two schools remain our friends. I appreciate them for doing that and for standing with us. It meant so much to me and gave me encouragement.

Now, years later, we have great sports' seasons. We host premier tournaments in volleyball and basketball. Teams come

The Dayspring Basketball Classic champs of 2013.
Finally, we won our own tournament again!

from all over the United States to play in our tournaments; and they all love to come and play and experience some of what is becoming famous: Quentin Road love and hospitality.

That's why I want to encourage you right now. You may be going through something as dark as what I was describing. Maybe you have had someone reject you, or an organization has said false things against you. Whatever the case, know that in the darkest of night the light of Christ shines the brightest. While you may not feel like it at the moment, know God is with you. He will use this difficult time in your life to eventually bring the greatest blessings.

I sure did not see any way this dark day could possibly be a blessing—but I did believe God is faithful and truth would prevail. If I could have known then what I know now, I wouldn't have had to have faith that God would work it out. We are now known for having strong sports teams with great testimonies and fantastic tournaments. God tests us; and in the darkest moments, we can be sure that He will always be with us, encouraging us and guiding us with His strong hand of power.

Soon after this, I took our school kids to our camp in Minnesota. I still felt torn up about what had happened when Mike Floyd and I took a ride down an old, logging road.

Then I saw it.

A moose. Standing in a field.

I asked, "Mike, what do you see?"

"I see a moose."

It was very unusual to see a moose in that part of Minnesota. As many times as I had taken our kids to that area, I had never seen one. Its size and beauty took my breath away. The game warden later told me that there was only one moose in the whole area. I can't believe I had been privileged to see it. I took the moose as a sign from God that the situation we faced would be fine. I always called this experience the "sign of the moose."

We called different schools to see if they would play us in basketball and volleyball, but they refused after the stigma of our being kicked out of the association. I looked in the directory and found Averyville Baptist

School. When I called, they said they couldn't play us, either. I was so discouraged. Then the athletic director called us back and said he had been wrong. Of course, they would love to play us. That was such a blessing, and I appreciated them so much. Ridgewood Christian School and South Side Baptist School stood by us as well. I was thankful to God for them.

❧

The Last Encouragement

Barnabas is most known for standing by someone who even the Apostle Paul didn't consider trustworthy, his relative John Mark. This man had forsaken Paul during one of Paul's journeys. Maybe John Mark got homesick, tired of traveling, or tired of the trials Paul kept going through, and so he ran home.

You can only imagine how deeply this must have wounded Paul. Think of how John Mark must have felt, probably utterly worthless and done. He most likely didn't want to continue.

Paul and Barnabas prepared for another missionary journey to spread the gospel. Barnabas, always the encourager, decided he wanted to take John Mark with them. Paul disagreed, not just a little bit, but a lot. He didn't want to give John Mark another shot. After all, the man had already proven his worthlessness for the Lord. (Honestly, I'm sure all of us can understand where Paul was coming from. There are many things that are difficult in ministry; but betrayal has to be the hardest, especially when it is by someone you loved and trusted. This has happened to me so many times in ministry. I can relate to how Paul was feeling.)

This is when I also admire Barnabas, who lives up to his name once again. He chooses to take John Mark and go on his own journey. Acts 15:36–41 says that contention was so sharp between the two that they split up for a time over it. The neat thing about that was it enabled the ministry to be doubled. Barnabas and John Mark went and shared the gospel, and so did Paul and Silas. The difficult time still allowed for God's work to flourish and grow stronger.

That's what I want to encourage you the most about. Don't let the stuff that happens all the time in churches get you down. You are always going to have hurt feelings and people who think they know more than the pastor. Know this, God is still working when you can't see His hand. You might be surprised what God will do in the future, using even your current, ugly trial as a starting point.

❧

God Wants the Pastor to Give

When we were in our first frame building, we asked Dr. Mark Cambron, one of the professors in my Bible college, to come preach. Dr. Cambron was the kind of person you couldn't be around without having fun. (We loved going out to eat with him at the Ground Round. He loved to throw the peanut shells on the floor as he ate peanuts.)

Dr. Cambron preached on giving that Sunday. I sat behind the pulpit as I always do, taking notes. I was excited he was preaching on such a subject, because I felt it was a message my people really needed to hear. But then he said something that completely challenged me personally. He said, "The preacher needs to give, too. The tithe is a minimum. The preacher should at least be doing that."

At the time, our church was barely giving me a salary. We weren't making enough to live on; but I took the challenge to heart, and gave a tithe and as much over as I could. I saw God bless so much.

Another time after I'd gotten back from leading an Israel trip and was extremely tired, I learned that a disgruntled group of former church members had written a letter that they had sent to every person in the church. They had also sent it to every one of our sister churches, family members of members, and business associates of people in our church. The letter was full of lies and bizarre things that didn't make sense. I read the letter to our whole church and answered it publicly. Even though it was really painful to have something like that happen, the letter had the opposite effect of what was intended. It united the church even more.

The hard times will unify your church to levels you won't believe. Know that people will say and do things you would not have believed they could do. Christians can do the same hurtful things that the world does, if not worse. Carnal Christians are fighting a battle inside. They have to prove they are right and the church is wrong. That's why they fight so hard and make it so difficult for those who love the Lord.

You need to hang on when the going gets tough. The Apostle Paul ends his letter to the Corinthians with the following encouragement: "Therefore, my beloved brethren, be ye steadfast, unmovable, always abounding in the work of the Lord, forasmuch as ye know that your labour is not in vain in the Lord." 1 Corinthians 15:58

Steadfast Job

We need to be steadfast. Consider the man Job in Scripture. Everything was taken away from him: his wealth, his children, and his health. The only thing left was his wife, who was not the most encouraging person in the world. In fact, she told him to "curse God and die." How would you like to be left with someone like that? He also had three friends who spent days telling him that surely he had committed some sin, and he was being punished by God.

Would you feel like continuing if this happened to you? Would you want to keep going? I doubt it. If all of this happened to you, I imagine you would feel pretty discouraged.

Yet we see Job continuing to be steadfast. He doesn't quit. Job 42:1–9 says,

> "Then Job answered the LORD, and said, I know that thou canst do every thing, and that no thought can be withholden from thee. Who is he that hideth counsel without knowledge? therefore have I uttered that I understood not; things too wonderful for me, which I knew not. Hear, I beseech thee, and I will speak: I will demand of thee, and declare thou unto me. I have heard of thee by the hearing of the ear: but now mine eye seeth thee. Wherefore I abhor myself, and repent in dust and ashes. And it was so, that after the LORD had spoken these words unto Job, the LORD said to Eliphaz the Temanite, My wrath is kindled against thee, and against thy two friends: for ye have not spoken of me the thing that is right, as my servant Job hath. Therefore take unto you now seven bullocks and seven rams, and go

to my servant Job, and offer up for yourselves a burnt offering; and my servant Job shall pray for you: for him will I accept: lest I deal with you after your folly, in that ye have not spoken of me the thing which is right, like my servant Job. So Eliphaz the Temanite and Bildad the Shuhite and Zophar the Naamathite went, and did according as the LORD commanded them: the LORD also accepted Job."

God wanted Job's three friends to offer up for themselves a burnt offering because they had not given Job wise counsel. God did not like what Job's friends had said to him.

Sometimes when you are going through a hard time, even your closest friends will say things to you that will deeply wound you. I don't know why in the darkest times, it is so difficult to find true encouragement. Sometimes people don't know what to say, or they are nervous so they end up saying something stupid. It's the last thing you would want to hear, and the thing that will hurt you deeply.

In those moments when you don't know what to do or say, you have to put your hope in the Lord. This is when I go through the Psalms day and night. They have become my comfort like no other book of Scripture. I read them through over and over. Even when I don't feel like hoping in the Lord, when I don't feel like trusting the Lord, the words of the Psalms become my hope and my help.

Psalm 16:8–11 is always a help. "I have set the LORD always before me: because he is at my right hand, I shall not be moved. Therefore my heart is glad, and my glory rejoiceth: my flesh also shall rest in hope. For thou wilt not leave my soul in hell; neither wilt thou suffer thine Holy One to see corruption. Thou wilt shew me the path of life: in thy presence is fulness of joy; at thy right hand there are pleasures for evermore."

Psalm 22:1–11 gives me strength in the darkest times.

"My God, my God, why hast thou forsaken me? why art thou so far from helping me, and from the words of my roaring? O my God, I cry in the daytime, but thou hearest not; and in the night season, and am not silent. But thou art holy, O thou that inhabitest the praises of Israel. Our fathers trusted in thee: they trusted, and thou didst deliver them. They cried unto thee, and were delivered: they trusted in thee, and were not confounded. But I am a worm, and no man; a reproach of men, and despised of the people. All they that see me laugh me to scorn: they shoot out the lip, they shake the head, saying, He trusted on the LORD that he would deliver him: let him deliver him, seeing he delighted in him. But thou art he that took me out of the womb: thou didst make me hope when I was upon my mother's breasts. I was cast upon thee from the womb: thou art my God from my mother's belly. Be not far from me; for trouble is near; for there is none to help."

The Psalms remind me that God is not far from me. He is near me and He is helping me.

Take a moment right now and think about something in your life that is difficult. Perhaps you have someone who has personally rejected you. Maybe your church has gone through a time when people are spreading lies. It could be you have faced a personal betrayal. You trusted someone and then found out you couldn't trust them after all.

Whatever the case, know this: in the middle of the deepest pain, God is there to encourage you, to give you your own "sign of the moose." God will guide you and give you the strength and peace you need to keep walking close to Him. I can guarantee you one thing that you might not believe right now: God will do great things, especially during the worst times. He always does.

Finish Line Strategies

- Be open to the church about your discouragement. Share with main people in the church what is going on. If necessary, go to the whole church and make the matter public, but only do this after getting counsel from other preachers.

- Be open with your wife and children about what is going on in the church. You don't need to shield your children from every discouragement. This will give them an unrealistic view of ministry and will also keep them from seeing the great hardship that ministry is. They want to help you and give you comfort, and they can't do that if they don't know what you are going through.

- Pray, pray, pray.

- Know God is listening to your prayers and doing a great work, even if you don't see it now.

- Continue to do God's work when it is the most difficult. I used to think that when I got to a certain point, there wouldn't be any more troubles in the ministry; but now I see that isn't true. There will always be troubles when there are people. But God is always there and will help and guide.

Chapter 31
Peace When You Need It

Then said Jesus to them again, Peace be unto you: as my Father hath sent me, even so send I you. John 20:21

The pain in my right arm started at 8,000 feet altitude in our small church plane. At first I ignored it, but the discomfort increased. I asked my son-in-law, Neal, who was flying the plane, to fly lower so I could get more oxygen. I resolved to have this pain checked out as soon as we touched down on land. When we got to the hospital, they did some tests. I learned I needed bypass surgery. I had rarely been sick in my life and had never been in the hospital, except when I was born and one other time for a few hours, but never for surgery.

The day before the bypass surgery, I woke up concerned and feeling troubled. I opened my Bible to the Psalms and read Psalm 34:6–10 which states,

"This poor man cried, and the LORD heard him, and saved him out of all his troubles. The angel of the LORD encampeth round about them that fear him, and delivereth them. O taste and see that the LORD is good: blessed is the man that trusteth in him. O fear the LORD, ye his saints: for there is no want to them that fear him. The young lions do lack, and suffer hunger: but they that seek the LORD shall not want any good thing."

"Lord," I prayed, "I don't know what to think about going through this surgery. I'm not sure what to think about them putting me on a machine that pumps my blood while they work on my heart. But I do trust in You, and I know You are holding me and taking care of me."

I also asked for peace when I went into surgery; because frankly, I was a little scared about what lay ahead. I know preachers aren't supposed to admit to being frightened or ever not trusting in the Lord. (Of course, the Lord has never let me down once and has proven Himself more than trustworthy.) But at that moment while waiting for my family to come see me before surgery and waiting for the nurses to come and prep me, I was nervous. Before I had the bypass surgery, people would come to me and say they were going to have some type of surgery; and I'd say, "The Lord will be with you." While I meant it, I have to admit I didn't have as much sympathy for what that person was going to face as I do now. That is one of the reasons we have to go through difficult things, so we can learn to be empathetic to others who are experiencing hard times.

I went to the Lord with my fears. The minute before my prayer I had fear, but now I had total peace. No fear at all. It was more than a miracle.

My family arrived and the hospital workers came to wheel me into surgery. While I had never doubted the Lord's presence, He gave me a strong feeling that He was with me. I had a peace like you wouldn't believe. I almost felt like I was going on vacation from that moment forward. That was how much peace I had. John 14:27 says, "Peace I leave with you, my peace I give unto you: not as the world giveth, give I unto you. Let not your heart be troubled, neither let it be afraid."

My soul wasn't troubled or afraid. I knew the Lord was with me, guiding me, and helping me. Philippians 4:7 certainly describes how I felt. "And the peace of God, which passeth all understanding, shall keep your hearts and minds through Christ Jesus." I can tell you this verse is real.

I came out of the surgery and found out they had done quintuple-bypass surgery. Apparently, I had an extra artery that needed to be replaced. (I could say to the people who didn't think I had a heart at all that I now had an extra artery for my heart.)

I recovered; and ten years later, I have never felt better. I exercise and enjoy life. And most of all, I appreciate the peace the Lord gave me that day.

Peace in Your Difficulty

Recently, I had some friends who were pastors go through very hard times in their churches. (A pastor often has to fight with one hand tied behind his back because he has so many people to protect.)

I understand the pain these pastors were going through since I have gone through it many times. There is no pain like the pain of ministry. There is no way to describe or understand the things that people will do or say that will hurt more than I could ever express.

And yet in the middle of the deepest pain, I have often seen God work in great ways. In the case of one of my friends, he was able to see one of his 13-year-old girls lead another seventh grader to Christ during his church's kids' program. This was so precious to him and made all the pain more than worth it.

When dealing with difficult situations in the church, my heart breaks for the people involved. Often they have made poor decisions through time and now are reaping the consequences of their actions. (I also have made poor decisions at times.)

It is hard to see them go through the hardship they have to experience. Most pastors get very little pay. Their pay is still to come as Pastor R.G. Lee said in his famous sermon, "Pay Day, Someday."

Our camp started very primitive, but the kids always loved it.

One year, our church bought a small piece of land in Northern Minnesota. We wanted to have a camp, but the land was in the middle of a forest and a swampy area. We would have to set up tents and do all of our cooking outside. We loaded up our church bus with city kids, and set out for the 12-hour drive to Minnesota. When we arrived, we were tired and ready to set up our tents and go to bed. There was only one problem: The moment I stepped off the bus, thousands (and I mean literally thousands) of mosquitoes landed on me from head to toe. Deer flies the size of skunks circled my head. I quickly stepped back onto the bus and closed the door, trying not to let in all the bugs. I looked at all the kids. Their eyes were wide, and I knew they were wondering what they had gotten themselves

into.

"This is the biggest mistake of my life, and I think you are all going to have a miserable time; but I guess we'll have to make the best of it," I said.

I don't think the kids really knew what to say. They stood up, got their stuff, and started to get off the bus. I waited for the mosquitoes and deer flies to attack them.

But they didn't.

Miraculously, the bugs didn't come on our property at all after that initial time. If the kids stepped off the camp property, they would immediately be attacked by mosquitoes and deer flies; but if they stayed on the property (and this was a great deterrent to keep kids from wandering off), they didn't get bitten. (Reminds me of the rain that didn't come during the building project.) God loves faith. Even our stupid faith.

We had the

Cindy (Pendelton) Holler was at our first camp.

time of our lives. Cindy Holler, who later became the director of our pre-school, was on that first trip to camp. She loved it, though she isn't exactly the camping type. That year she dedicated her life to Christ.

Just as the mosquitoes and the deer flies only attacked when the kids stepped off the property, so fear and discouragement will only attack you when you aren't firmly focused on the Lord Jesus Christ. He alone is our Focal Point; and when we look to Him, we can feel real encouragement and peace.

Hang On

Amber knew her friend, Kristine, was having a really tough year. The downturn in the housing market hit Kristine and her husband Paul very hard. They had been trying to sell their house for almost a year, and it had nearly drained their finances. To add to their worry, their six-year-old son had been diagnosed with autism.

For the past year, Amber has walked alongside Kristine. Several Sundays at church, she has slipped a couple gift certificates for Kristine's favorite restaurant in her purse. She has cooked up extra meals and delivered them to Kristine and Paul's house. She went online and looked up resources that were available for kids with autism.

But most of all, Amber took Kristine's burden as her own. A few times over coffee, the two have cried together. Amber has sent Kristine encouraging emails filled with Scripture verses. She and her husband have prayed intensely for their friends every single night. When Kristine talked of quitting church, Amber wouldn't let her do it. "Hang on," she said, "just hang on."

The Bible tells us in Galatians 6:2 to "Bear ye one another's burdens." But so often, we take that as a quick prayer and a pat on the back. Sometimes we may add a smug grin and a cliché like, "God will work it all out." That really helps someone who's suffering. Is that what you would want to hear?

"Bearing" a burden implies much more than this. Imagine your spouse climbing the stairs with an armful of groceries about to dump all over the ground. To help "bear" your spouse's burden, would you smile and say, "I'm praying for you—you can do it," but not step up and grab some of the bulging grocery sacks?

If you did this, you'd probably have to eat somewhere else for dinner. If you rushed over, scooped up some of your spouse's load, and carried it to the kitchen counter—now you're "bearing their burdens."

I really don't think you can truly encourage someone in their struggle until you try to make it a part of yourself. Weep when they weep. Rejoice when they rejoice. Pray specifically and spontaneously when they ask for it. Do kind, essential favors that ensure their spiritual survival.

Oh, and listen. Let your struggling friend vent without you offering solutions and sermons.

〰〰

The Lowest of the Lows

Many years ago, I suffered through a very serious trial. People I had helped quite a bit decided to turn their back on me.

This was probably the lowest point of my min-

The Cucuzza family and church have been a huge blessing to us.

istry. It was a time I harbored serious thoughts of quitting. My heart was heavy, and I found it hard to concentrate on anything else.

At that time Pastor Tom Cucuzza, who pastors a church in Minnesota, dropped everything and drove down to Illinois. He accompanied me to a basketball tournament our school was participating in. I'm not sure I remember much of what my friend said during those difficult days.

I do remember his presence, him listening, and his loyalty and kindness. I might not still be in the ministry were it not for his willingness to drop everything and rush to my side.

This pastor went beyond the norm to encourage me in a hard time. I have tried to do the same thing for the many hundreds of people who have walked through the doors of Quentin Road bearing heavy hearts. I've tried to make our ministry more than a collection of spiritual clichés, but something real.

Transferring God's Love

When you encourage a brother or sister in need, and you bear their burdens, what you are really doing is transferring God's love to them. You're a vessel of His grace. And it may be your presence that keeps them from giving up on their faith.

Can you think of someone in your world who is experiencing their own private pain? Can you help them? Maybe you have brushed them off and avoided hearing their needs. Maybe you have not wanted to be bothered with their litany of problems.

They need a friend. They need someone to talk them off the ledge. Will you step up and answer the call?

Whatever your situation—whether you are going to have surgery, are facing a problem in your church, or reaping something that you don't want to reap, know that God is still with you. He will not fail you or forsake you, ever!

One of the most important verses that Linda and I have clung to throughout the years is Deuteronomy 31:6. "Be strong and of a good courage, fear not, nor be afraid of them: for the LORD thy God, he it is that doth go with thee; he will not fail thee, nor forsake thee."

It is God who goes with us. We can trust in Him. We can know His peace, even when things are at their worst.

Take a moment and think about something in your life that is hard to face. Go to the Lord with your situation, and ask for His peace and comfort. Read through Deuteronomy 31:6 one more time. Read it prayerfully. Know that God is with you no matter what. Rest in that knowledge right now.

The Vote

After my bypass surgery, I knew it was important we start looking toward the future of Quentin Road and all the ministries of *Victory In Grace*. While I knew that I most likely still had many more years of service still left in me, I wanted everyone to be prepared for the future.

My son, Jim, was the pastor at Westchester Bible Church. I brought him to our board and to our church, and recommended he come alongside Quentin Road and be the Executive Pastor for a time of training so as to take over when I am gone.

It went to a vote of the congregation by secret ballot. Most of our votes have been public, but I felt it was important that this one be private. I wanted it to be a clear mandate for my son and for the future of our church.

I have to be honest, I sweated a little bit. Here were the people I had been the preacher of for over 30 years. They knew my faults. They knew everything about me. If they were not happy, they could express their displeasure with me against my son and remain anonymous. It would be an opportune time for people to vote no.

When they took the tally of the votes, the elders came out and told me the news. The vote was

My son Jim's ordination ceremony, January 2, 2001.

unanimous in favor of Jim. Tears came to my eyes. This meant so much to me. I really can't describe to you how much it meant. All the pain, all the hardship, all the suffering. It was all worth it. My honorary doctorates mean a lot to me, but nothing like this. They all voted yes. Anonymously. And that, my friends, is the greatest honor ever given to me.

A Paradigm Shift

What if you looked at the pain and hardship you or your church is suffering in a different way? Instead of being depressed and wondering if you can make it, what if you looked at these times as opportunities, chances to see God work in a bigger way than you thought possible?

That's what happened that day in our first camp. The mosquitoes and deer flies were still there, but they didn't bother us if we stayed in the right place.

Hard times and difficulties don't have to keep bothering you. Of course, you will feel pain and you will suffer—this is a part of the ministry. I'm not trying to minimize that. I'm suggesting you look at trials from an eternal perspective and look for God to use these hard times for His miraculous good.

Our camp eventually grew to hundreds of people each summer.

That first trip to camp led to many more. One day, I drove by a beautiful resort on the second-largest lake in Minnesota, and noticed it was for sale. Soon our church owned that resort. We had many wonderful years at that camp, enjoying the great fishing and the beautiful area. If we hadn't hauled those kids up to camp that first year, and if we hadn't endured all those hardships, we would never have bought the new camp.

We need a paradigm shift in our thinking when it comes to trials. We need to look for the opportunity in the adversity. Our struggles often force us to figure out new skills. They make us pick up the phone and ask someone to help us. They give us the impetus to learn something new, to do something we would never have thought of before. We need to look at trials not as strange and difficult, but instead thank God for them.

You might be thinking, *Pastor Scudder, I've gleaned a lot from this book of yours. But I draw the line at being happy that I'm going through trials.*

I'm not saying you have to be happy in the sense of you jumping up and down with excitement. I'm simply saying to rejoice in the biblical sense. Realize deep within that the hard things you go through in your life and in your church will eventually work out for your good and for God's glory. The hard times have always made our church and ministries stronger. The difficult times have made us see things we didn't see before. They have helped us come up with solutions that weren't there before. Rejoicing in the hard times is a way to encourage other people around you who are also going through difficulties.

Why don't you determine right now to look at trials in your personal life and in your church in a new way? To see them for what they really are: opportunities to grow your faith and for God to give you His peace.

Finish Line Strategies

- Our trials might be as big as a ship, but keep in mind the ship floats in the ocean of God's provision.

- How can your current struggle help you to see a new solution? Maybe this is time for some "out-of-the-box" thinking. I remember many early days sitting in a coffee shop with a friend and both of us thinking of ways the church could grow. Somehow, writing these ideas on the back of a napkin did wonders for our creativity.

- Consider taking your family to a different city to walk the mall, or go to a forest preserve and walk a new path. Doing something different will get your mind off your troubles and help you bond with your family. This is important, because your family loves you and wants to help you get through the trials you are facing.

- I refuse to let myself get depressed. Go somewhere away from the people who are causing you problems. Linda and I have done this countless times by taking long drives in the country.

- Be open with your family about what your church is going through. This will help your family pray for you and also help them understand what is bugging you. Dad was always open with me when I was a kid. He would tell me about his money troubles and was honest with me. I appreciated his openness, and it only made me love him more. His worries about money helped me always pay my bills and be a good steward of what God has entrusted to me.

Chapter 32
How to Finish Strong

Therefore, my beloved brethren, be ye stedfast, unmoveable, always abounding in the work of the Lord, forasmuch as ye know that your labour is not in vain in the Lord.
1 Corinthians 15:58

"I wouldn't want to go through my huge trial again," one preacher told me, "but I have to admit that I miss how close I felt to the Lord when I was going through the difficult time. I would love to have that again."

At the time, I wondered why the preacher said such a thing. This was in the middle years of my ministry, and I didn't fully comprehend the difficult trials that were still down the road. There isn't one of my trials that I would ever want to repeat for any reason.

As the years have gone by, I have slowly begun to understand what that preacher meant. There is no way to get through trials except by relying completely on God's power through prayer. I have to immerse myself in the Word of God to get through the day when I'm going through difficult times. In those dark times when we are relying completely on prayer, we feel the peace of God like never before. I finally understood what that preacher meant.

During one particular trial that personally hurt me very much, two people had left the church. My kids saw me crying so much I couldn't stop. These trials are so deep they are difficult to describe.

Yet in every one of those times, I discovered more about the power of prayer. The hardships have developed more compassion in me. Before I had quintuple-bypass surgery, I didn't really understand what others were facing when they were going to have surgery. Now, I truly understand what they are going to go through and I have great concern for them.

Going through trials does this for us. Hardships humble us as we keep moving forward.

Every trial furthers the church. Every hard time furthers the gospel. Every bit of suffering makes your congregation stronger, and the people who stay love you more than ever. When you are going through particularly nasty trials, the people who love you see the pain you are going through. They will get behind you even more, and you will see God work in a mighty way.

Would I want to go through any of these hard things again? While I can unequivocally say the trials have made me a better person, there is no way I want to go through them again. The "spiritual" thing might be to say, "I have arrived and would have no problem going through those difficult times again." That may be someone's anti-biblical definition of spiritual, but I'm not that kind of person. I'm human after all, bleeding like everyone else. There is no way I would want to go through those hard times again. Never ask for a trial. They will come automatically.

Looking back, I can tell you this: every trial has been a blessing; every trial has made a difference in my life; and every trial has taught me about walking close to my Savior.

Called to Endure

Gladys Aylward knew God had called her to China as a missionary; but when she was 27 years old, the dream of going to China faded when she failed her Bible class at missionary training school. She didn't have a formal education or a missionary organization to back her. She raised her own finances by serving tables and doing odd jobs, and started on a trip to China all by herself. Several months later, she found herself on a wooden train platform. Flashes of orange lit up the sky and the forest to the east. Loud cracks of gunfire and the

Gladys Aylward, missionary to China.

boom of cannons rolled through the darkness. The railroad tracks were covered with powdery snow that fell, blanketing everything.

Gladys didn't want to step off the platform and begin her trek, but she had no choice. The conductor had tried to get her to step off the train earlier before it wound its way through the Siberian forest, but Gladys had refused. She wanted to get to China to minister to the people there, and that was what she had been called to do. Before she had left Haymarket, London, a clerk at Muller's Shipping Agency had traced a route on a map.

"Over the English Channel by boat from Hull," he had said. "Board the train in the Hague, Holland, and overland through Germany, Poland, Russia, Siberia, and on to Tientsin in China."

The clerk had made it sound so easy at the time, but he also mentioned that there was a "little" war going on in Siberia. That had seemed like an unimportant detail to 28-year-old Gladys, since she was so impatient to get to China. Now she found herself in Siberia in the middle of a war, and the train wasn't going forward. It had stopped at the front line between the war going on between Russia and China, delivering fresh Russian soldiers. The trains now waited to pick up the dead and wounded and carry them away from the front.

The conductor said it might take weeks for the train to return. If Gladys was intent on going forward to China, he could do nothing for her except give her a cup of strong coffee and point back up the railroad tracks. Gladys was not welcome to stay and wait for the return train ride. She was going to have to walk back to Chita, the destination she had come from, and try to catch another train.

With her bags in hand, Gladys stepped down from the railroad tracks and began her trek. For thirty miles on the train, she had seen nothing but thick, dark forest. The icy wind whipped at Gladys' face. With each whip of the wind around her, she felt her strength ebb. Soon, she could no longer carry her bags, so she slid them through the snow. She heard growls around her and wondered if they were wolves or bears. She began wondering if she would ever make it to where God had called her. Surely, He wouldn't let her die in the snow in a Siberian forest.

Somehow in spite of a perilous journey through the Russian front, Gladys made it safely to the inland city of Yangchen, in the mountainous province of Shansi, a little south of Peking. She and another missionary set up an inn where the mule drivers could stay, and then they could tell them about the Lord.

Gladys went through many trials, even going through a war in China. By this time, she had over 100 children under her care. For their safety during the war, she led them for 27 days over the mountains, where they all endured many hardships. She suffered from typhus, pneumonia, a relapsing fever, malnutrition, and extreme exhaustion. When she arrived with the children at a safer city, she completely collapsed. She regained some strength, but never fully recovered. Yet this didn't stop her from continuing her ministry. She started a church and began to share the gospel again in the surrounding villages, earning the nickname, "Ai-wen-deh" (virtuous one) from the Chinese, who grew to love this woman whom they had initially distrusted.[xxiv]

We can learn from the endurance of Gladys Aylward. She endured when things kept going wrong. She was able to finish strong because she got her strength from the Lord.

∝◦◦∽

Continuing in Prayer

My wife, Linda, has gone through many surgeries. During one of them, the surgeons fixed her back, and then went through her stomach to fix her back on the other side. She was in some of the worst pain I have ever seen. As I sat at her bedside and prayed for relief from the pain, the throbbing only got worse. My prayers weren't working at all.

This is something we need to understand about trials and about prayer. As I've mentioned several times, trials are a part of the Christian life. There is no way around them. One of the ways to get through trials is through prayer. And you need to understand this about prayer: God always answers, but sometimes the answer is much different than we would have thought it should be. He is sovereign and always has the big picture in mind. Isaiah 55:8–9 says, "For my thoughts are not your thoughts, neither are your ways my ways, saith the LORD. For as the heavens are higher than the earth, so are my ways higher than your ways, and my thoughts than your thoughts."

Jeremiah 29:11 gives us more perspective on God's thoughts. "For I know the thoughts that I think toward you, saith the LORD, thoughts of peace, and not of evil, to give you an expected end."

God knows what is best for us and for the people we are praying for. He knows our congregations and their needs. When we as pastors pray for the people in our churches, we need to remember God is always working all things for good. (This doesn't mean all things are good, but rather that all things work together for good.)

Later, Linda recovered, and the doctor said she walked better than any of the other patients who had the surgery. God always answers, but the answers might be different than you thought they would be.

Prayer for a Friend

His friends wanted him out of prison. They spent the night praying. The death sentence awaited him. Only a miracle would stop it.

The next morning, William Tyndale was led to the stake. Everyone still wanted a miracle; but as the guards brought him forward, the Christians' hearts must have been seized with pain. They had expected

My wife has suffered through much pain. But God has seen us through.

God to answer their prayers. Tyndale looked up to Heaven before the first flame licked the straw at his feet.

"Lord, open the eyes of the King of England." His famous prayer echoes in our hearts today. His last words before he courageously withstood what none

William Tyndale.

of us could imagine: death by being burned at the stake.

Think about how Tyndale's friends must have felt. They had so wanted Tyndale to continue ministering and continue translating. Now it seemed all was lost.

Yet all of us who know about the King James Bible understand what really happened. It took time, but God really did open the eyes of the King of England. His order for an English translation of the Scriptures transformed the world. The translators used Tyndale's translation for much of the New Testament. This was not a coincidence. This was a much greater answer to prayer than anyone could contemplate at the time.

Prayer is not getting God to adjust His program to what we want; rather it is adjusting our lives to the revealed will of God. When we pray, it isn't God who changes, it is us. The purpose of prayer is to glorify God through His work here on earth. We are not to use prayer as a tool to try to change the will of God; rather it is a tool to see His will performed on this earth.

Keep on Keeping On

My encouragement to you is to keep on keeping on. Keep praying. Keep reading God's Word and studying it. Keep calling other godly Christians when you feel discouraged. Keep witnessing. Keep reaching out when it seems like you aren't really doing much good as a pastor or lay leader.

Don't allow yourself to be discouraged. Don't allow your church to get down. God is on the move. He is doing great things. 1 Corinthians 15:58 says, "Therefore, my beloved brethren, be ye stedfast, unmoveable, always abounding in the work of the Lord, forasmuch as ye know that your labour is not in vain in the Lord."

2 Corinthians 9:8 says, "And God is able to make all grace abound toward you; that ye, always having all sufficiency in all things, may abound to every good work."

You shouldn't be surprised

when Satan tries to stop you. You shouldn't be surprised when the hard times keep coming. You shouldn't be stunned when you finally start lifting those steel beams and they start to twist like spaghetti.

They may twist like spaghetti, but lower the problem back to the ground and ask God for wisdom. God has promised to give you wisdom and be with you every step of the way.

Sometimes I had to make hard decisions during our building projects. One time a man wanted to pull cupolas onto the roof of our new building using a truck. I felt that it was dangerous to do it. We got into an argument. Sometime later he left the church. He used another reason, but I suspect our disagreement was the real reason. The man had helped us a lot. I appreciated all he had done, but I couldn't go against my gut feeling that it was dangerous to do what he wanted to do. If people had gotten hurt because of my failure to stand up for what was right, I would never have gotten over it. (I'm sure in his opinion, people wouldn't have gotten hurt. I do understand; but in the end, I was the leader. If you aren't the pastor, you are to follow your pastor and support him as he does God's work.)

Hebrews 13:17 states, "Obey them that have the rule over you, and submit yourselves: for they watch for your souls, as they that must give account, that they may do it with joy, and not with grief: for that is unprofitable for you."

A pastor should never be a dictator, but a pastor is a leader. The pastor must give account for the spiritual well-being of his people, and this is a heavy responsibility. You have to make painful decisions if you are a leader. There hasn't been a leader who hasn't had to make decisions that are sometimes heart-breaking and gut-wrenching.

There are also times when you make decisions that you do not see the true impact that the decision will have. When we began our preschool, we started it mainly as a chance for the workers in our Christian school and other ministries to have a place for their children. After two years, the preschool started to grow like wildfire. In the beginning we had one class; then two. After the second year, we grew to three classes. The third year we had seven classes; the next year twelve. The preschool grew to the point that we set up preschool classes in our auditorium. We always found creative ways to make our building work.

For the past 20 years, we've averaged 1,200–1,400 kids a year in our preschool. We have some of the best facilities in the state with wonderful playgrounds, sports camps, language classes, swimming lessons, horseback riding, and more. We have the largest Christian preschool in the United States.

When kids come to our preschool, they are like sponges, soaking up knowledge from the Bible. Many times they go home and ask their mom and dad to start praying before meals. We have had many preschool families become members of our church. Cindy Holler did an excellent job heading up the preschool for many years. Her former assistant, Molly Julian, is now the head of the preschool, and she is doing an excellent job as well.

The nation's largest Christian preschool.

Sometimes ministries in churches grow when you least expect it. Other times it seems like ministries are never going to grow. It's important to look outside the box when it comes to ministry in the church.

The Best Is Yet to Come

A couple years ago, my son, Jim, who is now the president of Dayspring Bible College and Seminary, started to pray about a new campus. We had used up all our land at our current property, and buying land in our area would have been very expensive. Jim drove by a private school every day on his way to work at Quentin Road. He would pray that someday this beautiful, 13-acre property with seven buildings would be the answer to Dayspring's prayers.

One morning, Jim was listening to the radio as he was driving by the property, and heard that it was up for foreclosure. He immediately called about it and found they were willing to sell the whole school for a great price. Private land, dorms, common area, offices galore, brand-new gymnasium, and a commercial kitchen—a perfect site for our college. It was the answer to many prayers.

The buildings weren't in good condition, and the property was overgrown with weeds. The walls were covered with graffiti, and the roofs with stones. But hard work never scared anyone at Quentin Road. (In fact, the property reminded me a little bit of that first property God gave us in Palatine: lots of weeds, junked cars, and a dilapidated house with bad plumbing. All of that was absolutely perfect for our needs at the time.) Today, the campus is beyond our dreams, surrounded by hundreds of acres of county-owned forest. The perfect, quiet place to study the Word of God.

Another true miracle.

The future is bright. God isn't finished with Quentin Road, with Dayspring Bible College and Seminary, or with *Victory In Grace*. There is still a good bit of the journey left until Jesus Christ returns.

Our first property in Palatine was in worse shape than our new campus.

The Hardest Job in the World

Make no mistake, being a pastor is the hardest job in the world.

Why? Because you can never leave your work behind you. The care of the people, the care of the church, the spiritual pressure, the satanic battle, trying to stand strong when everything around you begs you to give up.

Some people ask me, "What is the hardest part of your job? Is it preaching?"

Preaching is a big part of what I do. I prepare four to five messages a week, and a lot of my time is spent doing that. But preaching isn't the hard part of my job.

Other people might think the administration of such a huge church/school is the hardest part of my occupation. I have to admit it isn't always easy to run a church, Christian school, Bible college, preschool, dyslexia program, horseback riding program, outreach events, food service kitchen, radio and television ministry, and more. Overseeing these ministries does take a large part of my time. (I have administrators, leaders, and workers who do a great job helping me with these ministries.) Besides this, other pastors often seek my counsel, and I seek theirs. Then I am constantly looking for new ideas, ways to improve, and ways to make everything better. But administration isn't the hardest part of what I do.

The most difficult part of what I do is to care for the spiritual well-being of the people. Caring for people's souls means I rely heavily on the Lord. The burden is more than I can bear. Our church is under attack. The devil wants to bring us down. We are in a culture that has completely lost its moral compass. Being a strong, biblically minded church is the hardest thing in the world. Charles Spurgeon once wrote, "I feel as though I had created a great machine and it is ever grinding, grinding, and that I may yet be its victim. No one knows the toil and care I have to bear."

Statistics say that 50% of ordained ministers across denominational lines are out of the pulpit within five years, which means 1,700 pastors leave the ministry each and every month in this country.

Marathon runners reach a point where they don't think they can keep going. They call this hitting the wall. Their muscles burn with pain. Their strength is gone. They feel defeated. They wonder if all the training they did has any bearing on the race they are running right now.

In the church, this happens to the faithful as well. Believers hit the wall. Even preachers hit the wall. You come to a point where you think you can't take even one more person getting upset about something trivial; one more board member not understanding the vision; one more visitor coming for awhile and building up your hopes, only to go to another church.

You <u>can</u> keep going. Your church <u>can</u> keep going. You run for an <u>eternal</u> prize. You are going <u>forward</u> for the greatest <u>reason</u> in the world, the <u>salvation of souls</u>. You aren't doing this for the day-to-day life of this world. <u>You are doing this for Heaven.</u> <u>You are doing this for souls.</u> Because of that, you will ultimately hit the wall physically. God will then gently and carefully continue helping you for the last mile of the race. As you limp along, He is hanging on to you, refusing to let you fall. As sweat pours down your face and you wonder if you have any ability left, know that God delights in availability rather than ability. He will give you and your church the grace to cross the finish line.

A crippled, elderly lady hobbled to church on her crutches. A friend observed her faithful attendance and asked, "Why do you continue to come to church even though it is so hard for you? How do you manage to get there for every service?"

"My heart gets there first, and then my old legs follow after," she said.

That's how it ends up being in the Christian life. Our hearts get there first because we know that Jesus will help us make it across the finish line.

Perhaps you are personally facing something you don't think you can ever make it through. Know this: God is with you. Pastor, God will strengthen you. Leader, God will empower His mighty Church. Believer, continue going forward. Never forget how close He is to you right in the middle of the worst situation. He will help you finish strong.

From the early days in the hills of Kentucky, to the skyscrapers of Chicago, to an elementary school in Mount Prospect, to 2 ½ acres in Palatine, to 40 acres in Lake Zurich, to a tiny village in India, my Savior has been with me every step of the way. I owe everything to Him. God has guided and established my every step.

He will do the same for you.

Finish Line Strategies

Here are some thoughts from Dr. Chuck Svoboda, founder of Bible Related Ministries, on how to keep your church on course. I thought they were fitting for our chapter on how to finish strong.

- Pray for God to help keep you as a clean instrument in His hands. Be sensitive to sin in your life. Psalm 19:12; Psalm 66:18; 1 Corinthians 11:28

- Pray faithfully for the church family if you are the pastor. If you are in a church, pray faithfully for the pastor, his family, the leadership in the church, and the people of the church. 1 Timothy 2:1; Ephesians 6:18–20

- Treat the pastor and leadership with respect. Teach your people to do this if you are the pastor. 1 Corinthians 11:1; Psalm 118:8[xxv]

More Finish Line Strategies

- Keep a prayer journal. Write down your prayers and the people you are praying for.

- When someone asks you for prayer, take a moment and pray for that person right away. Not necessarily out loud, but praying right away ensures that you did pray for that person, in case you forget to write down what he or she asked you to pray for.

- Get in the habit of praying before every handshake, every phone call, and every meeting. Don't leave prayer off until the last minute. Prioritize it.

Appendix A

There is nothing I like more than to use this simple illustration to share the gospel. Going to Heaven is not about what you do. It's about what Christ did.

Your good works can't get you to Heaven. If they could, then how would you know you've done enough good works? Eternal life is a free gift, paid for by Christ's death. He was buried and then rose again to give you new life — eternal life.

How can you know for sure that you have eternal life? Simply accept that Christ paid it all. He did 100% — you do 0%. Place your trust in Him alone.

You can never lose your eternal life because Christ not only saves you, He keeps you saved. (John 10:28–29)

If you've just trusted Christ, would you share the good news with someone else? Learn this simple illustration and use it today.

1. (Point to hand.) Let my hand represent you and me.

2. (Place wallet in hand. Point to wallet.) Let this wallet represent sin. We all have sin on us. In order to go to Heaven, we have to be sinless. "For all have sinned, and come short of the glory of God." Romans 3:23

3. (Point to hand.) God loves us....
"For God so loved the world, that he gave his only begotten Son, that whosoever believeth in him should not perish, but have everlasting life." John 3:16

4. (Point to wallet.) ...But He hates our sin. "For the wages of sin is death...."
Romans 6:23a

5. (Hold wallet between hands.) Our sin separates us from God. We cannot get rid of our sin by our good works. If we pay for our sin, we will have to spend eternity in Hell. "For the wages of sin is death...."
Romans 6:23a

6. (Raise other hand.) Let this hand represent the Lord Jesus Christ. He had no sin. He was perfect. "For he [God] hath made him [Christ] to be sin for us, who knew no sin...." 2 Corinthians 5:21a

7. (Place wallet in other hand.) Christ voluntarily took our sin and its penalty, death, upon Himself. "For he [God] hath made him [Christ] to be sin for us, who knew no sin...." 2 Corinthians 5:21a

8. (Point to wallet.) Jesus paid for our sin through His death and shed blood on the cross. His resurrection shows that God accepted His payment. "But God commendeth his love toward us, in that, while we were yet sinners, Christ died for us." Romans 5:8

9. (Put wallet away. Point to first hand.) Our sin is no longer on us because He took it and paid for it. He gives us His righteousness. "For he [God] hath made him [Christ] to be sin for us, who knew no sin; that we might be made the righteousness of God in him." 2 Corinthians 5:21

10. (Put hands together.) Trusting Christ removes the sin that separated you from God. You can know you have eternal life when you, by faith, accept the payment Christ made for you. "These things have I written unto you that believe on the name of the Son of God; that ye may KNOW that ye have eternal life, and that ye may believe on the name of the Son of God." 1 John 5:13 [emphasis added]

Ephesians 2:8–9

"For by grace are ye saved through faith;
and that not of yourselves: it is the gift of God:
Not of works, lest any man should boast."

Notes

Notes for Chapter 2:

i John Cloud, "The Survivor: A Miracle's Cost," *Time Magazine*, September 9, 2002, http://www.time.com/time/magazine/article/0,9171,1003216,00.html.

ii David Bauer, October Newsletter 2012, http://biblerelatedministries.org/newsletterOct2012.pdf.

iii George Barna, "The State of the Church," (Ventura, CA: Issachar Resources) 118.

Notes for Chapter 4:

iv Brad Mutchler, Western Kentucky University Basketball Hall of Fame, 1999, http://www.wkusports.com/ViewArticle.dbml?DB_OEM_ID=5400&ATCLID=1568601. For more information, see http://www.zoominfo.com/#!search/profile/person?personId=306170291&targetid=profile.

v Sermon Central Illustrations, http://www.sermoncentral.com/illustrations/sermon-illustration-paul-fritz-stories-7220.asp.

vi Sermon Central, http://www.sermoncentral.com/illustrations/sermon-illustration-scott-chambers-stories-11893.asp.

Notes for Chapter 5:

vii http://archive.ktkiwanian.org/CircleKDocs/KTHistory/ KTCKIPastGovs.html.

Notes for Chapter 6:

viii Charles Lindbergh, *Spirit of St. Louis*, (New York: Scribner, 1953), 5–7.

ix Hansi Lo Wang, "Father of the Cell Phone 'Unleashed' World's Callers from Copper Wires," NPR News, http://www.npr.org/blogs/ alltechconsidered/2012/07/09/156481784/father-of-the-cellphone- unleashed-worlds-callers-from-copper-wires.

Notes for Chapter 15:

x http://www.jellogallery.org/jellohistory.html, http://www.jellogallery .org/jelloHistory2.html, and http://www.jellogallery.org/jelloHistory3 .html.

xi http://biblerelatedministries.org/index.html.

xii George Barna, http://www.barna.org/faith-spirituality/504-barna- examines-trends-in-14-religious-factors-over-20-years-1991-to-2011.

Notes for Chapter 16:

xiii Robert Callovi, "Park Vista's Ryan White Overcame Stroke to Be One of Area's Top Cross-Country Runners," September 14, 2011, *Palm Beach Times*, http://pbgametime.com/news/park-vistas-ryan-white-overcame- stroke-to-be-one-of-areas-top-cross-country-runners/124576/.

xiv "In Alaska, Fast Food Often Can Take Days," Associated Press, March 1, 1992, http://articles.latimes.com/1992-03-01/local/me-5255_1_fast- food.

Notes for Chapter 17:

xv http://articles.ochristian.com/article491.shtml.

Notes for Chapter 18:

xvi Duke Study on Peace of Mind, May 14, 2012. http:// drdanabeezleysmith.com/home/Dr._Danas_Blog/Entries/2012/5/14_ Duke_University_Study_on_Peace_of_Mind.html.

Notes for Chapter 19:

xvii John Adams, http://www.innsofcourt.org/Content/Default.aspx?Id=5787.

Notes for Chapter 20:

xviii Sermon Central, http://www.sermoncentral.com/illustrations/illustrations-about-adoniram-judson.asp?Keyword=Adoniram Judson.

xix Robert Morrison, "I Felt as If I Were Walking with Destiny," May 10, 2011, http://www.americanthinker.com/2011/05/i_felt_as_if_i_were_walking_wi.html.

xx http://bible.org/illustration/practical-implications-consecration.

xxi Stan Toler and Mark Hollingsworth, *You Might Be a Preacher If...*, (Tulsa, OK: Albury Publishing, 1995).

Notes for Chapter 23:

xxii http://www.biblestudytools.com/history/foxs-book-of-martyrs/the-fourth-persecution-under-marcus-aurelius-antoninus-a-d-162.html.

Notes for Chapter 29:

xxiii http://www.brainyquote.com/quotes/quotes/m/michaeljor127660.html.

Notes for Chapter 32:

xxiv Janet Benge and Geoff Benge, *Gladys Aylward*, (Seattle, WA: Youth with a Mission Publishing), 31–52.

xxv Chuck Svoboda, *Who Would Believe It?*, (Hinsdale, IL: Bible Related Ministries, 2002) 100–102.